STATE

PL

Michael Calvin, one of the UK's most accomplished sportswriters, has worked in more than eighty countries, covering ever major sporting event, including seven Olympic Games and six World Cup finals. He was named Sports Writer of the Year for his despatches as a crew member in a round-the-world yacht race and has twice been named Sports Reporter of the Year.

He is a bestselling author, whose book *The Nowhere Men* won the Times Sports Book of the Year prize in 2014. He became the first author to receive the award in successive years, when *Proud*, his collaboration with former Wales and British Lions rugby captain Gareth Thomas, was named Sports Book of the Year in 2015.

In the same year the second book of his football trilogy, *Living on the Volcano* was shortlisted for the William Hill Book of the Year prize. *No Nonsense*, his collaboration with Joey Barton, was named Autobiography of the Year in the 2017 British Sports Book awards. *No Hunger In Paradise*, an insight into youth football, became an immediate *Sunday Times* bestseller when it was published, to critical acclaim, in April 2017.

Praise for State of Play

'Michael Calvin has always been a perceptive chronicler of how football operates on a human level. But *State of Play* is surely this award-winning writer's best book to date; a thought-provoking survey of all the characters who make the game ick and also exploit it for their own ends. Full of insight and genuine love for football.'

— **Ben East,** *The Observer*

'Calvin on searing form, once again shining light into overlooked corners of the game.'

Jonathan Northcroft, Sunday Times

'A grandstand view of the beautiful game. From mental-health issues to women's football, Calvin draws on his own frontline reporting as well as interviews with leading footballing figures to present an exhaustive portrait of the modern game.'

— *Radio Times*

'Calvin brilliantly shines light on overlooked issues permeating contemporary football. Every word written will resonate'

— **Stuart Horsfield,** *Shortlist*

'What Mike Calvin doesn't know about football could fit on the back of a postage stamp. He shows The Beautiful Game is anything but when you peel away the glamour and shovel aside the piles of money. A hard-hitting football must-read'

— **Jon Wise,** *Sunday Sport*

Also available by Michael Calvin

Life's a Pitch
Only Wind and Water
Family
The Nowhere Man
Proud: My Autobiography (with Gareth Thomas)
Living On The Volcano
No Nonsense: The Autobiography (with Joey Barton)
No Hunger In Paradise

MICHAEL CALVIN

STATE OF PLAY

arrow books

1 3 5 7 9 10 8 6 4 2

Arrow Books
20 Vauxhall Bridge Road
London SW1V 2SA

Arrow is part of the Penguin Random House group of companies
whose addresses can be found at global.penguinrandomhouse.com.

First published in Great Britain by Century in 2018
First published in paperback in Great Britain by Arrow Books in 2019

www.penguin.co.uk

A CIP catalogue record for this book is available
from the British Library.

ISBN 9781784756123

Printed and bound in Great Britain by Clays Ltd, Elcograf S.p.A.

Penguin Random House is committed to a
sustainable future for our business, our readers
and our planet. This book is made from Forest
Stewardship Council® certified paper.

For Marielli and Michael

Contents

INTRODUCTION

A Father's Gift

'The point about football in Britain is that it is not just a sport people take to, like cricket or tennis or running long distances. It is inherent in the people. It is built into the urban psyche, as much a common experience to our children as are uncles and school. The way we play the game, organise it and reward it reflects the kind of community we are.'
– Arthur Hopcraft

I miss my dad. As I write these words, senses heightened by rural stillness and seemingly impenetrable pre-dawn darkness, I summon the mental image of him cradling a newborn baby, Marielli, the only great-grandchild he would know. His life force is palpable. Blue eyes, radiance refracted by thick-lensed glasses, illuminate an open, expressive face.

Charlie Calvin was a big man, in all senses of the word. He passed away, surrounded by the family he nourished literally, spiritually and philosophically, on 23 October 2015, in the council house in which he had lived for more than half a century. We had lost Mum earlier in the year, in the same room that looked out into the back garden, and felt an orphan's emptiness.

Our grief was somehow softened by reminders of mortality: his smell, lingering on a recently worn suit; the sight of his shoes, lined up against the bedroom wall; and the sheen on the flat black leather cap he wore daily to Mass. He gave us values, ambition and hopefully a little compassion.

Perhaps the most cherished gift, from a personal point of view, came in the form of two books, scavenged from an empty house he helped secure as a cable jointer's mate for the Eastern Electricity Board. They shaped my attitudes and ultimately dictated the course of my life.

The first, with a green mock leather cover inset with gold inscription, was a glossary of the immediate post-war parliament of 1945. As someone whose own father was unemployed for ten years, from the 1929 Stock Market Crash until the outbreak of global hostilities, Dad passed down his belief in the benevolent socialism that led to Nye Bevan's National Health Service.

The book contained pen portraits of each of the 640 seats, and a summary of election results. I was in the first flush of adolescent idealism, devoured the detail, and can still recall, unbidden, the balance of power: Attlee's Labour, 395 seats; Churchill's Conservatives, 215; Mum's Liberals, 12; others, 18.

The second book – hard-backed, with a wraparound cover photograph of what I later discovered was a First Division match between Leeds United and Everton – should, by rights, have been returned to Watford Public Library. It was last lent out on 3 February 1971, nearly three years after its publication. As an adult I still have pangs of guilt at its illicit acceptance, but I was 13 years old, entranced, and kept it as treasure trove.

The Football Man, subtitled 'People and Passions in Soccer', was written by Arthur Hopcraft, a journalist, novelist and screenwriter, who, in an all too typical example of intellectual snobbery, is lionised more for his TV adaptations of John le Carré's *Tinker Tailor Soldier Spy* and Charles Dickens' *Hard Times* than his seminal summary of our national sport.

It took me, spellbound, from Old Trafford, where 'a thin old man with stubble on his chin and a neck like a cockerel's' sought benediction from a teenaged George Best, to the 1966 World Cup final at Wembley, where Sir Alf Ramsey's players were re-imagined as Battle of Britain pilots, setting out 'to whack the Hun again'.

I was never going to be a footballer, despite imaginary winning goals scored, volleying an old leather football against the wall of a prefabricated, flat-roofed block that included an outside toilet, a coal hole and a tool shed. My first, impulsive ambition, on watching grainy footage of the Moon landings in a friend's house across the road from our grammar school, had been to be an astronaut.

That was quickly overwhelmed by the romantic notion of becoming a working-class warrior in Westminster, fighting for social justice for the common man. Yet the moment I read the last line of Hopcraft's two-page introduction, lying on the top bunk in the bedroom I shared with three brothers, my path was set.

'I am a reporter trying to reach to the heart of what football is.'

He detected the game's heartbeat, celebrated its humanity. He spoke of football grounds as 'privileged places of working-class communion'. Many years later I would interview some of the book's central characters, knights of the realm like Bobby Charlton and Stanley Matthews. I came to appreciate Hopcraft's triumph in distilling heroism, revealing intimate foibles and frailties.

His book is a time capsule, containing items from a long-lost world, in which hope and perspective – signified by Earthrise, the photograph of our planet seen in all its ethereal beauty over a lunar horizon, taken by astronaut Bill Anders from Apollo 8 on Christmas Eve, 1968 – were neutralised by the horror of generational slaughter in Vietnam.

The year 1968 was one of convulsive sporting, political and societal change. In the UK Conservative politician Enoch Powell delivered his infamous 'rivers of blood' speech, a provocative vision of the consequences of immigration and racial integration. There were riots and revolutions in Europe. Martin Luther King and Robert Kennedy were assassinated in the United States. An African famine, exacerbated by civil war, claimed the lives of millions.

Two US athletes, Tommie Smith and John Carlos, offered a global platform for the civil rights movement by giving black power salutes as the 'Star-Spangled Banner' played in recognition of their gold and bronze medals in the 200 metres at the Mexico Olympics, where Bob Beamon made 'the great leap forward', setting a world long jump record that was to last for almost 23 years.

In England, football was stirring from the ration-book greyness of the 50s. Hopcraft, who died in 2004 aged 71, was remarkably prescient in highlighting the far-reaching consequences of hooliganism and predicting the formation of 'a domestic Premier League', yet even he could not have foreseen the impact of rapid, vapid, consumerism.

In 2018, top matches are no longer staged where 'the air is rancid with beer and onions and belching and worse'. Stadia creak under delusions of grandeur, rather than decades of decay. They are sanitised corporate fiefdoms, tourist traps in which it is possible, at exorbitant cost, to gawp at multi-millionaire footballers, assembling, unseen by the great unwashed, in glass-walled tunnels.

Remarkably, though, the final paragraph of Hopcraft's book still resonates: 'Even now, whenever I arrive at any football ground, or merely pass close to one when it is silent, I experience a unique alerting of the senses. The moment evokes my past in an instantaneous emotional rapport which is more certain, more secret, than memory.'

The Premier League is rapacious, as skyline-defining as the cylindrical glass eyesores that have changed the face of London, and so many other historic capitals. Largely unearned wealth allows it to exist in a moral vacuum, in which grass-roots funding is decreasing in real terms, despite the strident double-speak of its corporate social responsibility programming.

We have just reached the end of the longest and most lucrative season in history, with a World Cup finals staged in Russia, a nation listening to echoes of a dark, autocratic past. The next tournament, due to be staged in Qatar in 2022, is impossibly tainted by exploitative labour laws and sustained whispers of the corruption that continues to define Fifa, football's global governing body.

Innocence, we will discover, dies hard. There are uplifting stories to be told, from the front line of urban gang rivalries to the smaller clubs where players are unpaid and fans man the barricades. My job will be done if it sheds shards of light on the work of hidden heroes like Tajean Hutton, Errol Johnson, Dave Kelly, Doug Harper, Tony McCool, Albert Barnes and Pete Lowe.

This is not a cavalcade of champions, but a contemplation of personal challenge and a reflection of a love best passed down the generations. My aim is to humanise issues, examine the molecular structure of a game that has changed beyond all recognition in the last half century. An 18-month journey has been shared with remarkable people like Zigi Shipper, the Holocaust survivor who seared the soul of such football legends as Steven Gerrard and Wayne Rooney.

I realise the impudence of attempting to modernise Hopcraft's vision in these pages, but trust you will forgive the indulgence. I have limited myself to four sections, instead of his nine. Inevitably, and entirely understandably, there were omissions in the original that are incomprehensible to 21st-century society; Mary Fullaway, George Best's landlady, and Elizabeth Charlton, Bobby's mother, featured briefly as the book's only female presence.

To put that into bewildering perspective, women's football was banned at the time; its 50-year isolation by the Football Association did not end until 1971. My intention is to celebrate modern heroines like Dawn Astle, daughter of the man of 1968, Jeff Astle. Her campaign for football to recognise its wider responsibility for the brain injury that killed her father has irresistible force and huge long-term significance.

Football needs a mother's love, a woman's touch. Despite advances led by Jacqui Oatley in journalism and the late Sheila Spiers in supporter activism it has yet to evolve into a meritocracy that provides true equality of opportunity. If it does so, and Emma Hayes is judged on her own merits as a coach of relentless purpose and distinctive sensitivity, the men's game will have the chance to incorporate a powerful pioneer.

Of course, idealism is difficult to sustain. Agents have reshaped the landscape with their cynicism and desperation. Their most valuable players are increasingly projected through copy-approved, one-way conversations that purport to be interviews. Though England's World Cup squad sought successfully to reconnect with fans and the media, their communion with the public is too often restricted to a snatched selfie or a scribbled autograph.

That artificial airlock does footballers few favours, since their resilience in the face of the game's brutality and their elevated levels of performance deserve to be acclaimed. They are human beings, rather than X-Men. Cut them and they bleed. Doubt them and they worry. Drewe Broughton, whose mentorship of young players is shaped by the casual cruelty he experienced as a 22-club journeyman, knows they cry themselves to sleep.

This is an age of rancour and division. Managers are emperors who accept they will be naked, stripped of their last remaining rags, on the inevitable day of reckoning. Fans are persecutors, even their executioners, but are capable of great benevolence. Club owners who remain true to their roots are being picked off by a strange mixture of speculators and savants, yet their experience can still be life-affirming.

It is all too easy to craft a case for a dystopian future, in which players have personalised media platforms, games are compressed into 60-second digital snacks, and matches are staged between holograms across multiple venues. Men accustomed to wielding power from musty committee rooms must change, or die.

A new generation will shape its destiny, though the greed and opportunism driving football's development process carries the danger of greater distortion, and no one can predict with any certainty how a futuristic version of the game will be consumed. Commercially-run factory farms, producing teenaged superstars for four-a-side, laser-lit, live-streamed cage games are not entirely implausible; adolescent footballers with millions of followers on social media are already being pursued and promoted as style icons.

I might take an occasionally harsher line than Hopcraft, who suggested 'I have tried to salute football while remaining as watchful for its blemishes as affection allows', but he expresses eternal truths in prose that, unjustly in my view, is considered to have gone out of fashion, with black and white televisions and the Test Card.

The best footballers are products of time and place, the ebb and flow of professional sport. Clubs across Europe, and beyond, are prone to the wilful betrayal of their heritage. Institutions browbeat individuals, without killing their spirit. The modern game is not a one-size-fits-all exercise. It can still cater for all tastes, all creeds. It retains the power to captivate.

The boy who read that misappropriated library book all those years ago is still searching for a reason to believe. Perhaps that is why he finds himself in a low-ceilinged lounge in a house at the end of a country lane, sitting in the favourite chair of a man known as 'The King', who was killed by the game at which he excelled.

PART ONE

The Player

CHAPTER ONE

Martyr

'Dr Willie Stewart, the neuropathologist who re-examined Dad's brain, said it was so damaged that if he hadn't known it was the brain of a man of fifty-nine he would have thought he was looking at one from a man in his late eighties or early nineties. So, when I get down, or feel the pressure, I just remember I watched my dad choke to death on his own sick because of that. I dust myself off, give myself a kick up the backside, and I go again.' – Dawn Astle

The silence is filled by a miniature grandfather clock in the hallway, and a classic circular wall clock, half hidden in an alcove. Their unsynchronised rhythm has a strangely hypnotic quality, like a drum roll at a public execution. Dawn Astle is counting down the last seconds in the life of a man who dominates the room from beyond the grave.

I am sitting in her father's favourite spot, facing the wall on which a large framed photograph captures him at Wembley, arms aloft in a messianic gesture towards an unseen crowd. Jeff Astle has just scored the only goal in West Bromwich Albion's extra-time win over Everton in the 1968 FA Cup final, and paused in front of a gaggle of car-coated cameramen.

To my right, through the open doorway, there is another imposing image, hung over a chimney breast. It frames the fusion of instinct, technique and timing in his instant left-footed shot, following a rebound from an attempt with his right; his head is slightly tilted but still, and his body is unfolding as the ball begins its journey to the top left-hand corner of the net.

Around the corner, in the open-plan kitchen, magnetic tiles on an upright cream-coloured refrigerator proclaim him as 'the King'. The eye is drawn, irresistibly, to a black and white photograph, held in place by Blu Tack. Jeff Astle is standing in the surf, on a club tour to California. He is lean, tanned, poised; the picture of health and happiness.

The brain injury that killed him began to manifest itself when he was 54. He was physically fit, climbing ladders as a window cleaner and coping with arthritis in his knees. Yet he began to show signs of confusion, randomly and repeatedly asking whether his mother, who had died 16 years previously, was still alive. Diagnosed with early-onset Alzheimer's, his descent into incomprehension was swift and traumatic.

'Our lives changed for ever. The scans showed the cells at the front of his brain were dead or dying. We offered to sell the house, to fund treatment in America, but were told it was irreversible. When he was well he was like an electronic charge, the life and soul of our family. You just had to follow the sound of laughter to find him. He completely changed; it was horrific, the worst thing in the world to watch.

'He would steal food from his grandchildren as they sat in their high chairs, scoop a load of butter out of the fridge and stuff it into his mouth. Mum had to hide knives; he had no sense of danger and tried to get out of moving cars. He had his tea in a baby beaker, and lay on the settee in this big nappy thing. His hands used to shake, sometimes quite violently. He was gaunt and grey and never spoke.

'He didn't know who I was, and didn't know he had been a footballer, even though Mum tried desperately to ignite the smallest spark by surrounding him with all the things he had won – his FA Cup medal, his England caps, his trophies and mementoes from the 1970 World Cup. All these years on, I still fight the guilt that there were times when I couldn't bear to see him.

'He was a hero to others, but to me he was just Dad, this giant, this massive, massive, man with really dark, slicked-back hair. He was always very smart, but more than anything I remember his smile. He never lost that huge smile. That's what kills me. I feel his presence, you know. More when I get upset, because my dad didn't like to see anybody upset. I sense him saying, "come on, duck, you're all right". And I hope he's proud of us.'

A daughter's love lingers and intensifies, until it is preserved like a flower pressed between the pages of a favourite book. A single tear falls from Dawn's left eye, and is brushed away with the back of her hand. An inherited version of her father's smile – moist, wide and engaging – accompanies the refusal of an invitation to pause before returning to the terrible events of Saturday, 18 January 2002.

It was her 34th birthday, a birthdate she shared with her maternal grandfather, a deeply private man who had buried his wife the previous day. He didn't like fuss, but Dawn and her mother Laraine had organised a family dinner so that he was surrounded by love. The house, which adjoined a field lined with disintegrating remnants of diseased elm trees, hummed with four generations of the Astle clan.

'I'd set the table, and at the time Dad was really poorly. He had to have everything cut up really small for him. We had to watch him because he'd keep putting stuff in his mouth before he'd swallowed the last lot and he'd be like a bloody hamster. I can see him now. I can't say he walked in ... he sort of walked with a stoop. He just looked like a really, really old, old man.

'I was in the kitchen and he sat at the dining table. Someone said to him, "Don't start yet, Jeff, we're not ready". I said, "Oh he's fine". Everyone was watching him. And he was ever so careful, just doing little bits of meat. He started to cough and I had to lean back a little bit to check there was someone with him. Mum was there, with a few other adults, but he just kept coughing.

'Someone said, "Let's stand him up". Of course you had to help him up, and you could tell this coughing was getting worse. Somebody said, "Let's take him out-side". They opened the two doors, and we were on that little bit of a path out the front. It's private there, so there was nobody about to see him. He was heaving, and we got the kids away, took them upstairs.

'People were saying, "Spit it out, Jeff, whatever you've got in your mouth, spit it out". He gritted his teeth together, you could see it, he just wouldn't. His brain couldn't send the signal for him to throw up. My mum was trying to open his mouth. Alastair, my partner, shouted "watch your fingers" because he would have bitten her bloody fingers off. And then his legs went from under him.

'I shouted, "Go and fetch some cushions, bring my quilt, bring anything" because it was cold. I rang the ambulance service and was ratty with them because I just wanted help, immediately.

'I don't mention this a lot but years and years ago, in my grandma and grandad's house, I earwigged on a conversation my grandma was having with one of the neighbours, about this death rattle. I always remembered it but didn't really know what it was.

'And then I heard something … Dad had stopped heaving and coughing. He just lay there. His eyes were open, his teeth were still gritted together, and me and Alastair started to do CPR on him. I was ex-police and had been trained, but I just couldn't remember what to do. Alastair was very calm – do this, do that – and as I was doing it, I was going, "Please Dad, please Dad". Honest to God, it felt like hours and hours before the paramedics arrived.'

Dawn retreated to the side of the house, retrieved an emergency supply of cigarettes she had hidden on top of the refrigerator, and could barely bring herself to watch the tragic tableau that unfolded beneath a harsh security light. The paramedics, working in what is now a rose garden, used a defibrillator for another eternity.

'I was squinting because I didn't want to look, but knew I had to. I'm not particularly religious but I was thinking, "Please God, don't let him die". And then they took him in the ambulance. Mum and my sister Claire followed it. Everyone was in a state of shock and I collapsed at one point. Then suddenly the phone rang and my eldest sister Dorice answered it.

'I remember it like it was yesterday. She went, "Hello. Is he? All right. Bye." Put the phone down. I was sat by the table. I think the kids were still upstairs. And she just turned around and said, "My ...". That was it. I grabbed the tablecloth, for some mad reason, and pulled it, like a bloody magician does, and the food went bloody everywhere.

'I jumped straight in the car. I said to Alastair, "I don't care whether you get stopped. Get me there now. Just go as fast as you can." When I walked into the hospital all I wanted to do was to see my dad. They took me through to this room and there was nobody in there apart from him. I didn't know what he was going to look like.

'A nurse came by, asked me if I was OK, and pulled back the curtain that surrounded him. He was sitting slightly upright, with his mouth slightly open. I noticed the gold signet ring he used to wear was the wrong way round, so I turned it so that it was proper. When I saw him later I asked everyone to leave us, and spoke to him: "If football has done this to you, Dad, I promise you I'll make sure the whole world knows, and I'll get justice for you."'

Though his death has contemporary relevance, Astle was a man of his time, a working-class hero of mining stock whose father died in a pit accident when he was a toddler. He stuffed his hand-me-down football boots with paper to make them fit but could never afford a ball. He learned the art of heading at Notts County with his friend Tommy Lawton, who was also to die from dementia.

Those supporters who stood on graveyard walls to touch his coffin, as it was borne into a church funeral prior to cremation, related to his natural humility. He lived in a club-owned semi-detached, where an old goalpost was used to anchor a washing line. Before he returned triumphantly from Wembley, neighbours laid a red carpet to the front door, which could not be opened since it was blocked by hundreds of thank you cards. Jeff had to retrieve the key to the back door from underneath a plant pot.

Dawn's fulfilment of that private promise gave her father's life greater weight than a nostalgic yearning for lost innocence. The 'Justice for Jeff' campaign she launched in his name in 2014 has led to cravenly delayed but far-reaching research that promises to force football to confront the possibility that, to use her phrase, 'it is a killer'.

The football industry's ambivalence is camouflaged by professionally packaged promises of corporate commitment and stimulated by suspicions of financial consequence. Those in positions of authority were in denial from the initial inquest in 2002, when Andrew Hague, the coroner, found Astle had died from an 'industrial disease' – dementia brought on by the repeated trauma of heading the ball.

The family, invited into a side room by the coroner to compose themselves before addressing journalists who instinctively understood the ramifications of the verdict, were stunned by the clinical distillation of the damage inflicted by constant blows to the head.

Descriptions of a club legend and former England international suffering from so-called 'boxer's brain' demanded an official response.

The Football Association and Professional Footballers' Association (PFA) promised to prioritise a ten-year longitudinal study, which was never published after sustained prevarication. The Astles received two letters from the governing body during the mourning process. The first, from FA solicitors, counselled against legal action. The second offered tickets to an England friendly, but specified that Laraine could take only one of her three daughters to the match.

'Two tickets ... is that what my dad's life was worth?'

The enduring anger is palpable. Dawn sweeps her hands backwards through long, straight fair hair, emphasising a firm jaw and a steely gaze. The waxy pallor of PFA chief executive Gordon Taylor, when she condemned him in front of TV cameras for an egregious throwaway line that 'my mother's got dementia and she's never headed a ball', becomes instantly understandable.

It was the spring of 2014 before an examination of Jeff's brain, stored at Queen's Medical Centre in Nottingham, site of his post-mortem, led Dr Willie Stewart to conclude he had suffered from chronic traumatic encephalopathy (CTE), the degenerative condition that has reached epidemic proportions in American football.

The NFL, a totemic symbol of American society that has political influence beyond even the Premier League and its export-driven eminence, spent nearly 20 years fighting association with the disease before, with legal caveats, it promised $765 million to provide medical assistance to more than 18,000 former players, covered by a class action suit.

In a statement, the NFL stressed its commitment to 'supporting scientific research into CTE and advancing progress in the prevention and treatment of head injuries'. It pledged another $100 million 'for independent medical research and engineering advancements in neuroscience related topics'.

The parallels with Astle's case were portentous, but Dawn's motives were personal, since she was galvanised by a conviction that her father was a martyr to his sport. Though she had never previously written an email outside the workplace or owned a laptop, she became the figurehead of a media-conscious, strategically effective and emotionally inclusive campaign that broke down football's tribal loyalties and exposed the fears of generations of players.

There were flashes of dissidence, in which Dawn considered protesting at the FA's Wembley headquarters by 'smashing every window in the place', but her father's cause gained irresistible momentum through an inaugural Astle Day at the Hawthorns, which triggered nationwide support through the football supporters' movement.

A tipping point, of sorts, was reached when Greg Dyke, who adopted a conciliatory approach in the latter stages of his chairmanship of the FA, apologised for the conduct of his predecessors during an hour-long meeting. Dr Stewart, who accompanied the family, stressed the significance of the case, since the increasing incidence of accidental head injuries, together with the speed and physicality of the modern game, suggested the perils were not limited to the era of heavy, water-infused footballs.

To reinforce the point, he oversaw research at the University of Stirling in Scotland, in which players headed 20 balls fired from a machine calibrated to replicate the pace and power of a well-struck corner kick. The researchers recorded a reduction in memory function of up to two thirds in the 24 hours after the exercise.

Institutionalised caution, at odds with the common humanity that prompted Dyke to promise Jeff's widow 'we are listening now', continued to slow the rate of progress. In February 2017, Fifa, in an all too familiar gesture of expedience, insisted there was 'no true evidence' of the effects of constant, concussive blows to the head in the context of the game.

Almost simultaneously, however, Dr Helen Ling and Professor Huw Morris, of the Institute of Neurology at University College London, confirmed for the first time the presence of CTE in a clinical study of 14 retired footballers who had played from childhood for an average of 26 years and developed dementia in their mid-sixties, ten years earlier than the national average.

It was not until the autumn of that year that the FA and PFA finally commissioned an independent study, led by Dr Stewart, into the long-term effects on 15,000 former players. Its findings will not be available until 2020 at the earliest and the scenario is bleak. A study of 576 athletes by FIFPro, the global players' union, published in October 2017, found that those who had suffered more than six concussions were between two and five times more likely to report common mental disorders.

Researchers at the Albert Einstein College of Medicine in New York found that footballers in their thirties, who had headed a ball in excess of 1,800 times, struggled significantly in memory tests. They used advanced MRI scanning to detect damage to the brain's white matter, a key communication channel that consists of billions of nerve axons, or fibres.

The most influential CTE research is overseen by Dr Ann McKee at the Boston University School of Medicine, where the disease was found in 110 out of 111 deceased former NFL players, whose brains had been donated to scientific study. Symptoms included memory loss, confusion, impaired judgement, aggression, depression, anxiety, impulsive behaviour and suicidal tendencies.

Desperation for the truth can be expressed posthumously. One of the players in that study was Dave Duerson, twice a Super Bowl winner, who committed suicide by propping himself up in bed and shooting himself in the chest with a .38 Special handgun. He left a handwritten note, referring to Boston University, which read 'please see that my brain is given to the NFL's brain bank'.

The outlier in that brain bank (essentially a series of upright refrigerators in which remains are cryogenically frozen and stored in transparent bags) was that of Patrick Grange, a former college soccer player whose death, at 29, was originally misdiagnosed as being a result of Lou Gehrig's disease. Healthy cells are beige in colour; Dr McKee's microscopic examination of his brain tissue revealed dark blotches, a conclusive sign of CTE since it signals the presence of tau, an abnormal protein that kills cells.

Football has much to learn. Its warped tribalism and institutionalised ignorance led to medical fact and professional expertise being challenged when Dr Ross Zafonte, a leading US trauma specialist, confirmed that Liverpool goalkeeper Loris Karius had suffered concussion during the defeat to Real Madrid in the 2018 Champions League final.

His errors were decisive, prompting death threats and a tearful public apology. When Dr Zafonte concluded he had suffered from 'visual spatial dysfunction' rival supporters, amplified by pundits who should have known better, concocted the conspiracy theory that the process was part of a reputation management strategy.

Misplaced machismo is a recurring theme, expressed most starkly when Nordin Amarabat was allowed to play against Portugal, five days after suffering a concussion in a World Cup group match against Iran. Herve Renard, his manager, hailed him as "a warrior". The player removed a protective skull cap fifteen minutes into the game.

Concussion has more subtle, less visible, symptoms than other sports-related injuries. It can involve sensitivity to light and noise, violent headaches, memory impairment and temporary loss of balance. Yet, as Dr Ross Tucker, player welfare consultant to World Rugby, attests, 50 per cent of cases do not involve traditional symptoms, like dizziness, confusion and loss of consciousness.

Rugby's head injury assessment protocol allows a ten-minute substitution for a player to be assessed. Football is currently too consumed by the prospect of competitive advantage to follow suit. As Dr Stewart says: 'The practical reality is every sport interprets to suit their rule book, not the injury, and does pretty much their own thing.'

The sense of time being wasted, and a tragedy inexorably unfolding, is heightened when Dawn hands me a blue, ring-bound A4 notebook. It contains the names of nearly 400 footballers who have died from, or are in the final stages of, dementia. There is a heart-breaking eloquence to her spidery handwritten summaries of the fate of fathers, sons and teammates.

Death confers a strange solidarity. Some are household names, others are lesser lights who shone intermittently in the lower leagues. All mean something special to families, searching for answers to long-suppressed questions. The potential scale of the problem is so big these can only be regarded as token case studies.

They are referred through the charitable foundation Dawn has established in her father's name. Stricken relatives began contacting her immediately after details of Jeff's death were brought to public attention. Supplementary evidence – folders containing reports, research papers and personal testimonies – are stored in several cabinets in the dining room, which feels more like a CID incident room where documents are spread across a gate-legged table.

Dawn's police training has given her an eye for telling detail and historical context. She pulls out a delicate, yellowing cutting from 1958 and an article entitled 'Football's corridors full of punch-drunk footballers'. Delving further back, she produces a photocopy of a report from August 1939 of the death, aged 56, of Charlie Roberts, Manchester United's first superstar, after a seven and a half hour brain operation.

A commanding, broad-shouldered centre half, he had captained United to their first league titles, in 1908 and 1911. His obituary, in the *Manchester Guardian*, observed: 'It was his talent for heading a ball which maybe led to the injury to his skull and brain for which he had entered into the Manchester Royal Infirmary.'

History lends his life a certain irony, since he co-founded the Association of Football Players' and Trainers' Union, the forerunner of the PFA, in response to the penury of the family of his teammate Tommy Blackstock, who collapsed and died on the pitch, at the age of 25, after heading a ball during a reserve team match against St Helens.

The FA tried, briefly, to ban Roberts for life, and ensured he did not add to the three England caps he won before committing the cardinal sin of political pugnacity. Yet he was installed in the Hall of Fame at the National Football Museum in September 2017, and the PFA paid £30,000 to acquire the shirt he wore in leading United to their first FA Cup win, in 1909.

As calls to the Astle Foundation multiplied, a pattern began to emerge. Teammates were linked in death as intimately as they had been in the prime of life. Five of Aston Villa's 1957 FA Cup-winning team had died of Alzheimer's or dementia-related issues, as had five of the Kilmarnock team that won the Scottish League in 1965. Four of Tottenham Hotspur's Double-winning team from the 1960–61 season – Danny Blanchflower, Dave Mackay, Peter Baker and Ron Henry – succumbed similarly. The mortality of legends found its greatest symbolism in the plight of England's World Cup-winning team; Martin Peters, Nobby Stiles and the late Ray Wilson had their memories stolen by dementia-related disease.

Relatives reported less celebrated figures suffering in the shadows. A widow in Bristol revealed that ten former footballers, stricken with the disease, were receiving respite care in a single home. Haunted by the ramifications, Dawn found herself waking in the small hours, stealing downstairs, and conducting internet searches on her iPad until first light.

'It was like, what the bloody hell is happening? Half the team? That can't be right. It just blew my mind. I never thought in a million years it would involve this many people. I thought, Jesus Christ, how big is this? Have they covered this up? Is this why they don't want to do anything, because of what they might unravel? All these players are dying of dementia and they've done nothing about it? Oh, my life. It consumed me.'

She attended funerals at her own expense, found herself the conduit of so much pain, fear, anger and confusion. The line between a sense of duty and obsession became blurred. More anonymously supplied case studies came through the post. Her evenings were spent on the telephone, conducting what amounted to informal therapy sessions.

'They're not five-, ten-minute calls. I can be on the phone for two hours to someone who just wants to tell me about their dad. I hear, too many times, from families who are worried that they are going to lose their homes, or have to sell everything their dad has won in the game, to pay the care bills. It's just wrong, so wrong.

'Just think what those players meant to people. There's me, muddling along, not having a clue what I'm doing half the time. I've got the will, but not the resources to help. The authorities have got the resources, they've got the people, but they haven't got the will. All this could have been addressed years ago. In the meantime, all these poor players are dying, never knowing that they've been a footballer. It's just dreadful.

'You don't know who to turn to. You just don't know what to do. There are hundreds of families relying on us, but the sad thing is, and it makes me ill at times, is whatever I say to them, there's never any good news. These poor guys will never get better. I would have walked to the bloody Moon for my dad, but there's nothing I could have done. There's no glimmer of hope.

'I come off the phone at times absolutely drained, totally drained. I literally just go straight to bed. If I haven't eaten then I'm not bothered. I listen, give my honest opinion. They want to talk about the stages Dad went through, to compare or prepare. I have learned to gauge how upset they are, and whether I can broach the subject of brain donation, because that is vital.'

Dawn has a vision of establishing a brain bank, similar to that driving research in the United States, where Dr McKee has made a breakthrough in being able to detect CTE in living tissue, and a nationwide network of care homes for former footballers, along the lines of the Leonard Cheshire homes for former servicemen and women. More recent players, led by Alan Shearer, have pledged to donate.

She is scathing about the lack of pastoral care available through the PFA, and supported by the weight of evidence accumulated by Jeremy Wilson, the campaigning *Daily Telegraph* journalist. According to Dr Mike Sadler, who treated Southampton captain Kevin Moore, the first player from the Premier League era to die from dementia, Gordon Taylor was 'fairly dismissive' of evidence he provided to him in early 1994.

In mitigation, the union did lead lobbying for the UK to adopt the US policy of banning heading for children under the age of ten, and limiting it to 30 minutes a week for those aged between 11 and 13. The US Soccer Federation's Concussion Initiative was partially a response to a class action lawsuit, filed in a district court in California.

Taylor Twellman, a former US national team player with New England Revolution, received death threats when he advocated extending the ban to children under 14 because he was supposedly jeopardising the progress of 'a new generation of Messis'. Such reflexive rancour and grotesque ignorance may increasingly define social media, but it also hints at the sensitivity of the subject.

The long-term effect of activity-related concussion is a global issue that ensnares such diverse contact sports as rugby, wrestling and bull-riding, but football's ubiquity lends it unique significance. The debate triggered by Jeff Astle's case features uncomfortable challenges to those of us who have grown up in an era in which discomfort in the name of endeavour is soothed by rose-tinted romanticism.

The hungover Sunday morning footballer, ploughing through a peat-bog pitch in the pouring rain, giving and taking knocks without fear or favour, represents the fleeting triumph of a muddied oaf in a world obsessed by superficial perfection. Yet perversely, the coach who expects his players to play through the proverbial pain barrier, and thinks nothing of using moral blackmail as a motivational tool, is also lionised.

Many would balk at the sanitisation of a sport that trades on notions of sacrifice, collective commitment and a third party's pain. Iconic images, such as that of a wide-eyed, blood-drenched Terry Butcher, evoke visceral admiration. Professional football is inherently insecure, since a player is only ever one bad tackle, or incident of ill-fortune, away from retirement, but those who do succumb to serious injury have the mystique of fallen heroes.

The rules of the game, first drawn up in handwritten form by solicitor Ebenezer Cobb Morley and approved at a meeting of the newly founded Football Association at Lincoln's Inn Fields in London on 8 December 1863, would be substantially different if they were to be redrafted in today's risk-averse, health and safety conscious society.

Weight of evidence hangs heavily on those former players in their forties and fifties, who admit to being keenly aware of any sign of mental degradation. The current generation are better protected, through legislation enacted for the 2014–15 season, which decreed any player suffering a head injury would not be allowed to return to the pitch before assessment by a doctor.

A key ally of Dr McKee, former wrestler Chris Nowinski, founder of the Concussion Legacy Foundation, put the issue into sobering perspective when he told *National Geographic*: 'People are so concerned about the legal and financial implications that no one is going to admit it until we force them to. This is a threat to profits.

'The sports that can keep the spotlight off themselves the longest with regards to this issue are the ones which will attract the most children. I worry that part of the reason they are not owning up to the problem in soccer is because they want the sport to succeed potentially more than they want the players to succeed.'

Parallels between the Astles and the Hillsborough families are imperfect, yet inescapably relevant. The 96 faced a longer wait for truth and justice, and had arguably a greater wrong to excise, but both campaigns harnessed the power of ordinary people in the face of official interference and disdain to help change the system.

Dawn Astle is seized by the spirit of solidarity: 'Football owes football supporters a huge debt of gratitude, for their sheer determination and raw bloody-mindedness, in carrying our fight to the four corners. For refusing to be cowed, for not simply lapsing into silence and going away, when the game and its institutions seemingly didn't want to hear.

'It will always stand as an object lesson to us all, of the power that ordinary people, driven by an extraordinary cause, can still wield, even in the face of extraordinary odds. If I thanked those people, every day of my life, it wouldn't be enough. We were called scaremongers, compensation chasers, but I am fiercely loyal, very protective of my family.'

To reinforce the point, she invites her visitor to compare photographs of her father, early in his career at Notts County, and her 19-year-old son Matthew. 'Peas in a pod, aren't they? They both started on the left wing, and both had the habit of standing with their hands on hips during a break in play. Matt has his mannerisms, his laugh and, above all, his smile.'

I remark that her smile completes the set. 'I tend to be crying more than smiling these days,' she says, with a sadness that deserves to remain on the game's conscience until it is cleansed by the conclusion that Jeff Astle died so that others can live. As we will discover, football preys on many forms of weakness.

CHAPTER TWO

Perfectly Imperfect

'I've lost count of the number of times I've sat with young guys in tears. My conversations expose them to a ruthlessness that's paramount, a ruthlessness they don't understand. The lies, the insincerity, the constant lack of trust. The mental health issues that arise as players move through the system, and away from their God-given talent. It's the industry, so let's prepare them for brutal reality.' – Drewe Broughton

Ron Alfred led a life of quiet achievement after fleeing the Indo-Pakistani war of 1971. A successful figure in IT recruitment, he settled in Milton Keynes and followed football through his sons, whose natural talent was never fully realised in academies at Chelsea and Norwich City. Along the way he met a journeyman player named Drewe Broughton.

Over a decade, as Broughton eked out a 17-year career that encompassed 516 appearances for 22 clubs, the barriers came down. The footballer shared his fears and frustrations as he sought a deeper meaning to his struggle for self-worth. They developed a rare intimacy, a confessional relationship that defied the conventions of professional sport.

When Alfred was on his death bed, in the final stages of terminal cancer, he removed his oxygen mask to utter his last words to his friend: 'Make sure you lead. You are a leader of men.' The memory has lost none of its power; a framed photograph of the pair sits on the desk where Broughton organises his new life as a performance coach.

His work is so emotionally intense he limits himself to a maximum of ten clients; two are golfers, the rest footballers who pay him to provide holistic support they feel uncomfortable accessing at their clubs. Personalised fitness programmes address the wear and tear of an increasingly physical game; private soul-searching sessions coax deep-rooted mental health issues into the open.

Predictably, his words carry a contradictory sense of wistfulness and urgency. 'Ron made it all right to be me. He was my mentor, my crutch. He saw why I never really fitted in many dressing rooms. I was intelligent, sensitive, bright, but to survive I thought I needed to be aggressive and tough. They can throw as much money at football as they like, but you can't buy enlightenment.

'The great taboo in the game is its spiritual side. The minute we use that word, fucking hell, all hell breaks loose. You need an enlightened leader, saying "we need to change this". There's still a grey area in the human being that scientists can't fathom. For me, it's the spirit. What Ron and I had was a spiritual connection, complete alignment. It was beautiful.

'I'll be honest, I've always regarded myself as a natural leader. This is my crusade. Why are we haemorrhaging talent? Football will never change until coaches look into their deepest, darkest places and work through their issues. Players are going into coaching without addressing the shit they have had to go through in their careers. They're damaged. Sub-consciously, they go out and put that on the next generation.

'I think I can get inside young players and unlock their feelings. I lead people back to themselves. The one thing is to stay true to who you are. I went from club to club trying to find myself. I remember Ron saying to me once, "You keep saying that you're shit but have you ever thought you must be quite good? People keep buying you." And then I fell off the face of the earth.'

He landed in a lay-by, just outside Stevenage, trying to sleep in his car, a black VW Passat. He had reached crisis point, personally and professionally. His marriage had collapsed and he had been thrown out of the family home. He had failed to keep Lincoln City in the Football League, a definitive low in a career that promised so much when he scored on his Norwich debut at Wolves at the age of 17.

He sought help through the PFA and was admitted to the Sporting Chance clinic, where his addictive personality was quickly defined. The process of self-discovery began immediately when, in a familiar ritual at the Hampshire retreat, a therapist encouraged him to acknowledge his powerlessness. It was a form of rebirth, the first step in reconfiguring an ego-driven existence.

'I can't go, well, I'm a footballer – no you're not. I've got my flash car – no, you haven't. I've got my house – no, you haven't. I couldn't grab on to anything. I was left in a room with me. Bones. Muscles. Spirit. That was it. I was clearly an addict. The next fix, the next game, the next club. What transpired was that had developed into a sex and love addiction, the Tiger Woods syndrome.

'The most powerful part of the process of recovery is sitting in a room and baring your soul, saying to the group "this is me". It's very freeing to take a cloak off and say "I'm human". You realise you are not alone when you hear people responding, saying "yeah, I was feeling the same". Mental health and high performance, excellence, are, for me, bedfellows.

'A talented kid is a couple of bad decisions away from life-changing failure. If he has poor mental health he will start to second-guess himself, lose trust in who he is. The biggest problem is that loss of self. The ego creates a false sense of who you are. I was walking around going, I'm Drewe Broughton. People know who I am. I elbowed him, I smashed his jaw. They're not going to mess me around. It was something that I held myself up to be, because I didn't know who the fuck I was.'

He studied biomechanics for four years, specialising in movement patterns and injury prevention, and abandoned a psychotherapy degree after a year because he failed to see its practical relevance. Football had already given him a bitter insight into human behaviour; the game took little pity on him as he funded his education by playing part-time at four non-League clubs.

'The word on me was "a fucking good pro. Tough. First here, last away." People would go, "you wouldn't fuck with him would you? Was he lazy? No, he was fucking crazy." I did yoga before yoga became fashionable. I ran in the Alps by myself, training three times a day for three summers so I could get back for pre-season and humiliate my teammates.

'When I was eighteen, pre-season against Man City at Carrow Road, I was walking across the edge of the box, and bang. I got Gerry Taggart's right hook. He said something like "you little fucker". The shame is, I did that to people when I got older. I apologise for that because it's wrong, but that's how lost I was. I was thinking I had to do that to show I was tough.

'At the end I was depressed, broken, empty. There was just no fuel left in the tank. It felt like I was running around with a caravan-load of crap on my back. I was mentally, emotionally gone. I was getting bullied by kids in the Conference South, kids I would have eaten up and spat out a couple of years earlier. I used to drive home and my soul was broken.'

The scars are difficult to detect. Approaching 40, he is lean, open-faced, soft-voiced and naturally engaging. Delve deeper into the consequences of football's expedient dishonesty, however, and the eyes narrow. There is a hint of exasperation, a suggestion of a quick temper. For all his inside knowledge, he has an outsider's restlessness.

Football's dream factories depend on a suspension of disbelief, an acceptance that the game's lacerating edges can be smoothed by welfare programmes that fail to address private fear and institutionalised insecurity. Even the survivors of the system are so wary of others equating vulnerability with weakness they carefully construct an alternative reality.

One of Broughton's clients, an England Under-21 international, regularly cries himself to sleep at night; his social media profile, an achingly fashionable mixture of street smarts and knowing humour, gives no indication of the inner struggle.

It is no surprise to learn that a competitively successful season coaching the under-14s in Luton's academy earmarked Broughton as an iconoclast: 'I remember sitting in the dressing room with the group. The director of football was in there, and three or four others with clipboards. I didn't know who they were. A London representative team was coming down to play. It was horrific: pissing it down, freezing, gale force winds. The Champions League was on TV that night.

'I sat the lads down and explained that, rather than training, we would be playing. I said, "Look, boys, the truth is it is shit out there. I'll be honest, when I used to play in these games on Tuesday nights, and others said they loved it under the lights, I fucking hated it. It's freezing cold. I just want to be at home: sofa, film, some chocolate biscuits and a cup of tea. Does anyone feel like that?

'Well, one of the brave ones, Jack, a full back, a tough little bastard, he put his hand up and said "I do". So I said, "Anyone else? Because I'll be honest with you, I don't really want to be here tonight either."

'Everyone had a bit of a laugh about it, but I saw the coaches shuffling around nervously and gestured towards them: "Boys, these fuckers will judge you, say you're not good enough, not tough enough, don't want it enough. And it's all bullshit really. I don't want to be out there, you don't want to be out there, so it's a choice you've got to make. It looks like for the next hour and a half you've got to switch your head on, you've got to run and you've got to push. I'm trying to validate the truth here.

'"You want to be a footballer. What makes you stand out is desire, hunger, the games on crap pitches where you have to drive yourselves on, and run, and get your lungs burning. Never forget or disrespect those values. A nice flick or turn, or staying in the shape, that ain't it. Zero crowd, get after people, press, tackle, win the ball. Get through the voice that says, you can't make the box, I'm fucked, and drive through it. That's what makes a pro.'"

A powerful point had been made, with scant regard for professional convention. Broughton accepted he would have to work as a self-styled 'lone wolf' because he could not come to terms with the concept of compromise. 'I didn't have the stomach for the internal fight. In the system it would have been day after day, disagreeing, falling out. I didn't have the energy for it after seventeen years of playing. I was like, fuck it. At least if I do it myself, I don't have to answer to anyone.'

His aim is to empower, manage emotion and nurture creativity. It requires mutual trust and reflects the disconnect that exists in elite sport, where material reward and superficial celebrity are not the panacea to deepseated personal problems. Football's uneasy relationship with mental health issues, triggered by the suicide of Gary Speed in November 2011, has yet to be reconciled.

The dangers posed by the dynamics of a globally celebrated game played by rich young men are subtle but self-fulfilling. Millennial lifestyles are based on the perception of perfectionism, magnified by a culture of digital deceit. Elite sport encourages obsession and introspection. In its most extreme form, fear of failure, or exposure to criticism, is life-threatening. Even in milder forms, it is insidious.

Football's timeline of self-destruction runs from George Best to Paul Gascoigne, for whom the game held its breath when he re-emerged as a brittle, blindly enthusiastic public figure in early 2018. The searing testimonies of players like former England goalkeeper Chris Kirkland and footballer-turned-boxer Leon McKenzie, who trained normally the morning he was discharged from hospital following an attempted overdose, have helped to encourage an understanding of depression.

Dermot Drummy, whom I knew as a warm, kind and caring man, was found dead in woodland behind his home in the Hertfordshire town of Hoddesdon in November 2017, six months after he had been sacked as Crawley Town manager. He had been undergoing counselling for his 'low mood' and left a letter for his family which ended with the entreaty 'I hope you forgive me'.

England Under-19 footballer Zoe Tynan, a 'vibrant, generous and fun-loving girl' according to her grief-stricken family, died from multiple injuries when she stepped in front of a Birmingham to Liverpool train at West Allerton station in August 2017, soon after she had moved from Manchester City to Fylde Ladies. Her legacy is 'Zoe's rule', an informal reminder to FA coaches to be sensitive when passing on bad news.

Clarke Carlisle, diagnosed as suffering from Complex Depressive Disorder for 13 of his 17 years as a pro, survived two extensively publicised suicide attempts before setting up a charitable foundation that has as its founding goal the establishment of a treatment facility by 2022. His description of 'a duplicitous life of external lauding and internal loathing' will strike a chord with many of his peers.

'There are many, many people out there who feel exactly as I do,' he told ITV's *This Morning* programme. 'They feel they are a burden to their family, that they're not worthy of oxygen, never mind space on the earth. You need to know that other people feel like that and it is not true. It is your illness telling you a lie.'

Achievement offers no protection from the demon of self-doubt; one of the greatest Olympians, American swimmer Michael Phelps, winner of 23 gold medals, sought help after several suicidal episodes. Awareness is another flimsy shield; rugby union player Dan Vickerman, who oversaw player welfare programmes after representing Australia 63 times, was 37 when he took his own life in February 2017, on the day he was due to give a keynote address on hidden stresses assailing the retired athlete.

Extravagant praise and obvious promise applies its own pressure. Washington State quarterback Tyler

Hilinski, acclaimed as a future NFL draft pick at the age of 21, took a former teammate's .223 calibre rifle and shot himself in January 2018. He was found to have been in the early stages of CTE. Madison Holleran, a college track star, leapt to her death at the age of 19; the first line of her suicide note, released by her parents, read: 'I don't know who I am anymore. trying. trying. trying.'

It is the ubiquity of depression, and the instructive memory of his struggle to compartmentalise the conflicting stresses of professional sport, that convinces Broughton of the need to prioritise mental health. He works in a vale of tears; the breakthrough in many of the relationships he forms tends to occur when his client summons the moral courage to cry in front of him.

'It's emotional. I can see the fear in their eyes, because I know it. I still experience fear every day. I'm human. You can't ignore fear. It's an energy, which you need to get rid of. So you go drinking. You sit in a casino. You visit a brothel. Or you over-train. You ignore everything and you push yourself harder. When that fear manifests itself, I try to look at the worst-case scenario.

'Your train of thought goes, shit, if I don't play well tonight I'm dropped.

'The next thought will be, well, if I'm dropped it's going to be weeks before I get back in the team.

'The next thought goes, if it's weeks before I'm in the team and I'm in the reserves on Tuesday nights, fuck, I'm never going to get there. It's another wasted season.

'The thoughts keep coming: my contract runs out in a year; who's going to want me because I've been on the bench for seven months? I'm going to lose confidence and I'm going to have to get another job; the missus won't want that and then she'll leave me . . . .

'All of a sudden you're in a place where the last thought is, well, what's the point?'

Recognising and responding to physical signs of stress, such as shortness of breath and muscular tension, is relatively easy. Many athletes struggle with the complementary approach, which involves combatting the destructive power of the imagination by challenging its logic. To reinforce the point, Broughton acts out a comparatively straightforward coping strategy.

'Let's go back to that first thought, "Well, what if I get dropped tonight?" Well, what if you don't? Why would you get dropped? "Well, if I give the ball away." Why would you give the ball away? I've seen you, your touch is unbelievable, your link-up play is top. Technically you can't trap a ball and pass it? "Well, yeah, I can." So why would you give the ball away then? "Err . . . well, OK. I guess I can't give it away."

'But you can't control that. "What do you mean I can't control that?" Well you can't. Just control what you can. "So what's that?" Well, just fucking run. Be part of the team. Don't isolate yourself with your own thoughts and think, I've got to do this tonight. Go and talk to someone. Say to that midfielder, "If I give that ball away tonight I'll get it back and I'll run". We can't do things by ourselves. We're a pack animal, and we need to be in a collective, be part of something.'

The dressing room is the crucible in which team spirit is supposedly forged by the white heat of anticipation. It is a place of sacramental urgency, desperate desire, ceremonial pretence. Painkillers are swallowed, nasal passages are cleared, voices are raised, huddles are formed. Bellowed protestations of loyalty to a benighted band of brothers are, so often, the manifestation of private insecurity.

Broughton laughs, fondly. 'Ah, that's it. That's the dressing room. The zoo. I thought that was what I had to do. I'd be watching movies on a Saturday morning – *Any Given Sunday* or *Gladiator*, trying to find something. What was I looking for? I had that conversation with one of my players – what are you looking for at that time? They are actually looking for themselves, funnily enough.

'I played with Stuart Nethercott at Wycombe, and he's a legend. He used to vomit before a game. It is what it is. I did it all. I stood in tunnels shouting. I'm embarrassed today really. What was I doing? I wasn't doing that when I was eight, or nine, coming off with the match ball. So why was I doing it at twenty-five?

'Looking back, my best games were when the buzzer went at five to three, and everyone went "rahhh". I just sat there and transcended it. I'd almost go the other way. I'd take my time, have a flapjack or a banana, and watch the chaos. It was almost like I was outside myself. People shouting "come on!". I was sat in the middle of them and it went over my head.

'I'd delay it, walk over to the sink, put some water on my face. Now we're being shouted at to get in the tunnel. I'd be like, I'll be there, there's no rush. And you can hear the assistants whispering, "Is he all right?" Yeah, I'm good. You? Into the tunnel, lean against the wall, arms crossed, just really in a comfortable place with myself. Those were my best games. Probably thirty of them in five hundred odd. What's that, five per cent at best? Tragic, really.

'What was I doing? I was basically going, I'm good enough. There's nothing I'm going to find by shouting. There's nothing I'm going to find by standing in the tunnel eyeballing the centre half. I had a great week, trained my bollocks off Monday, Tuesday. I trained extra until three, went to the gym. Yesterday I got an hour and a half massage at home with a guy that came over. Physically, I'm like a fucking racehorse. I'm ready. So there's nothing to be worried about.

'If you look at the best players in the world, that's how they stand in the tunnel. Ibrahimović, Messi, those kinds of characters. They're not frightened of anything. Study the Champions League tunnels, the elite of the elite. They are shaking hands and hugging and completely comfortable. That's why they are the best of the best. Everyone else is trying to find something.'

Broughton's search for self, in the seven years since he reached his lowest point, has incorporated organised religion. He attended church services for a year, consulted with a priest to clarify his beliefs. Conscious of the tranquillity of worship and the relevance of spirituality in personal and professional relationships, he studied the Bible.

'It's the most published book in the history of mankind, so there's got to be something in there. It aligned with everything I believed, but for me it was a series of stories. I couldn't sign up for miracles, water turning into wine and people walking across water. But we can't ignore the lines in there by this teacher, mentor of his time, who was saying, "Be still, I am God. Be still."

'That's what I say to players. Be still. There's nothing for you to go and find. Me in the dressing room? Be still. I'm at peace. The great meditators, great theologians, all these people down the years are saying the same things. Chill. But the academy system won't let you chill. Football won't let you chill, because it is run by people who need to win. It just creates such pressure. I talk about the illusion of need. You don't need to win, in the literal sense. You need to eat. You need to breathe.'

Supporters see the fripperies of fame, the superficialities of a footballer's social status. What truths are obscured by the fluorescent boots and the fashionable bling? What flaws are hidden by shallow protestations of confidence and the endless flattery of the entourage?

Who is the person Broughton recognises when the player's mask is removed?

'We're all human. And I think we're all perfectly imperfect. We're all going to feel, regardless of how intelligent you are perceived to be, or how successful people think you are. I grew up watching Wayne Rooney. He was the next great hope at eighteen, when he broke out at Euro 2004. When he broke his metatarsal before the 2006 World Cup, for me, as a fan, he never hit that form again.

'That ability to just go past people? Gone. That fleetness of foot, power, acceleration? Gone. People will say, "Oh, it's because of the wear and tear, the games under his belt". I studied biomechanics so I'm qualified to talk about that, and that's not true. How then can you still have players playing well in their thirties who have had as much wear and tear?

'It's a mental freedom I think. And far be it for me to judge Wayne Rooney, because the pressures he must have carried are frightening, but I think we'll lose a player, because at some point that child-like spontaneity that he walked in with at eighteen, it's gone. I've learned along the way that we can only give what we've got to give.

'Life is an education. My daughter is six, and I try to validate her feelings. When we were walking to school on her first day I asked her how she felt. "A bit scared, in my tummy." That's OK, I used to be scared all the time.

"What, when you played football, Daddy?" All the time. And I said, you've got to take a deep breath and just go in there and see what happens.

'We live in a world where it's not all right to feel. It's ridiculous. They talk in football all the time about how they have teams of experts who build the body, and psychologists who build the mind. They have tacticians who teach young players about shapes and formations, so they will have knowledge and wisdom. But what about the other side: spontaneity, creativity, sensitivity?'

Football fetishises toughness, elevates sacrifice beyond rationality. Players are conditioned to suppress their true selves. They may pull up in the car park in a personalised Range Rover and appear to relish the bitter humour of the dressing room, but coaches do not take enough time to strip away the layers of bravado.

'There's this great myth about what's tough. I get pissed off when I hear people regurgitate the view that modern kids are too weak. The best are strong, self-driven. They've been the best from the age of nine, and they've pushed themselves hard. They may get too much too young, but don't waste your breath on that. That ain't going to change. It's going to get worse.

'Take, as an example, the young lad I work with from the England Under-21s. Sure, he's got his house, his contract, his car. But that doesn't take away who he is. That hasn't dulled his desire. We've got him to the point where his running stats are the best at the football club.

Yet his manager says to him, "I look at you; nice watch, you've got a lot of money for a young guy".

'Why is he even saying that? He's inviting the lad to a dark place. Does the manager know he cries himself to sleep? This lad is a natural. He wants to be one of the best in the world. He spends his evenings in his bedroom watching clips of Ronaldinho, pausing it, looking at moves, trying to work them out. But the word on him in football is that he's a big-time Charlie.

'The lack of emotional intelligence in the way players are treated blows me away. Should the ex-player be the coach? I've played with a million players who are completely unaware of their own emotions, because they are locked down. I've sat with too many coaches who say it is always someone else's fault ....'

He tails off and exhales deeply. Dilemmas drain him. He drives more than 50,000 miles a year to supervise sessions, watch matches, provide moral support. He mainlines the anguish of his clients and takes calls at all hours. He is a confessor, surrogate brother, and occasionally the deliverer of uncomfortable truths.

One of his players, a former teammate, is an ex-international whose career, launched in the Premier League, is winding down, inexorably, in League One. He is 30 and talks urgently and optimistically about his goals. The easy option would have been to foster the illusion of renewal; the following conversation, as recounted by Broughton, had brutal clarity:

'This is hard for me because you're not a kid. You've got kids. I don't really want to go here because we're mates. But let me tell you. It's not going to happen. I watch you train and you're not working hard enough.'

'Yeah? … Mate, you're killing me, but I respect you. What am I not doing?'

'You're spending money on this coach, and that guru, but you've stopped chasing and chasing and chasing. I remember when I was a senior pro. When you came into the team at seventeen you were brilliant. You'd chase everything down, run off the bench with fifteen minutes to go. I'm playing up front by myself trying to take on two big centre halves and you're like, "I'll do your running!".

'Now you're coming on and you're flicking at things. You think you've earned the right. And it breaks my heart because you're going to end up like me, thirty-three, thirty-four, you'll retire, you'll look back and you'll go, fucking hell, if only I'd known. You've lost that humility to go and do what you used to do.'

That tableau of tough love finds as its counterpoint the tenderness in Broughton's relationship with Steve Caulker, the former England defender who lost hundreds of thousands of pounds, as well as the last vestiges of self-respect, when he was in denial of the consequences of an addictive, depressive personality that took him to the brink of suicide.

Football views cynically Caulker's determination to rebuild his career and life through Broughton's additional training, which has enabled him to overcome long-standing hip and groin injuries. He attends meetings with both Gamblers and Alcoholics Anonymous, having made his last bet in December 2016 and taken his last drink in March 2017.

He speaks compellingly of the perspective acquired during low-key charity work in Sierra Leone, yet an admission that his ability 'is a gift but also a curse', and his refusal to disguise the damage inflicted by sequential, chaotic behaviour, appeared to count against him when he left Queens Park Rangers by mutual consent just before the transfer window opened in January 2018.

'It was a terrible set of circumstances,' reported Broughton, who refuses to accept payment for what are, in effect, counselling sessions with a close friend. 'Someone put the word around, "He's a bad egg, don't touch him". The reality is that Steve is an exceptional character. He is only twenty-five and I enjoy having him in my life. He is one of the few people in my career I have felt simpatico with.'

Caulker, theoretically an attractive proposition as a free agent, found that four separate deals to play in Italy suddenly evaporated. English clubs maintained their distance, though Karl Robinson offered him the chance to train with Charlton Athletic, and he signed for Dundee following an unsuccessful trial in Germany.

In many ways, football magnifies a dislocated society. A UK Government commission reported in 2017 that more than nine million British adults admitted to being 'often or always lonely'. A complementary study by UC Berkeley found that, despite having larger social networks, adults between the ages of 20 and 30 reported twice as many days feeling lonely or isolated than a similar group aged between 50 and 70.

These are the themes to which Broughton returns, as he talks to youth groups about depression and the danger of retreating into oneself. He is affronted that, in an age in which Premier League clubs are starting to employ DNA testing as a means of confirming physical potential, the mind is seen as being as distant and forbidding as the dark side of the Moon.

'I felt so fucking lonely as a player. I still feel lonely today. It is my overriding emotion every day. I have complete identification with Steve. I told him I was driving through Starbucks the other day. There was this guy taking his time, and this voice went through my head: "Get out, drag him out of his car and knock him out. Leave him there, smash his car and drive past him."

'I don't like that voice. Steve said it had spoken to him at QPR, two days after he returned to training. This new forward dropped his hips left and right and shifted the ball. The voice said, "Who the fuck are you?" Steve left him in a heap and walked back to the centre. You can do that with your boots on and even if that was a foul, you'd still get a well done. In real life, of course, you can't start doing that, but that voice was certainly there for me, as a player.'

I wonder whether it ever says 'well done' to him, as he fights the system, prejudice and the complexities of the human condition? He laughs loudly before pausing for what seems an eternity.

'There's your answer, in the silence . . . .'

CHAPTER THREE

Banged Up

'My daughter is sixteen months old. She's too young to know where Daddy is but I am missing her life, her first step, her first word. I've not changed her nappy. This place is full of spies, and I tell no one that I used to be a footballer. If they ask, I was a bricklayer. If I told them the truth they'd think I was completely stupid, because they'd kill for the chance I had.' – David Manton

The eyes are drawn naturally to the goalkeeper's hands. His fingers, long, broad and rough-skinned, are intertwined. It is only when they are opened, to express a point, that they reveal their secrets: two rudimentary tattoos that deface rather than decorate. The first, on his right palm, screams 'Fuck You'. The second, along the inside of the left index finger, warns a stranger to 'Jog On'.

The air is sucked out of the bare, small room by David Manton's professions of remorse. He leans forward, with an unwavering gaze; comfortingly, my field of vision expands to include a green, bulbous panic button on the wall. A white-shirted prison officer is at the end of the corridor; in the opposite cubicle a dreadlocked probation officer is meeting his client.

Rochester jail in Kent had been in lockdown on our arrival, owing to 'an incident in the grounds'. We were ushered through a series of secure zones, across a court-yard and along the back of a football pitch protected by a high wire fence to a functional two-storey building. A poster in the entrance hall proclaimed: 'Count the days. Make the days count.'

Manton, convicted of conspiracy to wound with intent, has five months to serve before he is released on licence. Albert Barnes, the charity worker who will ease his transition into the outside world, is soft-voiced but knowing and, above all, purposeful: 'Tell me the truth. I will not hold it against you.' The mood eases when Manton starts to tell his story.

He was taken on by a Premier League club after excelling in a trial against Ajax but released at 15 because of a poor attitude exacerbated by an adolescent experimentation with marijuana. He played well enough in a six-week trial at a League One club to be taken on as a scholar, but was rejected at the end of his second season because of his lifestyle.

48

'When they called me into the office to tell me, I was devastated. I was too busy in that first year, going out drinking and stuff. I really pulled my finger out in the second year, and took things seriously, but that first impression ruined my chances. I had nice boots, good gloves, the best kit, but I didn't understand the privilege of my position.'

His life began to disintegrate when he attempted to revive his football career by lodging with relatives and playing in Australia's second tier. Drugs were too easy an escape, too available. Weed, speed and cocaine blurred the boundaries. He began to miss training sessions and plunged into full-scale addiction when his new girlfriend urged him to try crystal meth.

Methamphetamine, also known by such street names as Ice, Crank, Glass, Yaba, Tina and Christine, is mainly smoked and insidiously addictive. The high is intense, exhilarating and gives the impression of hyper-alertness. The comedown is ruinous and leaves the user feeling agitated, paranoid, confused and aggressive.

'We weren't getting drug-tested at the club and I thought I could take the piss a little bit. I'd had a good pre-season but within two weeks I was hooked. I took my wages a week early until they were stopped because I missed matches. I ignored advice from everyone, had no money, and began to lose weight.

'I was in this circle of addiction, with the wrong people in the wrong place. My girlfriend came with baggage;

she had been a heroin addict since the age of fourteen. I started stealing, fighting, robbing, to feed the habit. I was not earning any legitimate money. Football wasn't even in the back of my mind for twelve months.'

Acting as an enforcer for a drug gang, he was arrested for inflicting actual bodily harm, convicted and deported. He tried to get clean in a rehabilitation unit in Bournemouth but was arrested for an historic offence in the UK and given three years. The pain in his eyes when Barnes tells him 'you have to demonstrate you are willing to change' is intense and convincing.

He served the first part of his sentence in High Down prison, built on the site of a former mental hospital in Banstead, Surrey. There was 'lots of bang-up, lots of time behind the doors'. Denied privileges for using a smuggled mobile phone, he lost his income from a prison job and could not afford to keep in contact with his family until a friend sent small amounts of money.

He pauses and admits 'it's been a long time since I thought of anything positive'. His eyes flick self-defensively towards the ceiling, where two fluorescent strip lights emphasise the pallor of his broad face, and the severity of his cropped hair. Having lost two and a half stones in the previous three months by purging himself in the gymnasium, he estimates he needs to lose a similar amount again before his release.

At 25, he hopes to play part-time and gain coaching qualifications. When I ask what three values, rediscovered through football, would ease his rehabilitation, he chooses hard work, loyalty and motivation. 'I know I have to get my head down and show a good work ethic. I need to repay my mum, who has been brilliant for me. I know I need to change because I want more than this.'

There are parallels between a prison wing and a dressing room. Information is power within each; communication is haphazard and instinctive. New players quickly take stock of their status. They assess who wields influence, gravitate towards them, and adjust to the environment. Similarly, new inmates must quickly learn who sets the unwritten rules and where it is safe to go. Problems tend to be deep-seated and profound.

Ryan Inniss has cut all ties with his father. By the time he captained England at under-16 level he had been homeless, to all intents and purposes, for two years. He lived on his wits, slept on the sofa in a succession of houses occupied by friends, extended family and football people. The precocity of his talent offered a modicum of protection; when the authorities threatened to put him into care, Crystal Palace placed him in club-funded accommodation.

Human warmth, of the kind provided by Errol Johnson, the youth worker, mentor and scout who allowed him to lodge in his home in Catford and ferried him to matches, was a rarity. Johnson is another understated enabler and founder of MAD About Kidz, an 'off the streets' programme of social engagement. Its success is reflected not just by the boys it ushered into professional football, but those it steered into careers in marketing, product development and the law.

Though Johnson works within conventional models, providing sporting opportunity 'in a safe and inclusive environment' for young people deemed at risk of anti-social behaviour, he also has an unofficial role as counsellor to emerging footballers, such as Liverpool's Joe Gomez, who made his England senior debut against Germany in November 2017.

'My mother told me that the best thing I could do in life is serve others, and I have learned that the more you give the more you receive. People in football have found out I am not interested in money. I am not interested in taking the glory. My reward is switching on the TV and seeing someone fulfilling their dream.

'For some, I am the dad they never knew. For others I am a mentor. I understand the vacuum in the lives of so many young people. I go to their level. I was from the streets myself. I know what they are going through. If their mum can't afford a pair of boots I will get them. If they have to travel across England to a trial I will drive them. I am nothing special. There are a lot of unsung heroes out there, doing what they can for their communities, by helping young people to broaden their horizons.'

Johnson sends Gomez daily homilies on WhatsApp. Those delivered on the day he reported for England's World Cup warm-up matches against the Netherlands and Italy in March 2018 were typical. 'Your past does not define you. It prepares you,' read one. 'Integrity isn't something you show others. It is how you behave behind their back,' proclaimed another.

The garlanded young footballer smiled as he showed me them on his mobile phone. 'Errol is an uncle figure. When I was younger he would do anything for me; getting me boots, helping me out, taking me to training. He had a massive impact. He is someone who does it out of the kindness of his heart.

'So many people try to get close to you as a young player. It can be evil. It is down to your judgement of character and what you think their angle is. Why are they doing it? From day one I could read Errol as being clean-hearted and honest. There has never been any business-oriented aspect to it. He is honestly just trying to help and see people progress.

'You have to give credit to the people around you, your family and so on. When you are younger they are the ones who protect you from all that, but as you get older you have to make your own decisions. It is about keeping a solid foundation, a core; my family, my girlfriend, people like Errol. It is about life and being a good person.

'I was eighteen when I left Charlton and moved away from my friends and family; in a new environment and you don't really know what to do or who to be around. It is difficult, but as time passes you adapt. It is part of starting a new life. You just do the things you can to focus on the pitch. Off it things will fall into place, hopefully.'

Inniss readily acknowledges his debt to Johnson, and a degree of guilt. 'I was just bouncing around, getting by on simple trial and error. I didn't know what I was doing, to be honest. But when you're good at football, people start to fawn around you. I'd been the best in my class, my youth team. I'd got an early pro contract and was playing for England. I didn't see the pitfalls. I wasn't on a lot of money, a couple of hundred quid a week, but when you've got by on nothing that's a lot.

'It was manic. I had no real male figure in my life and Errol was fantastic to me. I was in so deep, though, that I started to hide things from him; the gambling, drinking, girls, not applying myself at training. Getting my own flat was the worst decision I've ever made. The way I was living began to contribute to my injuries, and things became ten times worse. I was still going out, getting obliterated. I'd spend whole days in the bookies, spunking my money.'

Inniss turned a £5 stake into a pot worth £995, yet refused to take his winnings until he had exceeded £1,000. Inevitably, given the recurring reality of gambling and the indication it often provides of underlying depression, he lost everything. He received five police cautions for fighting before he was jailed for fourteen weeks for his part in a nightclub brawl.

Instead of making his debut for Southend, his sixth loan club, he spent a week in Belmarsh prison before winning his appeal and being reassigned to community service. Had he not had the foresight to confess to Alan Pardew, his then manager, before his court appearance was confirmed he would have been sacked. Steve Parish, Palace's co-owner, stood by him as he went through a private rite of passage.

'As I sat there, going to Belmarsh in the meat wagon, I hadn't really processed it. My mind was racing. I was put in the top bunk in a three-man bang-up; the two other guys in the cell didn't speak much English and simply gave me the TV remote. Maybe the fear factor made me tired, maybe the door being shut made me feel safe, but I slept like a kid tucked up on Christmas Eve.'

He slept for almost 24 hours and began to write poems and log life lessons on scraps of paper. He set personal targets, fantasised about the places he would visit when freedom was restored. It was a form of emotional healing, re-programming. It gave him a sense of who he was, and what he was in the process of losing.

'Everyone has troubles and I had to come to terms with mine. I knew right from wrong. I'd been in such a cycle of decline that I was oblivious to those who were outright using me. I'd put time into people who didn't give a fuck about me. I finally realised in football that they are going to lick your arse when you do well, but as long as you are aware of that, it doesn't matter.

'I'm a heavy, heavy thinker. I don't want to be that "what if" guy, the one in the pub who tells everyone, "I was a top, top player, you know". The core problem is still out there, because I see younger pros on more money than me making the same mistakes, but no one admits to it because no one wants to be seen as being vulnerable.'

His is a search for male guidance in a rootless world. Other good men have filled the role of surrogate father, from a one-armed neighbour he knew simply as Martin, who paid his subs for his first club, Seymour Villa, to Fred and Bernie Dillon, a father and son who bought his boots and provided hot meals when required.

Inniss's career stabilised briefly at Colchester United, where he began impressively before suffering a recurring shoulder injury in early 2018. He continues to lean on Albert Barnes, as a confidant and counsellor, and has been drawn towards Michael Bennett, the PFA's head of welfare. They identify as players from different generations, from similar backgrounds.

Inniss has the street wisdom to contextualise the weaknesses of conventional support programmes. 'A generic white guy in a suit comes in and is confronted with twenty kids, from different backgrounds, who feel they're being judged. One of them might have not been able to afford to eat the night before. Another one's mum will not have a pot to piss in. A few will have struggled to sleep because they are so worried about their career. Some will sit there, switch off, and think about getting home to play FIFA. No one will stand up and tell the truth.

'Young footballers depend on other people, but trust is hard to establish. If you're not one hundred per cent honest, because you are afraid to get things off your chest, you're not gonna get the help you need. Football is so macho, and players are so proud. They don't know whether they are going to be there for three months or three years. The insecurity of being injured is frightening. There definitely needs to be more of a support system.

'I'm trying to build myself towards being a good person. I want to be a good father, better than the one I had. I want to leave my mark on my family in a positive way. I now wake up in the morning and look forward to football. I might have taken it for granted before and moaned, Oh my God, we don't get this, we don't get that, but I just want to make the most of every opportunity.'

Kevin George is utilising the experience of an eight-year playing career, principally at West Ham and Charlton, in a secondary career as a human performance consultant. He works in clubs, schools and prisons, seeking to develop emotional literacy and a sense of accountability. Coaches, he believes, too often fail to appreciate the social sensitivities of their role.

'Lives outside football affect lives inside football. A kid is used to surviving on the street. If someone stares at him for too long there is an unwritten law that he refuses to look away. To do so would signal that he's someone's whipping boy. This same kid, a talented player, then finds a manager or coach shouting at him.

'There's a clash of cultures. The player feels he has to defend his honour. He either bites back or internalises his resentment. He is seen as having a bad attitude. It is really hard not to criticise the coach in that situation. The boy, who is conditioned to thinking society doesn't think much of him anyway, will not take that sort of treatment without explanation.

'It is sad to see the game lose potentially great players because it does not understand the environment that produces them. Players read the signs; if they are not given a starting team bib in training, for example, they tend to withdraw into themselves. One of my friends struggled to adapt, so that whenever he was dropped, or transferred, he would create an argument so that everything was done on his terms. That way, he felt he justified himself.'

This is not a generation of scabby-kneed urchins who kick a tennis ball, or a tin can, around terraced streets. Football is a wider form of cultural expression, as much of a personal statement as the clothes a young man wears, or the music to which he listens. In this age of official disdain, where signs that demand 'No Ball

Games' are erected on so many estates, modern youth extemporises, and creates football in a new image.

Urban football is closer in spirit to its basketball equivalent in the United States than the traditional 11-a-side model. Freedom is cherished in cages, where congregations are as likely to divide into 20-a-side free-for-alls as definitive two v two games, in which personal pride, peacock pose and exhibitionist skill are paramount. The urban player uses unconventional parts of the foot and values the three-card trickery of the sudden tomahawk chop of a drag-back as much as a spectacular goal from distance.

Colin Omogbehin, head coach of Fulham's Under-18s, has consistently recruited from the cages and amplifies George in stressing the need to marry social and sporting realities. 'The kids are developing their own way of playing football, doing things that might not be seen as expected, or normal in a structured football environment. A lot is self-learnt. What people don't understand is that the kids entering that structured environment are not used to rules, boundaries and discipline.

'A lot of young players with real potential find that difficult, and end up failing, maybe because a coach hadn't understood where they were coming from. No one is prepared to budge. As a coach you have to show patience, an interest in managing the individual, because everyone is different. It is important you let the player know you want to support him to do what is best for him.

'I'm not saying make allowances for bad behaviour but there might be an underlying issue going on. You don't scream and shout at that player in front of everyone; you use a little strategy. You might take him to the side and say quietly, "Look, that's not OK; that's not OK at all. That isn't how we do things." All of a sudden, the player knows you're on his side. He will end up running through brick walls for you.

'It is not a one-size-fits-all approach. Players have different things that make them happy, different things that make them sad. They have different things that affect them. It's up to you, as a coach, to be in a position where you're learning with them and identifying with them. Mentoring is very important because the background a lot of these kids come from is tough.

'There is a real hunger and desire to succeed, but let's not make any bones about it, when you're in an inner city there are so many directions you can turn to. You can get caught up in gang culture. You can get easily influenced, easily distracted and drop out of school.

'We've lost players with fantastic talents. We've lost players that have gone on to play on people's first teams but haven't been able to keep it together. When you try and reach them, even if you've had great relationships with them, they seem oblivious to the message you're trying to get to them until it is too late. They get involved in the wrong things and end potentially a great career.'

Football can be a venal, unprincipled world, but the instinct to help is strong. Five thousand young players have gone through Waterloo FC in the 20 years since it was formed by Arnie Reynolds. His vision is 'of a world where young people are no longer disadvantaged by their financial, geographic or family circumstances, where they can develop their skills and abilities to be successful in the world in their own right and belong to a supportive and inclusive community'.

Broadwater Farm, a calamitous experiment in high-density housing from the late 1960s, has become synonymous with racial tension and urban decay. Home to 4,000 people in Tottenham, in north London, it is such a stigmatised community that milkmen and post-men once refused to operate on the estate, yet football has become a source of positivity and unity.

This is due, almost entirely, to the work of Clasford Stirling. His Broadwater United football academy was set up from an abandoned shop unit in the wake of the 1985 riot, which led to the brutal murder of PC Keith Blakelock. Boys as young as three flock to the so-called Magic Man, who has ushered more than 100 boys into professional clubs and provided a source of stability and discipline for countless more.

'We maximise football as a vehicle to develop youth, mentor and all kinds of different things,' he says.

'Obviously, if they are good enough, I have a very good network with the professional clubs. The ones who aren't, they are in a safe environment where they can learn. I have been given the gift of talking to young people. It is a joy for me to look at people I trained and turned around.'

He is attuned to the rhythms of a community he has served for 38 years. He predicted the 2011 riots, pointing to a combination of aggressive stop-and-search policing and a 75 per cent cut in funding for youth services. The so-called postcode gang war between Broadwater Farm's N17 address and Wood Green (N15) is vicious and liable to flare up without warning.

Victor Olisa, who retired in 2018 as one of the Metropolitan Police's most senior black officers, dealt with the aftermath of the fatal police shooting of Mark Duggan when he became Borough Commander in the area in 2013. He ignored the advice of his colleagues, never to enter the estate unaccompanied, and found social salvation in a football tournament.

'People hear the name Broadwater Farm and think it is a den of iniquity. The notion is that it is dysfunctional. Yet the reality is contrary to that. There are families from a wide variety of backgrounds, just enjoying normality.

'Clasford has been our sounding board, a source of guidance, advice and credibility. He develops a sense of ownership through sport. People are not going to destroy their own environment. Through him, young people have something to do. Football is affordable, constructive and pleasurable. He engages different ages, boys and girls. His tournament, held over a weekend, brings everyone together.'

It takes a rare form of moral courage to trust when the evidence is dispiriting. Albert Barnes has been fighting leukaemia for two years but refuses to shift his focus from those he sees in straitened circumstances. Typically, he shared this ungrammatical text message, from a former England youth international, asking for '£800 or £900', supposedly for Christmas presents: 'I feel really bad in asking, but I don't know who else to turn too cos someone has fucked me over for a lot of money and I'm struggling a lot. Would it be possible if I could lend some of you. And I will pay it back monthly. If not then I do understand. I'm happy to sign a contract for it. Because I would never fuck you over like that. I feel really embarrassed about this . . . .'

Barnes summed up the bleakness of the teenager's existence in six words: 'Broken home. Abandoned. Gambler. Drug user.' The plea invited cynicism, but inspired kindness and generosity. Barnes promised to help, while recognising the signs of probable deception. 'Why isn't his club seeing the signs, as his performance has dipped over the last year?' he asked, plaintively.

The question lingered on a cold winter's morning soon afterwards when we visited Thamesmead, a privately run category B prison close to Belmarsh in the London borough of Greenwich. Three newly released prisoners, clutching black bin bags and radiating a poignant sense of hesitancy, lingered in the car park, awaiting their lifts.

It is hardly a Victorian vision of penal servitude; each cell has a shower, telephone and internet access to a 'virtual campus' offering education, training and employment opportunities. Yet it reflects the tension of an overstretched system. An unannounced inspection in May 2017 found that, despite a slight decrease in gang-related offences, violence levels were high. It housed 1,200 prisoners at the time; a quarter said it was easy to obtain illicit drugs. Three former staff members were serving custodial sentences for corruption, and oversight of the use of force was deemed to be poor. Since the threat of smuggling is constant, I should not have been so startled by a sign that asked, 'Are you wearing more than one pair of trousers?'.

Barnes has been seeing Ognen Bozinovski since the summer of 2017. The son of Macedonian asylum seekers, he is serving 11 years for running a drug-dealing operation, involving cocaine and heroin worth an estimated £4 million. Building a relationship with a long-term inmate is a delicate process, which must begin with the prisoner accepting the logic of his punishment.

Bozinovski has become a model prisoner, a so-called 'listener' trained in counselling techniques, but still struggles to acknowledge the wider impact of his crime. He speaks of never having smoked a cigarette, as if this has a moral equivalence to supervising the distribution of substances that wreck lives. Such self-possession accompanies him into a private room, off a visitors' hall where prison officers, on an elevated platform that incorporates a bank of CCTV screens, watch fractured families huddle around small circular tables.

A formidable figure in his late twenties, with a heavily muscled upper body emphasised by a purple-fringed Armani T-shirt, he is superficially friendly but cautious and keenly observant. 'Am I nervous?' he asks, as if he has noticed that his habit of constantly braiding his fingers has been second guessed. 'Of course.'

He has an air of authority, evidently applied beyond the tournaments he referees on the prison's AstroTurf pitch, which is in near-constant use. He admits he intervenes on his prison wing if he sees 'something going wrong' that 'I am not allowing'. The sense of a natural survivor working the system to his best advantage is stark.

'I'm sticking my head down,' he says, firmly but reasonably. 'I'm not going to lose my temper. I've never had a warning and I have followed my sentence plan to the letter. I am bright, proud and smart. They've said I'm a low risk to the public, and there is a low risk of me reoffending, but this is depressing.'

The crux of the matter becomes obvious when we discuss football, a common frame of reference. It is a welcome diversion but also a reminder of fundamental regret. He speaks of being spotted as a schoolboy centre half by Wolverhampton Wanderers, who offered him a scholarship at 16. His immigration status prevented him from signing and, in his eyes, denied him a stellar career.

'I had no right to work, no right to travel. I was raised not to ask people for things. You look after yourself. It's not about why, but how. One thing led to another. I was in love with football and lost without it. I didn't care about anything else. It was my chance to get respect, get a better life for my family. When you love something like that it doesn't leave you.'

He is scheduled to be transferred to an open prison before the end of 2018. David Manton was released, with an electronic tag, in the spring. He returned to his home town in the Midlands, secured an engineering apprenticeship, and set out to reward his mother by rebuilding his life. His local League Two club allowed him to train with them, to regain fitness and confidence. He accepts his football career is unlikely to be revived, but where once there was despair, there is now measured optimism. He no longer has to stare at the wall and beat himself into submission.

CHAPTER FOUR

Quiet Voices

'I say to the kids, whatever you do don't hate. Hate will ruin your life. Eventually you will hate everything and everyone, including yourself. But I do not have the right to forgive. Only the dead people can forgive. Only God can forgive.' – Zigi Shipper

The walls of the bungalow are lined with miracles, photographs of three generations of a family that would not exist without Zigi Shipper's survival of the Holocaust. It is his duty to tell of death, of babies wrenched from their mothers' arms and shot, or deliberately drowned in ice cold water, but he takes delight in celebrating the lives of his descendants.

The photographs capture images of domestic normality: births, bar mitzvahs, marriages and university degree ceremonies. Two daughters have raised six children, who in turn have given Zigi and his wife

Jeannette three great-grandchildren. They represent hope, and the ultimate defeat of Adolf Hitler's extermination programme, which reduced him to a number, 84303.

There is another wall filled with photographs, at the Auschwitz-Birkenau extermination camp, where he arrived aged 14. These, too, are family portraits in which infants are held to their mothers' bosoms, or clustered around their fathers' feet. Parents stand proudly, looking out into oblivion. These images were snatched from victims as they were being herded towards the gas chambers.

Zigi is 88 now, living history. His destiny is to share his story, of a boy from the Jewish ghetto of Łódź, in Poland, who endured the horrors of five concentration camps. He completed a death march while suffering from typhus, only because friends sustained him by feeding him snow. Those who faltered and fell had their suffering ended with a bullet to the brain.

He has cheated death on too many occasions to count. He leapt from a lorry during one ghetto clearance programme, hid and was saved because the bureaucracy of butchery didn't register his return to the metal factory in which he worked. He changed his date of birth four times to ensure he was deemed old enough for work parties away from Auschwitz, where the slogan at its entrance, 'Arbeit Macht Frei' (work sets you free), had a grotesque sliver of personalised truth.

He leaves briefly, as if to allow my imagination to do its worst, and returns from a bedroom with another sheaf of photographs. One, blown up to poster size, depicts him with Steven Gerrard. They are holding an England shirt, with his name and another number, 1, on the back. 'Pah, I was never a goalkeeper,' Zigi says, with a practised air of self-deprecation. When I chuckle, he catches my eye and says, 'I love to make people laugh.'

A second image is of him addressing the England squad before the 2012 European Championship in Poland. Ashley Cole is in the front row, leaning forward from his chair as if drawn towards Zigi by the force field of his dignity. 'Mesmerised,' the old man remembers, with a hint of pride. This was no normal team-building exercise, but it was a typical audience; around 75 per cent of the players admitted they had little or no knowledge of the Holocaust.

Joe Hart approached him afterwards and said, 'I want to know more.' The goalkeeper promised Zigi he would share his experience of Auschwitz, where tears were shed at the sight of small shoes and locks of hair, taken from those whose bodies were burned in the ovens. Wayne Rooney was also affected deeply and has subsequently bought books and videos to expand his knowledge of the institutionalised slaughter of six million Jews.

Gerrard was instrumental in extending an invitation to speak to Liverpool's academy footballers, in

November 2017. Zigi was heard in awestruck silence in a series of talks for the under-14s, under-15s, and Gerrard's under-18 squad. He was presented with another football shirt, with his name and the number 1 on the back. The questions took time to coax but were familiar and answered readily. As he said: 'Who is going to speak for the people who did not survive?'

He is spared nightmares but wells up when he recalls babies, subjected to inhuman experiments by the doctor who embodied evil, Josef Mengele, whom he describes as a terrible, distant presence. He dabs his eyes occasionally, primarily because age has taken its toll on his tear ducts. His voice has a lilting, strangely soothing quality, but the pressure points of his speech are difficult to endure.

He speaks of five boys in a work detail in Pomerania, caught stealing a couple of cigarettes earmarked for German soldiers on the Russian front. Slave workers were rounded up to watch their deaths; strung up on a makeshift gallows in a railway yard, they leapt from their stools before their sentences could be announced in a final act of defiance against their Nazi oppressors.

'It is like it happened yesterday,' Zigi says quietly. 'Those poor boys. So many horrors. All this killing, for no reason at all. I know I can't get an answer but how can these people do these things, kill babies during the day, and go home at night and listen to music, or have dinner with their wives and families?'

Football attracts publicity central to the mission of the dwindling band of Holocaust survivors. Their testimony is more valuable than ever, in a dangerous age where moral compasses are askew and the far right is on the rise. The Community Security Trust reported in February 2018 that there had been a 34 per cent rise in violent anti-Semitic assaults in the UK in the previous 12 months.

Zigi loves football and took part in games in the ghetto with an old leather football. Yet he stepped over dead bodies on those streets without a moment's thought. 'Can you imagine what hunger does to you?' he asks. 'You will do anything for that drop of watery soup. You will eat cats and dogs. I am ashamed because I stole small pieces of bread. Hunger takes away your humanity.'

He was brought up by his grandparents because his father fled on the eve of war. He was told his mother had died, because his parents' divorce was a source of shame in an Orthodox community. His grandfather, whose faith demanded a strict diet, quickly died from malnutrition in the ghetto. His grandmother, tragically, passed away on the day of her liberation.

'I would have liked to have held her in my arms and said thank you,' he says, pain finally clouding eyes that have seen too much. 'What I am I owe to her. Why was she not given one day as a free person? I lost faith in God and religion for so long but as I got older I started reading and thinking. Why the hell do we always blame God for what human beings do?'

His father returned from Russia in 1941 but failed in his attempt to reunite with his only son because he could not break into the Łódź ghetto. He disappeared after moving to Warsaw. His mother, who moved to England via Belgium, recognised Zigi's name on a Red Cross list when he was liberated, on 3 May 1945, by British troops in the naval town of Neustadt.

Identified by a childhood burn mark on his left wrist, he moved to London's Tottenham Court Road, where he endured a traumatic six months learning English and trying to piece together the missing years with the guilt-ridden stranger who was his mother. Football eased his rehabilitation; he watched Chelsea, Tottenham and Charlton, but became an Arsenal supporter out of convenience because an early girlfriend lived near Highbury.

A conversation with Zigi is a series of emotional depth charges. Nearly a week after we met, the announcement of Chelsea's anti-Semitism campaign triggered a long-buried memory, of walking to Stamford Bridge, from Fulham Broadway Tube station, for a match against Tottenham. I passed a crowded bar on the corner of a side street, where fans were singing, 'One man went to gas, went to gas a Yiddo.'

To their credit, Chelsea have been proactive in condemning such abuse, with record signing Álvaro

Morata urging supporters to stop offensive chants, delivered as a warped form of tribute. The club did much to raise the profile of the #WeRemember initiative, launched by the World Jewish Congress in January 2018. Chelsea owner Roman Abramovich, in a rare public pronouncement, said: 'We can all do something to challenge discrimination at our club, as well as within the world around us.'

Their players were addressed by another 88-year-old survivor, Harry Spiro, who lent on his walking stick and told of avoiding his family's annihilation at the Treblinka extermination camp because of his mother's premonition, which led to her pushing him out of the house against his will during a ghetto liquidation programme with the plea, 'Let one of us survive.'

The room incongruously contained the paraphernalia of football analysis, including a whiteboard and a pattern-of-play flip chart. England international Gary Cahill captured its mood: 'You could see everyone was fixated on his story. It's incredible to imagine for someone like myself, who has grown up in a normal environment, the things he has gone through and the pictures he must have in his head growing up as a young boy, which you should never, ever see.'

Football's ubiquity gives it a unique opportunity to challenge social consciences, but can the game itself, engorged by money and tainted by greed, deliver more than arid promises of solidarity? The progress of Juan

Mata's Common Goal project, launched in September 2017, will provide telling answers.

Already engaged by township visits in South Africa when he helped Spain win the World Cup in 2010, Mata was inspired by a visit to Ambedkar Nagar, a slum in Mumbai, in the summer of 2017. He coached boys under the auspices of the Oscar Foundation, which seeks to educate the poor and develop long-term role models for a disadvantaged community.

It crystallised his vision of football as a tool for social progress, since the sense of proportion was overpowering. 'I still get angry if I lose or if I don't play well. But there are other things in life that are much more important. Seeing those kids and the way that they live, and the way that football has changed their life, it gives you as a footballer a deeper meaning of what your profession is. It gives you a different perspective about how big football is as a power for uniting people.'

Mata is the public face of Common Goal, engaging and earnest. Co-founder Jürgen Griesbeck, a German whose streetfootballworld alliance involves 125 charitable organisations operating in 80 countries, provides strategic direction. Their overarching ambition is for 1 per cent of the proceeds from the multi-billion-pound football industry to be donated to good causes.

These have astonishing range, from trauma coaching in refugee camps and host communities along the border between Syria and Jordan to football-based gender equality programmes in Cambodia, Colombia and India. Community pitches have been introduced to Brazilian favelas, and 250,000 disadvantaged German youngsters play mixed-gender matches, without a referee to encourage dispute resolution, in football3, a programme overseen by Borussia Dortmund's Sebastian Rode.

Mata's formative gesture, in donating 1 per cent of his income to personally selected charities, was repeated by such luminaries as Mats Hummels, Giorgio Chiellini and Shinji Kagawa. Leading women footballers were represented in Common Goal by Alex Morgan and Megan Rapinoe. Hoffenheim's Julian Nagelsmann, the rising star of European management, was the first head coach to pledge. Aleksander Ceferin, the Uefa president, followed suit.

Ceferin's commitment was significant since political heft is required if Common Goal is to evolve into football's Live Aid, as a globally galvanising crusade. That's why, on the evening of 24 January 2018, Mata made a five-hour flying visit to the World Economic Forum in the Swiss ski resort of Davos, where the great, good and chronically self-important gathered, alongside 70 heads of state.

The tone of the day's debates was hardly auspicious. Angela Merkel, the German Chancellor, warned that the world order was under threat. Emmanuel Macron, the French President, highlighted the 'major crisis' facing globalisation. David Cameron, the former British prime minister, was caught off-camera making a virtue of Brexit 'going less badly than we thought'.

Mata was delayed by a huge security operation, launched owing to Donald Trump becoming the first US president to attend the event for nearly two decades. Mata's charm offensive began with an endearingly self-conscious Facebook Live event alongside Griesbeck, whose work in football was inspired by the murder of Andrés Escobar, the Colombia captain, after he scored an own goal at the 1994 World Cup.

The footballer spoke of 'opening my eyes and ears' to those in positions of influence, and pledged support for the UN's sustainable development goals. He emphasised that 'football is the biggest force for good in society these days'. He might not have power-dressed, in grey thigh-length cardigan and black roll-neck sweater, but his networking group had huge economic, cultural and charitable reach.

He attended a gathering organised by the Bill & Melinda Gates Foundation, which has endowments in excess of $44 billion and focuses globally on healthcare and poverty prevention. He played table football with Malala Yousafzai, the Pakistani education activist who, at the age of 17, became the youngest winner of the Nobel Peace Prize after being shot in the head for defying the Taliban. He discussed social reach with Sundar Pichai, chief executive of Google.

Politicians and business leaders admitted their surprise at the honesty and transparency of Common Goal's approach, since they are conditioned to whittling away at artfully concealed agendas. Perhaps the most relevant advice came from British film director Richard Curtis, the driving force behind the Comic Relief and Red Nose Day fundraising campaigns in the UK and US.

'When you say "here is a way in which you, a powerful person, can make a difference" they say yes,' Curtis told Mata during a seven-minute interview for CNBC, the North American business channel. 'People want to help. They'd be monsters not to. When you open the door that says "you can be generous, you can change other people's lives, you can fight for what's right", my experience is that people like to do it.

'These football projects you are supporting are miraculous. Kids who are unreachable, uninterested in education, come from very tough lives. When you bring them together by playing football, suddenly you create an environment where they are willing to change, willing to learn, willing to be helped.'

The profile of the players associated with Common Goal will inevitably generate awareness, but they are prone to insecurity and sudden misfortune. One of the movement's most convincing ambassadors is England Under-21 international Duncan Watmore, whose career was threatened just days after joining Swansea's Alfie

Mawson and Bournemouth's Charlie Daniels in the first batch of English advocates.

We met, in an anteroom at Sunderland's Academy of Light, seven weeks to the day after Watmore underwent successful surgery on his second serious knee injury in 11 months, a ruptured anterior cruciate ligament. The weather – fine rain and clinging mist that partially obscured training pitches beyond brown-hued hedges – was suitably bleak, yet his mood was measured.

He was tackled ruinously by Millwall defender James Meredith in the sixth match of his comeback from an identical injury, the one footballers fear most. His foot was planted as they fell together, so the force of the challenge was transmitted through his left knee. His surgeon had used the patella tendon to strengthen the joint in a previous operation, so compensated by using a piece of his hamstring to replace the ACL.

The pain was familiar but the shock was instant and overwhelming. Watmore broke down in tears when he reached the dressing room, where he was quickly joined by his parents, brother and girlfriend. The club's medical staff had four minutes to secure his privacy before his teammates arrived for the half-time break, so he was closeted in an adjacent physiotherapy room.

Such setbacks are treated like a death in the family. Immediately after the match, his teammates filed in, to offer their condolences and promises of support. One, Paddy McNair, was spotted lingering outside, fighting back tears. He had just recovered from a similar injury and had formed a special bond with Watmore during long, painful hours in the gymnasium.

'All the lads at the club were unbelievable, so supportive. Nobody knew what to say, because they all knew what that kind of injury means to a footballer. I knew what it meant to Paddy. I would have felt the same about him, had the roles been reversed. You can't comprehend it, really, but your body knows what you've done to it, if that makes sense.

'I knew what it meant for my career, as I'd done it once before. I knew what it took to get back. I knew that as soon as you do it a second time you can recover, but everyone starts asking questions, including yourself. Will it ever be the same again? I was in a very bad way initially. Football can be hard and you can sometimes forget how lucky you are to be playing it.

'For our club at this time, at the bottom of the table, it is not an easy game. When you are in that tough position, you can get bogged down in all the negativity. An injury is one of the best ways of making you realise how grateful you should be when you're fit and playing, even if you're losing and getting booed. You still need to remember that you are playing football for a living.'

The subconscious still plays tricks, yearns for the impossible. He woke from one vivid dream, in which he scored a hat-trick for Sunderland at the Stadium of Light, to reconnect to the reality that he had been sleeping in a knee brace to aid recovery. He spent the spring of 2018 closeted with physiotherapist David Binningsley, riding static bikes to build muscle mass and maintaining his balance by trampolining and playing the Wii indoor game.

'So many players are moody and mope around the place, because they just want to be playing, but I don't see the point in that. Why worry about the things that you can't control? You have to be mentally strong, because there's nothing worse than coming in each morning, knowing what you've got to do, and all the lads are getting their strapping done to go training, getting ready for the game.

'I know this sounds bad but sometimes it is better if you are in a bubble, away from them. As soon as you start thinking about the game you miss it. I tell myself this is my career and I'd love to continue playing but I'm healthy. There are a lot worse things in the world than getting a bad ACL. You can get tunnel vision in football and sometimes you have to step out of the game.'

Watmore is a distinctive footballer, a late developer who earned a first-class honours degree in economics and business management, but his universal popularity was underlined when he received a letter from Real Madrid wishing him 'a smooth and speedy recovery'. His reading tastes, designed to satisfy an inquisitive mind during the rehabilitation process, are indicative of his character. At the time of our meeting he was captivated by *Red Notice*, an insight into Vladimir Putin's Russia by Bill Browder, the largest foreign investor in the country until 2005. He has been leading a campaign to expose endemic corruption and human rights abuses since the death in prison in 2009 of his lawyer, Sergei Magnitsky, who had uncovered a $230 million fraud by government officials.

Such intrigue was, at least, a little more accessible to his teammates than Watmore's alternative brain candy, *Seven Brief Lessons on Physics*, in which Carlo Rovelli explains Einstein's theory of general relativity, quantum mechanics, black holes, the complex architecture of the universe, elementary particles, gravity and the nature of the mind.

Watmore's eyes light up. 'Do you know the closer you are to a gravitational source the slower time is, because gravity slows down time? So even though we're talking milliseconds here, if two twins were born at the same time, and one lived at sea level and one lived in the mountains, and they met when they were eighty, the guy who lived in the mountains would be a little bit older, because he's further away from the gravitational centre of the Earth. I find stuff like that really interesting, fascinating.

'Football in general can be a bit of a bubble. And sometimes it has to be, to protect your own interests. In terms of social media and going out and about, as a footballer you know that you're an easy target. The modern-day player closes himself off, and so it becomes "I get to football, do my job and go home". People say that we're like robots. Fans would love us to go for a pint with them, but you can't really do that now.'

Players do not exist in a social vacuum. They are sons, fathers, husbands; they cry, they care, they question. Watmore appreciates Common Goal's success will depend on the dismantling of distrust, and the simplicity of the message that 1 per cent of an individual's salary is enough to change the lives of thousands of strangers.

'One per cent is a really, really clever number, because it doesn't sound too daunting. Imagine if this gets going, and all kinds of people in football contribute. It would have such a big effect. My philosophy is that it gives my career a lot more meaning. We have a choice to nominate which charities our money supports, so I know at least I am giving something back to the game.

'I want to look at education, because education in football can be a lot, lot better. When you see kids missing school when they are so young, to play football on day release, that's hard. Miss one day a week at school and you're twenty per cent behind everyone else. Then it is two, three days a week and you don't have the incentive to catch up.

'It's a cycle. A boy starts to feel he has given so much to football he has to make it. That's where the tunnel vision comes in. I know there are programmes out there designed to help, but education has enabled me to look at the bigger picture when I am down. It's global – look at the story of Malala. That is the power of education at its greatest.

'Loads of people were really positive with me when I announced my support for Common Goal. Others have a cynical view of charities and it is idealistic to think that everyone in football will be doing it because they have worked very hard for their money. You are brought up not to trust in football and you just have to get over that.'

Like everyone at Sunderland, Watmore was intimately involved with Bradley Lowery, whose short life ended at 1.35 p.m. on 7 July 2017, when he succumbed to the cumulative ravages of neuroblastoma, a rare form of cancer. The boy's intense relationship with Jermain Defoe was a transcendent love story. They even led the England team out together for a World Cup qualifier at Wembley; the boy clung to Defoe, burying his face into his midriff, because he was overwhelmed by the noise.

One image, among many examples of compassion, stands out. Defoe is lying on a hospital bed, propping his head up with his left hand. Bradley is asleep in a foetal position, with his right arm across the chest of the famous footballer who became his firmest friend. Defoe appears to be lost in the moment, glassy-eyed. The boy's plight is captured by the contrast between his red, square Sunderland pillow and the tubes, compressed by a large rectangular plaster, leading to his neck.

When Bradley died, aged only six, Defoe poured his grief into a message on social media: 'Goodbye my friend, gonna miss you lots. I feel so blessed God brought u into my life and had some amazing moments with you and for that I'm so grateful. I'll never ever forget the way u looked at me when I met u for the first time, the genuine love in those cute eyes. Really finding it hard to find words to express what u mean to me.

'The way u say my name, ur little smiles when the cameras come out like a little superstar and the love I felt when I was with u. Your courage and bravery will continue to inspire me for the rest of my life. You will never know what a difference you made to me as a person. God has you in his arms and I will always carry you in my heart. Sleep tight little one. My best friend.'

Defoe broke down at the funeral, to which he wore an England shirt with Bradley's name on the back. He recognised the profundity of the occasion during his march behind the tiny coffin to the church at Blackhall Colliery in County Durham; he saw Sunderland and Newcastle fans hugging in the streets and understood the symbolism of supposed rivals being moved beyond tribal loyalties and diverse traditions.

He was 'blessed and humbled' to receive an OBE for his charitable work in the Queen's Birthday Honours in June 2018. Bradley lives on, in a charitable foundation that bears his name. It was inaugurated four months earlier and has, as its founding aim, the provision of medical support for vulnerable children that is not available on the NHS. The litany of need is heart-wrenching; to cite a typical example, two-year-old Poppy Martin needs £300,000 for proton beam therapy on an inoperable tumour that continues to grow behind her right eye. It is available only in the Children's Hospital of Philadelphia.

Watmore has felt the power of a child's pain. 'Bradley had a big impact on our club, and it obviously spread across the country. His relationship with JD was football at its best, because it highlighted its ability to bring people together. Football has a responsibility to give back to society, whether it is giving someone your boots, signing autographs or donating to charity.

'There's not much worse in life than seeing a sick child, and Bradley had the biggest smile. Everyone at the club had an emotional connection with him. He was so positive and happy, and that has a huge effect on you as a person. It puts football into perspective. It touches you and makes you take a step back. When I think of him I feel his positivity and see that thumbs up ... .'

It is human nature to support such causes but what are the limits of sport's influence, beyond instinctive, high-profile sympathy and extraordinary wealth? Should football be as conscious of its flaws as its potential benefits? Before concentrating on its capacity for benevolence, should it confront a culture founded on the often crude imposition of authority?

The questions were posed indirectly in a CNN interview with John Amaechi, the former NBA basketball player who has become a compelling social and sporting commentator on both sides of the Atlantic. He was responding to the sexual abuse scandals in US gymnastics and British football, the latter involving Barry Bennell, a paedophilic former youth coach at Crewe Alexandra and Manchester City who was sentenced to 31 years in prison.

Amaechi argued: 'People underestimate the almost supernatural position of sport in our society. It is like church. We know people have forgiven the church for similarly egregious acts. If you look at the institutions that have had significant challenges, they tend to be insular, closed, governed in a way that is less than transparent, setting themselves up as paragons of virtue.

'We have a different set of standards in sport. It's really dangerous. If your kid came home from school saying my French teacher stood three inches from my face, their breath and spittle hitting me, yelling at me because I didn't understand how to conjugate a verb, you'd be down in that school the next day, saying "unacceptable teaching methods. If this ever happens again I'm suing you." That is the daily experience of young people in sport.

'Sport is an empty vessel if we allow it to be filled with rogue elements, the gymnastics scandal, the football scandal. We can change this but we have to stop mythologising sport. We have to stop pretending that it's out for the best for our young people and realise that, with our great vigilance and oversight, we can use sport for great things.

'We can make sure our coaches are educated to a much higher level. We can make sure that it delivers the outcomes that it promises. They promise your daughter and son will come out with leadership skills and trans-formational interpersonal skills, and most sport does not teach that. In fact, not only do they not teach these great skills, they actually cause harm to our young people. We can do something about that but we have to stop pretending that, in of itself, sport is good.'

At its most pure, though, football has a capacity to shrink the world, transcend boundaries and unite contrasting cultures. Mata's movement will need to nourish such an idealistic vision of the sport, which he first shared in a *Guardian* interview with Donald McRae, when he used the cosmopolitan Chelsea team that won the Champions League in 2012 as a practical example of the game's pervasiveness. 'We came from all over the world, from different circumstances and spoke many different languages. Some had grown up during wartime. Some had grown up in poverty. But there we were, all standing together in Germany as champions of Europe. The way we had come together from all around the world to work for a common goal was more meaningful to me than the trophy. To me, that is something that can change the world for the better.'

Such sentiments take us back to the great survivor, sharing the lessons of man's inhumanity to man. Zigi Shipper says goodbye with a firm handshake, a final plea for reassurance about Arsenal's future without Arsène Wenger, and a promise to tell his story 'until the day I die'. In a shrill world, we should cherish such quiet voices, for soon they will be still.

CHAPTER FIVE

Deaf, Dumb and Blind Kids

'Creativity has always been the difference maker for Paul Pogba in all facets of his life, on and off the pitch. Since childhood, his imagination has been the catalyst to defying the norm in the world of football. Pogba's story mirrors our belief that creativity will take you further than your mind or body alone. There is only one Pogba, but all athletes can look to him for inspiration to use one's own creativity to make new rules in their sport.' – Ryan Morlan, Adidas

Dele Alli was having difficulty sleeping. Life, with its private pressures and hidden strains, lacked the reassuring simplicity of football, the game that rooted him to his childhood. He turned towards Simon Edwards in his search for perspective because he was a manifestly good man, whose instinct was to give rather than receive.

He worked with him at MK Dons, long before he became an England international. A source of invaluable advice, Edwards was a behavioural specialist, whose unyielding faith in human nature prompted him to obey the instructions of an international centre forward, who insisted he talk to him through his football boots, since they were his means of communication with the outside world.

I also knew of Simon's warmth, intuitiveness, tolerance and endless curiosity. He gave up a day of his limited time when I sought to understand the psyche of a young player, coming to terms with being a commodity in a cold, exploitative environment. He explained the distinctly different lessons of nature and nurture, and trusted me to use his insight sensitively.

A confidential case study, in which he effectively saved the career of a midfield player who suffered from agoraphobia, confirmed him as a People Whisperer. It is a more complex condition than simply a dread of open spaces; it incorporates a fear of panic, being trapped, helpless or embarrassed. Edwards's genius was to convince the footballer that the pitch was his haven, rather than a place of harsh judgement and perpetual vulnerability.

It was not until early January 2018, weeks before his death aged 60, that Simon's secret emerged. He had been diagnosed with terminal cancer three and a half years previously, with the prognosis that he would survive for a year. He had spoken to no one of his illness outside his closest family until he shared his plight with Karl Robinson, who had become a friend as well as a client.

Robinson, managing Charlton Athletic at that stage, visited him at the Hertfordshire Hospice with Dele and Benik Afobe, the striker who had returned to Wolverhampton Wanderers on loan from Bournemouth before confirming a £12.5million transfer. Despite its profound subtext, it was a light-hearted occasion. Dele led the laughter at stories that illustrated football's fundamental absurdity, and spoke of where his life might lead.

'As soon as Karl told me Simon wanted to see me I went straight away,' Dele remembered. 'It was good to see him and show support to his family. He was a great person, amazing. I felt very fortunate to know him and work with him. You could see he was just a genuinely nice person. He was one of the people you could trust and open up to. I could speak to him about anything. It's sad. You have to try and celebrate his life.'

The tall, earnest young man in conversation at St George's Park during an England camp bore no resemblance to the public perception of a provocative and immature character, whose career had hit unexpected turbulence. Players of Dele's potential live in gilded cages, behind bars locked and bolted by relative strangers with a vested interest in their status.

So many people feel they have skin in this particular game. Clubs, sponsors and agents attempt to create self-serving narratives with players of global renown. Celebrity seekers, rumour mongers and PR advisers approach them from a bewildering arc of angles. Families either fracture or solidify under scrutiny. Coaches and managers attempt to apply authority while maintaining a delicate balance of power.

The player himself, encircled, is faced with the paradox of being simultaneously isolated and over-exposed. Many come from difficult backgrounds; Dele, estranged from his Nigerian father and English mother, is understandably sensitive about the circumstances that led to his disassociation with the family name. That is a lot for someone who has just turned 22 to come to terms with.

Dele's sensitivity, in saying his last goodbye to a man who meant a lot to him, stimulated in Robinson a paternal sense of pride: 'It just shows you, most of these kids that come through, they are good kids, really good kids. You just hope that the game doesn't smother them and doesn't suffocate them, because all of a sudden you become a commercial enterprise.'

Coincidentally, I happened to be a witness at his coming of age, in a football sense. Dele was 16 and approached Robinson as we chatted outside the pavilion at the council-owned facility at which MK Dons train. He wanted to know whether he should join the other scholars doing their obligatory study for a level two coaching badge in the nearby dome.

'No,' said Robinson. 'Go and tell them you're staying with me. This is your job now.' Dele permitted himself a slow, thin smile of satisfaction at the time; he positively beams at a memory that gives focus to a blur of subsequent incident and opportunity. He is at his best at his most natural, interacting with children in community programmes run by Tottenham's charitable foundation, but has learned to be guarded.

'To be honest you can plan as much as you want but you never know what's going to happen in the next game, how things are going to change. When I went to Tottenham my life changed completely in the sense of how serious it became. Football has always been my life but it is hard to prepare for this life, the stuff other than playing, because playing is all you want to do.

'It is important to have people around you who you trust fully. A lot of kids who make it have parents who weren't involved in the game. It is hard for them to tell you what to do because they have no experience of this world. They haven't lived it. Karl was always great at that. It is the same with [Mauricio] Pochettino at Tottenham.

'I have been very fortunate to have had two managers you can speak to about anything. They are also not scared to tell you anything. Dan Micciche worked with me at MK from the under-elevens to the under-sixteens.

He saw me growing up as a kid and helped me a lot. All kids go through their own journey. At one point I didn't know whether I was good enough to make it. I didn't grow as much as the other kids. He moved me tactically, to get in a position where I was on the ball more.'

Football is the easy bit, even at the exalted level that involves highly speculative links to £100 million transfers to Real Madrid. Dele is paparazzi fodder in an age of duplicity and banality, where mundanities are distorted and distributed through cynical, click-based opportunism by media outlets that feed a climate of jealousy and ignorance.

This leads to the self-protective charade of leading players conversing behind their hands because they know they are on camera, and that any exchange, however innocent or humdrum, will be monitored, deciphered and sensationalised. They live in a world of fragile friendships, where strangers stare, open-mouthed, or slyly capture their unguarded moments and rank stupidity on camera phones.

Dele has been burned. 'You have to be sensible but it is difficult. I am in a position where I have to be careful. Naturally you look after yourself, do things the right way, but it is important to have the right people around you, to stop you doing stupid things. You can lose your head and be dragged into things that you should not be a part of.

'When you become a role model for younger kids you have to think a lot more. The football is the simple stuff. You know what you are doing. You grow up wanting to be a footballer; you don't learn too much about the other stuff around it. You always grow up looking up to people. You never think people will be looking up to you. Preparing for that is difficult.

'It becomes hard to trust people. You have outsiders around you and never know what their intentions are. That is a shame but that's the way the world is. Obviously, I am still young and I have made a few mistakes, either during games or off the pitch. I have done a few stupid things. You have always got to improve. Although I have achieved a lot now for my age, it's hard.'

Context is everything. Here is an athlete who could not afford £1 for a childhood coaching session, who has just bought a £4 million house. Life has come at him fast and he insists he is 'numb' to criticism. His gaze is unwavering, though there is a twitch of amusement at the corner of his mouth when I ask him to sum up, in a couple of sentences, the advice he would give his 11-year-old self: 'Just be ready for anything. Always enjoy it. When you make it in the Premier League, and play in front of all these people, try to be like a kid, play naturally and have fun. Sometimes it is easy to lose that sense of how amazing it can be, because of how much it means to other people. You can put too much pressure on yourself and focus on the wrong things.'

England manager Gareth Southgate, who admits he emerged as a player when 'the world was very different', makes the wider point, without dwelling on Dele in particular, that the art of survival is timeless. 'You have to dig in. It is a fight. Everybody looks at the glamour of professional football but it's a bloody hard world and you've got to really be resilient to make it.

'Am I fit enough to play, am I ready to play, am I good enough to play? I don't care who they are, pretty much every player in the world has been through that at some point. Even the very best have those moments of turmoil, when they doubt themselves. They are the really tough bits, because it's your voice. External stuff can bring pressure if you allow it, but normally the struggle is with yourself.'

The ramifications of Dele's decision to leave his long-term agent Rob Segal are being worked through. His day-to-day affairs are overseen by Harry Hickford, his adoptive brother, whose close-knit family helped Dele through adolescent issues. Dele's commercial portfolio is managed by the Los Angeles-based Creative Artists Agency, which has negotiated player contracts worth $3.3 billion in the NFL. The team is completed by a PR agency and a lawyer. Their challenge is to guide without sycophancy, to prevent prudence becoming paranoia. Though the best marketing campaign he could mount will be conducted on the grass, through consistency of performance, the making of a modern icon requires an understanding of millennial trends and attitudes.

Oliver Bierhoff, Germany's team manager, worked with head coaches Jürgen Klinsmann and Joachim Löw to create a culture that complemented the entrepreneurial nature of the modern footballer. 'The most important thing for me is to keep checking the players' mentality,' Bierhoff told Nina Weihrauch of Adidas. 'The new generation does not just want to execute, they want to shape things themselves, understand them, and tackle challenges.

'We give the players the tools to do so, because that's sometimes missing. In the areas where they feel comfortable they are very creative. But as soon as they might find themselves out of this comfort zone, they suddenly feel very trapped. The manager has to find a connection to the players, move them emotionally and then win their mind and rational thought.

'The fundamental attitude has not changed. It's about giving your best every day, trying to become better and never resting on your laurels. I've had the chance to be with very successful people. The really successful ones are truly unpretentious and uncomplicated, but they simply have an inner drive to want to do things better. You need to start your own fire in yourself and keep it burning. The biggest danger is feeling you've made it.

'Professional soccer players are a kind of independent entrepreneur and have to think about the path they're taking. Are they going to hire a chef or physiotherapist? How are they going to position themselves in their personal marketing? How do they organise their private life? Getting out of their own surroundings and meeting other young entrepreneurs who are taking a risk and have their own convictions is immensely important.'

Weihrauch manages social media channels for Adidas, who promote high-profile clients like Dele and Paul Pogba as 'content creators', capable of establishing their own media channels. The stunt transporting them through central London on a double decker bus, to launch the latest laceless boot, was deceptively retroactive.

Pogba, senior partner of the pair, has become an emoji in human form. His transfer to Manchester United was a masterclass in digital penetration, organised by the sports manufacturers and We Are Social, a global marketing agency that promises to 'win the thumbs and minds of sports fans by reinventing the old and creating the new'.

A convenient leak of a video featuring the footballer and Stormzy, the grime MC, generated more than 30 million views and 400 news articles. Impressive, but scratching the surface, given that almost 3.3 billion people consume social media, an increase of more than 100 million in the first quarter of 2018.

The target audience is young, urban and inhabits the intersection between sport, music, fashion and the arts.

The follow-up campaign, 'Calling All Creators', is seen as a showcase for 'those who have a bias for action, who flip the script and break boundaries'. They 'are the ones who influence how things are done on the field, track, court, stage or street'.

Launched initially in 33 countries, it features Pogba, Lionel Messi and David Beckham alongside Green Bay Packers quarterback Aaron Rodgers, Chicago Cubs third baseman Kris Bryant, Houston Rockets guard James Harden, Wimbledon champion Garbiñe Muguruza, rapper Pusha T, producer Pharrell Williams, fashion designer Alexander Wang and supermodel Karlie Kloss.

The corporate pretension is easy to deride, but the value of promotional contracts is soaring and traditional commercial relationships are splintering, as sport is treated more as a cultural phenomenon than an athletic pursuit. Adidas paid $200 million to lure Harden, the NBA's MVP, from Nike. Roc Nation Sports, Jay-Z's sports agency, signed Romelu Lukaku, who cited 'the depth of opportunities they create for their clients, be it marketing, media, philanthropy or brand building'. Tidal, the music streaming service owned by the rapper, his wife Beyoncé and such investors as Madonna, moved into the Premier League in the summer of 2018 by announcing a partnership with Arsenal.

Adidas expect to sell £1.5 billion worth of merchandise during their ten-year, £750 million deal with

Manchester United, which is, according to Deloitte's latest 'money league' report, the world's highest-earning club. Revenues totalled €676.3 million during the 2016–17 season; Ed Woodward, United's executive vice-chairman, has prioritised the commercial exploitation of its online presence.

Football has been slow to respond to initiatives in the NFL, NBA and UFC, where individuals and franchises seek to own their online content, and control data from huge social media audiences. United, one of the last clubs to respond to digital opportunity, claims 659 million international fans. It has 140 million followers and accounted for half of the Premier League's interactions on social media in the first quarter of 2018.

Steve Martin, chief executive of M&C Saatchi Sport and Entertainment, suggests data 'is like their oil'. He predicts 'if you fast track this over the next few years and beyond, this landscape is going to be about how you personalise content. The data allows clubs to know each fan individually and how they're spending.'

The digital football platform Dugout incorporates the non-match content of 174 clubs, including such high-profile investors as Manchester City, Liverpool, Paris Saint-German, Barcelona, Real Madrid and Bayern Munich. Advertising revenues are shared and, according to the organisation's president Matthew Baxter, growth is likely because the average user supports 4.6 clubs.

They probably refer to the game as 'footy'. The cult of monetisation means that a child's version of the latest England kit costs £86, without socks. Supporters pay more to be used as goods and chattels in cyberspace. They represent football's piggy bank, should traditional broadcasting revenues peak, plateau, or, heaven forfend, plummet.

The increasing resistance to independent scrutiny has led to clubs employing so-called journalists, who litter social media and in-house platforms with 'exclusive interviews' that are the digital equivalent of papier mâché creations by the infant class. The annihilation of traditional media outlets seems to suit everyone, including the players.

According to a senior executive at a top-six Premier League club, who has rare respect for those writers who look beyond the trivial and the tasteless, one of his leading players no longer has any interest in giving orthodox interviews. The player, an international and a household name, refuses to 'give away my content' because he has 'millions' more followers than the journalists and newspaper groups that pursue him.

The Players' Tribune cuts out the media middleman. The online platform, created with funding from venture capitalists in October 2014 by baseball legend Derek Jeter and sports marketing executive Jaymee Messler, communicates directly to the public through AGC, 'athlete-generated content'. Its first-person articles are well crafted, usually ghost-written, and potentially agenda-setting.

The site has provided an outlet for 1,800 athletes. It has broken major news stories, such as the retirement of Kobe Bryant, who did so through a poem entitled 'Dear Basketball'. Some contributions have a press release's lack of objectivity and creativity but, like the modern sports autobiography, many are revelatory, intelligent and insightful.

There are simultaneous ironies in operation. Jeter was notoriously reticent with the media as a player with the New York Yankees. The internet has irrevocably changed rules of engagement. Athletes appreciate the instant access to the public but have been alienated by its side-effect, the prioritisation of speed over taste and accuracy in online stories designed to maximise page views.

Football is central to the platform's strategic expansion in Europe, in partnership with Gerard Piqué and his investment group, Kosmos, which has also agreed a 25-year, £2.2 billion deal to stage a week-long tennis World Cup. The Barcelona defender embodies Bierhoff's notion of a modern player: entrepreneurial, independent and politically aware.

Piqué best expressed his credo when tap-dancing through the minefield of the Catalan constitutional crisis. 'Politics is a drag, but why shouldn't I express myself? I understand those players who don't want to say anything. We're footballers but we're people too. Why can a journalist or a mechanic express themselves but not a footballer?'

In his first post on the Tribune, in March 2018, Piqué broadened his scope. 'It's funny, I noticed some people in America have started telling the NBA players to "just shut up and dribble" when they express their opinions on real problems in society. It's ridiculous, no? It's the same here in Spain. They say, "just shut up and play football. It's all you know." Sorry, but I will not just shut up and play. It's not all I know.

'There's a lot more depth to footballers than most people realise, and I think it's important that we express ourselves and our views. Footballers are human beings, and that is something that is being lost in the media world that we live in today. There are things going on in our lives that the public has no idea about. Yes, you can google match results, and you can google transfer rumours, but you can't google how a person feels, or what motivates them, or what they fear.'

His initial interviews, with Luis Suárez and Neymar, were low-key, but the list of stars already signed up is telling. It includes Lionel Messi, Cristiano Ronaldo, Marcelo, Gabriel Jesus, Harry Kane, Antoine Griezmann, Gianluigi Buffon, James Rodríguez, Robert Lewandowski, Ivan Rakitić, Dani Alves, Thibaut Courtois, David Villa, Ronaldinho and Francesco Totti.

The genie is out of the bottle. In the week Piqué sounded the death knell for the quick quote for the back page, Wasserman, the sports agency, was unveiling Unlock, Mammon's equivalent of online dating. The platform uses real-time data, involving 200 variables and 330 million social media accounts, to highlight potential partnership opportunities for athletes. Thierry Henry, although not a client, was recommended to front a campaign selling Guinness in three African nations.

Where is all this heading? Football's fragmentation, like climate change, is an irreversible fact. Just as the spectator's scarf, bobble hat and rattle of my youth has the relevance of a ration book, a new generation has little interest in attending matches, and possesses the technological skills to circumvent payment for traditional satellite channels.

Clubs are complicit, since their ticket pricing policy is exploitative and short-sighted, but the audience is changing. Juan Mata, whose weekly blog and accessibility to more traditional forms of media gives him a notable independence of thought, observed the emphasis on superficialities during an interview with *Panenka* magazine: 'I see children now and many things surprise me: they ask me about my boots and why I don't dye my hair. I wonder, "Why don't you talk to me about how to cross the ball, control it, the position of the body when I strike the ball?" Previously, kids wanted a ball; nowadays they want boots and jerseys, they don't have a ball and they cannot play too much. Yet they don't mind because they can show off their boots and shirt and that's enough.

'Football is losing its essence, people talk about celebrations instead of goals. I am not criticising people talking about boots or haircuts but I would ask that people talk more about the other stuff, about the game itself. New boots and videos filmed by players have the biggest reach and I get it to a certain extent but the footballer has changed.

'I am not so old but when I started out, we had none of this. We did not have the need to show the things we do and the good life we lead. That is dangerous. Social networks can be very positive because it's a great vehicle to communicate but perhaps things need to be done in a different way. It's about taking football back to its roots. If not, all that is left is to start training with a mobile phone in our hands and filming us doing freestyle touches.'

Twitter has made everyone a pundit. Opinion takes precedence over action. If today's football icons are being homogenised by the image industry it stands to reason unlikely new heroes will emerge. E-sports are Richard Scudamore's worst nightmare, since they engage a youthful audience that prefers fantasy and imitation to the real thing.

The future is located in a white-walled semi-detached house in the Birmingham suburb of Smethwick, where a wan-faced 21-year-old better known by his tag, 'Gorilla', makes a mean cup of tea. Since it is just after 11 a.m., Spencer Ealing apologises for his probable inarticulacy, 'because I'm not usually up yet'.

He is primarily nocturnal, and invariably plays FIFA 18 in his bedroom until 3 a.m. It is a distinctive way of living the dream, since he won $200,000 on becoming the game's world champion. He has a traditional club allegiance, to West Bromwich Albion, but is a new type of professional sportsman. His transfer to FaZe Clan in May 2018 was the e-equivalent of Pogba joining Manchester United.

'With this generation, social media is the norm,' Ealing explained. 'I don't watch TV any more. It is about YouTube, and streaming. If I want to watch a programme at two in the morning I use Netflix. A lot is changing, quickly, but gaming will have a big role in the future. Winning the 200k opened up avenues to sponsors and made me realise the brand deals that are out there.'

He began playing FIFA on his Xbox console at the age of seven. He turned professional when he was 18 and has attracted more than 500,000 subscribers to his personalised YouTube channel. He has in excess of 100,000 followers on Twitter and builds his profile by offering impromptu online clinics 'because people want to watch my game play'. The average viewer identifies more easily with his lifestyle than that of a multi-millionaire footballer.

Prize money in virtual football is increasing, though dwarfed by the fantasy game Dota 2, where total tournament earnings in 2018 will be $138 million. Intriguingly, crowdfunding is a form of fan engagement undertaken by leading franchises such as Evil Geniuses, Newbee and Team Liquid, which is co-owned by basketball legend Magic Johnson. The global e-sports industry is projected to generate at least $1.5 billion a year by 2020.

Those are the sorts of figures, and type of customer commitment, that appeal to Fifa president Gianni Infantino. Football's global governing body co-owns the eponymous game with EA Sports. Their Ultimate Team Championship Series is widely televised. Infantino envisages game players eventually filling arenas; Tottenham's new stadium has been designed with e-sports in mind.

Ealing is personable, and marketable, but must contend with nervousness created by the alien culture he represents. Manchester United took a conscious decision not to recruit an e-player because, in the words of a senior club figure, 'we didn't know who or what we were getting into'. Manchester City has employed two in the UK, and five across its global network.

Their latest recruit, an 18-year-old Dane who used to represent Brondby, is Marcus 'ExpectSporting' Jorgensen. That is perhaps the least inspirational handle since, in a long-forgotten spirit of self-deprecation, snooker world champion Steve Davis answered to the nickname 'Interesting'. City have diversified into China, entering a five-man team in the Online Star League, headed by Zhang Jun, who appears to be known as Most Valuable Player.

West Ham are the only other Premier League club to enlist an e-player, Sean 'Dragonn' Allen. Wolfsburg employed the first English virtual footballer, David 'DaveBtw' Bytheway, and are exploring the potential of a pan-European competition involving clubs such as Roma, Ajax, PSV Eindhoven, Paris Saint-Germain, Schalke and Sporting Lisbon.

Matt Vincent, from the UNILAD team, gives hope to clubs that e-sports can be a youth recruitment tool. He is an Arsenal fan as a result of a traditional supporter's upbringing, having been taken to Highbury at the age of eight by his father, who went through an identical bonding ritual with his father.

Things have changed. 'Now young boys are getting into football through picking up FIFA 18. They have consoles from the age of five and the game is safe and sterile. As a parent it is the type of game I'd want my child to play. The great thing about e-sport is there are no barriers. Playing traditional football is so much less accessible; parents need to drop their sons and daughters off at training. If they become good at it their social life will suffer.'

Even those of us of a certain vintage can appreciate that these deaf, dumb and blind kids sure play a mean pinball. Watching Ealing at work is hypnotic. He leans forward, eyes as wide as his forehead is high. In a black, branded T-shirt, he has the air of a replacement keyboard player in Depeche Mode. His hands sweat profusely, so he has a towel constantly within reach, and his thumb-eye co-ordination is peerless.

His Midlands monotone fails to match the speed of play, and the dexterity of his actions. 'I like to play in the dark. I can't put my finger on why but as soon as I hit 7 p.m. I get in the mood to play. I can't play to my full potential in the morning. People always want to know the difference between me and the average player, but honestly, I don't know why I am good. I wish I did. It is not one particular thing. I suppose mentally I have learned not to buckle under pressure. People try to keep the ball against me, to frustrate me, but I press. When I get the ball, bang, I go. I'm a bit like Liverpool – I have no defence. People say I'll always score more than my opponent. I know the different angles. It is like second nature to me.'

His muscle memory is obviously acute, yet in a world of 25-year-old veterans he is conscious of a marginal decrease in reaction times. He has cut down on practising, reasoning that his regime of playing up to 12 hours a day had to be adapted because 'otherwise I would burn out'. The mental toll is such that Brazilian club Santos provides its e-players with a psychologist.

The new kid on the block, Donovan 'DhTekKz' Hunt, is 16 and a student from Exeter. A frail, pale figure in a black hoodie, he won his first tournament in Barcelona in January 2018. His prize money, $22,000, paid for his mother's holiday in San Francisco and Anfield season tickets, for him and his father.

Ruud Gullit has launched his own academy, featuring three players aged between 16 and 18. They are trained in FIFA and advised on brand building through social media. The former Chelsea and Newcastle manager was in the front row when Ealing won his world title; his virtual self was in the imaginary team. When the facsimile 'scored', the e-player pointed him out in the crowd with his index finger as a mark of respect.

'It was pretty surreal,' Ealing admitted, conscious of the inevitability of occasional trips down the wormhole when fantasy co-exists with reality. Ronaldo signed his winning shirt; Crystal Palace's Wilfried Zaha was his partner in a pairs event. Chelsea's César Azpilicueta and Hull City's David Meyler are accomplished FIFA players.

There are anomalies; Messi has the highest e-rating possible, 99, yet when he receives the ball in FIFA his first touch is loose. Ratings prick sensitive egos; Lukaku demanded an upgrade on his acceleration statistics and Dele refuses to play as himself because he is so disgusted by his rating of 84, two more than Anthony Martial and two fewer than Harry Kane.

The banality of blanket media coverage of Dele's streaming debut on Twitch, the video platform, seemed somehow symbolic. More than 25,000 viewers watched him playing Fortnite Battle Royale, as delstroyer14, with Tottenham teammate Kyle Walker-Peters. The churlish criticised him for playing bare-chested for a time, in contravention of online protocols, and wondered, slyly, why he was not watching simultaneous live TV coverage of the Champions League semi-final between Bayern Munch and Real Madrid. Maybe he was just having fun. Even multi-millionaire footballers have the right to be kids, at heart.

PART TWO

The Manager

CHAPTER SIX

Footsteps

'When I approached the ground and moved over the bridge along which our supporters had squeezed fifty abreast in their tens of thousands to shout for us I could scarcely bear to look. I knew the ghosts of the babes would still be there, and there they are still, and they will always be there as long as those who saw them still cross the bridge, young, gay, red ghosts on the green grass of Old Trafford.' – Sir Matt Busby

The imagination of the four-year-old boy who went to work with his dad at Old Trafford was seized by a pervasive smell that hinted at greatness. Only later, as a young man, did he learn that it was created by a special five-oil liniment, with hints of menthol, wintergreen, eucalyptus and lavender, being lovingly applied to the limbs of legends.

Memory magnifies and isolates, teases and beguiles. Manchester United was a playground for Paul McGuinness long before it shaped his coaching philosophy and, in its original incarnation, reinforced his personal values. He used Sir Matt Busby's old leather swivel chair as a roundabout. His favourite uncle, Bobby Charlton, threatened to throw him in the players' bath.

His father, Wilf, succeeded Busby as United manager. He is 80 now, a lucid link to a storied past. Paul ended a lifelong association with United and joined the Football Association as a coach educator in October 2017. The club's history is woven into that of their family, irrespective of its evolution into a marketing monolith that refers to the Cayman Islands as 'our home country' in its annual report.

The era of Busby and Ferguson has become a tourist trap, helping the club's new powerbrokers to sell romanticism to a global audience from the genteel anonymity of offices in Mayfair. Where once football was a release from the drudgery of manual labour on Salford Docks, it is now celebrated in United's statement to shareholders as a measurement of social media penetration.

A brief rebellion against the Glazer family petered out, signalling grudging acceptance of the men whose rapacious capitalism overwhelmed patrician owners. A game rooted in working-class escapism allows executive vice-chairman Ed Glazer to charge like-minded souls $250,000 to attend a fundraising event for the re-election of Donald Trump at his $22.7 million home in Beverly Hills.

Paul McGuinness was struck by the lack of reference to the history of football on FA coaching courses. His reputation in youth development was based upon a culture that took, as its major theme, 'following in footsteps'. United coaches were regarded as 'guardians of a legacy'; they preached pride in the club's past. The reference point, that individuals are the essence of any institution, formed a checklist to guide decisions.

Father and son owe their lives, in different ways, to random acts of chance. But for a knee injury sustained in a reserve-team match the previous Saturday, Wilf would have been on British European Airways Flight 609, which crashed on its third attempt to take off from a slush-covered runway at Munich-Riem Airport on 6 February 1958 and killed eight fellow Busby Babes.

Paul had agreed to coach in the United States when, on impulse, he visited Eric Harrison and Brian Whitehouse, who had schooled him in United's youth team. He was 22. Having left full-time football to study for a sports science degree at Loughborough University, he was asked to answer an injury crisis that had left United's reserve team short of players.

He filled in for eight games before Sir Alex Ferguson offered him a two-year contract as second-team captain. The manager recognised a figure of quiet authority, a natural link to teenagers learning their trade alongside senior internationals on the fringe of the first team. When that contract expired, Ferguson watched him struggle to build a playing career at Chester before offering him a part-time role as United's education and welfare officer.

It was a portentous apprenticeship. McGuinness found digs for the Class of '92 before they found fame and became another silicon-enhanced football brand. He put Gary Neville, pundit, property developer and right-on politician, on to a good thing by organising his first media training course.

The boys' dreams were developed by the proximity of their predecessors. 'They understood the history. They'd been coached by Nobby Stiles, Brian Kidd, Eric Harrison. Sir Alex made sure he had a core of home-grown people around the place. That's probably why he brought me back. He knew my dad, and he knew my feeling for it. I can see now what he was doing; establishing connectivity through people who knew the club.

'The modern owner is detached. The CEO is more of a financial man than a football man. Of course, the money is much bigger. Managers are sacked at the first sign of any problem. But to have a good team in any business, or any sense, you need people who are connected together so that the sum of the parts is worth more than the individual.

'That takes time for people to get to know each other. I remember once being in the directors' box at United and there was an American guy next to me. He said, "Gee man, are these set moves?" I explained many of the players had been brought up together, so they almost knew what each other was going to do before it happened.

'You had Beckham and Gary Neville playing down the right, Butt and Scholes working together, Phil Neville linking with Giggs. They had very good players around them, Yorke and Cole up front, doing all these overs and unders, but they knew each other inside out, on and off the field. When that connection is so strong you can keep it rolling.

'Look back over the years, beyond Sir Alex, to Sir Matt. He and Jimmy Murphy, who coached the players, were the key members of staff. After the crash they brought in Jack Crompton and Johnny Aston, ex-players, so they already knew the system. Then my dad broke his leg and went on the staff, so that's another person who knows what he's doing.

'My dad coached Nobby Stiles, Brian Kidd, Tony Whelan, John Cooke and Jim Ryan, who all went on to the staff at United. Then I'm brought in, Jim Ryan's son comes on, and my dad's telling me about Jimmy Murphy. Sir Alex brought in Brian McClair, Mick Phelan. These are people who live and breathe United. It's a way of life that they are already into.

'Even those who come from outside, like Denis Law, Cantona and Solskjær, fall in love. It wasn't a monolithic club to us. It was like a family, because of the way Sir Alex ran it. Bobby Charlton used to come to our house every year at Christmas; it was Uncle Bobby and Auntie Norma, so I can only imagine it would have been Uncle Eddie Colman, or Uncle Duncan Edwards.

'All these young players, playing fantastic, exciting football, lost. My mum talked about them more than my dad, so for me it wasn't just a piece of history. I wonder how much people know about the crash now, and the romanticism of the recovery, but it is still embedded in the club. It meant more to us, of course, because dad was a Babe.'

His father remembers the immediate aftermath of Munich as 'a thick fog'. He and Gordon Clayton, a young goalkeeper, represented surviving players at the funerals. The victims are ghosts, gliding down the corridor between generations. Black and white photographs and jerky, sepia-toned moving images aid veneration, but it is the turf they trod that reminds us of a way of life, and the deeper meaning of the manner of their deaths.

'As coaches, we reminded the boys they were actually running in the footsteps of Edwards, Charlton, Best and Law at the Cliff training ground. There was an even stronger message when they pulled the red shirt on and played at Old Trafford in the FA Youth Cup, which the Babes won for its first five years. We'd infer they were guardians of the tradition, the playing style, the behaviour, the whole thing.'

The association extended to particular tournaments. United have a special affinity with the Blue Stars youth tournament in Zurich, won 16 times between 1954 and 1982. Youth teams return annually to the week-long Milk Cup in Northern Ireland, where football is almost secondary to a ritual enacted each Tuesday, for as long as anyone can remember.

United's boys stage races in the sand dunes before wading deeper into the cold, grey sea until someone loses his balance and is submerged. Every player must then swim up to their neck, at least. It is an example of the tangential influence of John Hattie, a New Zealand academic whose concept of Visible Teaching, developed over 15 years and meta-analysis of 800 instances of achievement, involves students being helped to become their own teachers.

'Hattie grades the most important things that affect learning. One of the best, in schools, is Outward Bound courses, because you're out of your comfort zone. You've got to learn new skills quickly, listen to instructions, and watch your teammates. You've got to work with them. It's so life-enhancing. In terms of football, tournaments and tours can do that.'

McGuinness hails Ferguson as 'a cultural architect'. He drilled deeper, demanded attention to the smallest details. His lessons were harshly delivered at times, but his emotional intelligence belied the martinet's caricature. When a point was made to an individual, it swept across the club like a series of after-shocks from a tightly centred earthquake.

'I was twenty-seven, very young to be in charge of the Centre of Excellence. It was the first time I had run a development week. I had to organise the coaching, the timetable and the trial games, which had to be in the afternoon because Sir Alex wanted to watch the four-teen-year-olds. There was kit to sort, minibuses to organise, drinks to provide, a lot of running about to do.

'All the scouts were invited. Some were a bit scary, because they'd been there when I had my trial as a kid. It went down really well, but on the Monday morning the manager called me into his office. He said, "Right, sit down. Some of the scouts said they think you're arro-gant." Honestly, it was like he'd kicked me in the balls. I was like, I can't believe that, I've been so humble. I've been working so hard.

'And he said, "Yeah, but you've been that busy you're forgetting to speak to them. These guys have come from all over the country, they've brought these kids, and they're working like hell all the time. You need to give them a pat on the back and tell them how good the player is. That is so important." He's not given me a bol-locking. That's great advice. From then on, that's exactly what I did.

'You've got to pay attention. You've got to show you care. I've seen managers walk straight past the youth team guy at clubs, because he doesn't have time to know

122

him. That youth guy might just buy him a little time. It is a massive lesson, to be interested in what everybody is doing. We were building a staff, a club within a club, based on the manager's values.'

Another aspect of the humanity of Ferguson's management is hidden in the small print of United's first title win in 26 years, in the Premier League's inaugural season, 1992–93. His team were in the relegation zone after failing to win any of their first three games when he emerged from the dressing room and shouted at McGuinness to 'get in here now'. The tone of the summons prompted a tremor of self-doubt: 'I'm thinking, I'm going to get it in the neck now for something. And he says, "Get me Paul Gibson's telephone number, now." Paul Gibson was a goalkeeper, under-sixteen, who'd had a boot right in his face. It had knocked his nose back, and they were saying he might not play again. He was in hospital with his parents.

'So ten minutes after the first-team game he rang him and said, "Look, don't worry, you're going to be fine. We're going to get the best treatment for you, there won't be a problem. You'll be back training soon." That's one example of thousands, probably, that people don't know about. He wasn't just this guy on TV shaking his fist at the ref.

'And of course, what happens then is a ripple effect. The boy's parents tell other parents. I go and speak to the other coaches, so they go, "Oh, so I need to do that for the under-tens". Sir Alex gives people his time. That's why when he went into hospital for a minor operation he woke up at 7 a.m. to find a load of managers there, checking how he was.'

The outpouring of concern, goodwill and respect when Ferguson suffered a brain haemorrhage in May 2018 underlined his impact, but he has been retired for five years. United's credo has changed under José Mourinho, who has corporate permission to defy convention and elevate cloying, minutely organised resistance over freedom of spirit and boldness of expression.

Mourinho doubled down on such heresy by referring acidly to United's 'football heritage', as if the term represented a simple summary of results. Enmeshed in his own ego, Mourinho ignored the inconvenient truth that the best clubs gauge their impact by something more substantial than the league table. They seek to remain community assets in a globalised economy. They value the empirical evidence of tradition, and express themselves with a certain style, an emotionally engaging panache. They prioritise tomorrow without patronising the achievements of yesterday.

Who can protect the purity of the bloodline? The Neville brothers are characteristically 'busy', to use Jaap Stam's immortal description of their irritating ubiquity. Brand Beckham owns an MLS expansion club in Miami. Ryan Giggs manages Wales. Paul Scholes applied to manage United's under-23 team in the summer of 2017 but was rejected in favour of Ricky Sbragia. Michael Carrick was integrated into the first-team coaching squad in the summer of 2018 but only Nicky Butt, as head of United's academy, represents immediate continuity.

'We do things the Manchester United way because we think we are pioneers in what we do,' Butt told Mark Ogden of ESPN. 'We move forward, we don't stand still. We have coaches and people at the club who don't suck up to kids. Instead, they help them learn how to do things in life.'

It was impossible, then, to avoid the symbolism of United's 2–0 defeat to Liverpool in the last 16 of the 2018 Uefa Youth League on a cold, dull winter's afternoon at Tranmere Rovers, where roughly 300 spectators huddled in three sections of the main stand. Butt was self-contained on the touchline, but poor tactical and positional awareness, aligned to a lack of aggression, clearly stung.

The identity of the former England teammate in the opposition dugout hardly eased the angst. Steven Gerrard has learned quickly, as a coach, to be deliberately low-key. His satisfaction came, not in the breathlessness of combat he once relished as a player, but in the intelligence of his team's pressing, their fluidity and width when in possession.

Youth football is a twilight world, and the tie lacked the toxicity of the Old Trafford fixture between the senior teams three weeks later, when United won 2–1 after being let off the leash by Mourinho for the opening half hour. Mindless chants about Munich and murderers defiled a rivalry between two great neighbouring cities that encompasses art, science, commerce and culture.

For some players, the transition into coaching is an indulgence, a reflexive response to waning powers. Gerrard is driven by a sense of duty, rather than destiny. The dark circles around his narrow eyes suggest that the anxiety he suppressed as a player, due to his overwhelming sense of responsibility to both club and community, has been renewed.

This is a man known to a city by his given name, Steven. He cherished the footsteps he followed, as Liverpool captain. Yeats, Hughes, Thompson, Souness, Hansen; their surnames were shorthand for strength, passion, intelligence and professional vindictiveness. To fulfil predictions that he will become Liverpool's next great manager, he must prove worthy of walking a mile in the boots of Shankly, Paisley, Fagan, Benítez and Dalglish.

Jürgen Klopp, the German extrovert making a cogent case to be considered worthy of admission to that group, advised Gerrard that 'after a couple of years you will know if this gig is for you'. The sense of succession planning is enhanced by a club video that captures them together on a long, vanilla-coloured leather sofa in the manager's office, overlooking the Melwood training ground.

Klopp reminisces about his first match as a manager, two days after he retired as a player. He still saw everything as a right back, and bluffed his way through a press conference, where 'they obviously don't listen because I have no clue what I am talking about', before running home to watch the match four times, so that he would be prepared for the following morning's training.

'Opinion is what you have as a player,' he tells Gerrard. 'As a coach you have to tell the truth. You will see it, and then you have to think about how you can achieve it for your boys. We all have our different ways. It is all about trial and error. No one knows how it works at the beginning. That's why it is so difficult to start on a public level, where people are talking about you all the time.

'We are human beings. We have doubts, questions. What am I doing? How can I deal with this player, this problem? Losing feels the same at every level but not having outside pressure helps. If you want to learn you don't need to be a genius, you need to be busy and interested. Then, when you know how it works, it will be a big help that you have been a world-class player.'

Gerrard is clearly captivated by his search for greater understanding and has taken a profound gamble in signing a four-year contract to manage Rangers. The acid bath of Old Firm rivalry strips away logic and reason; joining a storied club with such obviously unrealised internal issues was the football equivalent of running into a burning building.

At Liverpool, in the first stage of his managerial apprenticeship, he learned to watch a match through the prism of his players' personalities, to study patterns of play and project the consequences of his decisions. He found a voice, settled on a philosophy. Watching him oversee a coaching session for his under-18 squad in fine rain was a reminder of the humility that so often accompanies greatness.

He hauled mannequins around the pitch, carried miniature goals on his shoulder, and made an unnecessary diversion to introduce himself. Two French coaches watched him reverentially, at a distance. Once the session had concluded, he delighted parents with shy, understated gestures of recognition. Fittingly, for someone who constantly projected his ambition on to others, he made a point of stressing his debt to Phil Roscoe, an 'absolutely brilliant' education and welfare officer.

A wry smile creased that pale, familiarly pinched face when I asked him to expand on lessons delivered by his former managers and coaches. 'How long have you got? I've probably had 25 years of those messages drilled into me. They always relate to the club, the values, the attitude and the mentality you've got to have to get to the top.

'You're not just getting judged as a footballer, you're getting judged as a person. You've got to have something within you that wants to learn, wants to earn the right. I keep using the word obsessed but if you're obsessed and you've got ability and talent, you've got a better chance.

'I'll be honest. Coaching is a lot more difficult than I thought it would be before I started doing my qualifications. There's a lot more to it. Preparation's key. When you're a player, you automatically think your coach and his staff are doing an easy job. But when you've got to go out there yourself, out of your comfort zone with twenty-five players around you, it's tough, very tough.

'As a player I could switch off when the game was done. That is very difficult as a coach. Now after a game I'm thinking what went well, what didn't go well, what individuals do I need to work on this week, who do I need to praise, who do I need to speak to, who's been naughty at school? Having to handle that side of it has been very different for me.'

The pathway stretching before an emerging player is strewn with more obstacles than in Gerrard's youth. Criticism is more virulent because of social media; premature wealth brings intensity of scrutiny and constant temptation. Gerrard can offer only so much protection from random opinion and unwanted external opportunism. Warning signs, lack of punctuality despite being ferried to training by taxi, are leaped upon.

Do boys understand the basic brutality of the game? 'Some do, and the penny drops with them a lot earlier than others. Some come in and just think it's a game of football and it's a training session. They don't realise the harsh reality maybe until they're told it's over, that they're released and getting moved on from the football club.

'Then I bet you it hits them very, very hard and they're saying to themselves, why didn't I switch on earlier? Kids can be ruined by giving them too much too soon. Kids can be ruined by getting an agent too soon. Kids can be ruined by parents being too strong and too forceful. You have to be very careful when there's a lot of money, a lot of pressure, involved. I ask myself as a parent, what would I do in that situation? Just try and be patient and make the right decision for football reasons.

'There is pressure, but you hope not to see it in the kids. It is important that we, as staff, take fear away from them, if we can. If you go on to the pitch with worries and insecurities on your mind you are not going to be able to perform to your level. We want them to express themselves, do themselves justice with a clear mind.

'It is sink or swim at the top. It is cut-throat and it is brutal. Talent gets you a certain distance but the way the game has gone, you've got to be world class and really, really hungry. I've been saying it for a short while now, if you're a very good player at the top six, eight clubs in the Premier League you're probably not going to get in and stay in. A manager has to be immensely brave to play a young lad when he has an experienced professional in the same position.'

Gerrard consciously restricted the force field of his fame when working with young players. The easy option of using his own career as a convenient storyboard was resisted because 'I'm done'. Dealing with senior players, spared the consequences of serial under-achievement, required a different approach.

Gerrard the manager demanded the virtues of Gerrard the player, intensity, pride in performance, unyielding commitment. He promised to root out those who failed 'to empty the tank' because he expects nothing less from himself.

'If you don't work hard away from the training pitch, you get found out. The session will not flow as you want it to. As soon as I've finished my day's work I've got to be thinking straight away, how am I going to progress from today into tomorrow? I'm making tons of mistakes and trying to improve each day.'

Libraries have entire shelves devoted to deconstruction of the mysteries of personal motivation. Ultimately perhaps, it comes from the dreams we had as children. Gerrard relished the rawness of street football on Ironside Road, Huyton; Paul McGuinness, his brother by another football mother, was captivated by the tension of 'Knockout Wembley', one-on-one contests in the playground at St Hugh's primary school in Altrincham.

McGuinness was infatuated with his father's England caps and shirts; he would put them on, with permission, and pose in front of the bedroom mirror. From the age of 11 he spent an hour each Friday night sitting on a stool and scraping the mud off his boots before sponging them down and lovingly wiping the three stripes so they regained their lustre.

Gerrard took time to confirm his allegiance; he wore kits from Tottenham, Norwich, Real Madrid, Barcelona and even Manchester United. Once on the Kop, though, he found his calling in the seething, swaying masses. The skinny kid with close-cropped hair, who idolised Ian Rush, would truly live the game, through and for the common man.

His impassioned plea to teammates before the 'Miracle of Istanbul' confers immortality: 'Just look at our fans. It means the world. Don't fucking well let them down. You don't realise the reaction you will get from these fans if you win. You will be a hero for the rest of your life. Make every challenge count, every run count, every shot count. Otherwise you will fucking regret it for the rest of your lives.'

McGuinness understands the sentiments because he, too, has seen the game seize control of the central nervous system. Old Trafford celebrating a 3–0 win over Diego Maradona's Barcelona in 1984 'felt like an aircraft taking off'. Ole Gunnar Solskjær's 93rd-minute goal at the Camp Nou, which won United the Champions League in 1999, 'was how I imagine being on drugs is like'.

The best memories have a human thread. At the staff party after that victory, players' wives and girlfriends compared bruises to their calves, sustained when they instinctively threw themselves out of bucket seats to celebrate. Johan Cruyff, Barcelona's manager in 1994, was seduced by the smell of hot dogs at Old Trafford; United's kitman Norman Davies brought him one to eat in the tunnel, like a naughty schoolboy.

'So, what do we want from football?' asks McGuinness. 'Raw excitement and songs, tribalism transferred to the pitch. When the flags are going and United are playing in Europe, or going to Anfield, you tingle when you go to the ground. Surely that's something you have to be aiming for. Otherwise your product is going to die a death, if you're not careful.

'Over the last year or so, I've been going to youth games, schoolboy games, non-League games. I went to FC United with my dad. They mobbed him in the bar and I couldn't get him out. It feels more like football there. Everyone says hello to you. I can't tell you how much I enjoyed the pies at half-time, the Bovril. It was like, this is pure football.

'You can't pass on a way of life unless everyone lives it. One of the new guys who came to the club said to me,

"What's so special about United then?" It was as if he couldn't see it. When I gave my answer it was the truth, but it was probably a truth he was never going to understand, because as I said, it's a feeling. It's a feeling. You feel like you belong.'

He pulls out a scrapbook from what he wryly refers to as 'a royal visit' to Kenya with United's youth team. They visited HIV clinics, orphanages, and staged training sessions in Kibera, the largest urban slum in Africa, four miles from the centre of Nairobi. The poverty was oppressive; the average income was less than $1 a day, and there was no running water.

Football felt tangential, but it brought temporary joy into blighted lives. A wooden carving on the wall of the assembly room at the Starehe boys' school, which began as a rescue centre, prodded the conscience: 'From those to whom much has been given, much will be required.'

The innocence was appealing but begged a follow-up question, relevant to the modern game: are those demands getting out of hand? When legends are denigrated, and leaders are belittled, the answer has to be in the affirmative.

CHAPTER SEVEN

Angry Britain

'I get moaned at for fucking voicing my opinion. When is it acceptable to say this can't continue any more, and for people to shut the fuck up and actually realise I am saying it for a reason? Arsène Wenger is finished, finished. What the fuck? I don't need to speak eight languages, and I don't have to have been a manager before to see we are a fucking shambles.' – Mr DT, Arsenal Fan TV

The stars of Fan TV, uniformly self-regarding and inevitably self-appointed, emphasise the coarseness of what passes as public debate in a world without the constraint of truth, fairness and balance. Their narcissism is as overpowering as their ignorance, yet they set the tone, purport to speak for those who lack the intellect or inclination to think for themselves.

Professional reputations are shredded, conspiracy theories are concocted, and incoherent agendas are pursued. They shout into the void because they fear silence or a lull in ferocity will strip them of their imaginary legitimacy. They are shallow, manipulative, cowardly and perpetually angry. They are football's sound and fury, which swirls and echoes in the wind tunnels of social media.

'Angry England. Angry Britain.'

The sandpaper scrape of Sean Dyche's voice fills the open-plan lounge of his home, on the fringe of a golf course in Northamptonshire. He may be judged externally on such superficialities as the deceptive menace of his bearing, that of a recently retired regimental sergeant major, but here, perched on a long, deep sofa, he can be himself: acute, intelligent and knowing.

Taking Burnley into Europe, after establishing them in the Premier League, is a substantial achievement, yet elements of the metropolitan elite still regard him as the managerial equivalent of a tin bath in front of a coal fire. The realities of which he speaks, of football's earthiness, relentlessness and rigour, is so out of context with the times that the sophistication of his approach is routinely overlooked.

'There is definitely a case that football, and how it's run and the view of it, often mirrors life. This is Angry Britain. I notice it because I'm old enough to have children. They're growing up in a different world than I grew up in. I'm not really on about the national media. I'm on about people gravitating to bad news, spreading stories via social media.

'There's a thirst for blame. Everyone wants a reason. It's an undertone of life. There are some great things about life but there's not much responsibility being taken for your own actions. It's mainly about blaming someone else. Look at football – blame the managers, blame the players, blame the club, blame this, blame that.

'Demand is instant. Managers' heads are on the block every single week, whereas there used to be a belief in the manager, the board and the owner, and a sense of where the club could go. The best example is Arsène Wenger. You know and I know, when he first started, everyone went, "Who?" But the Arsenal fans trusted the club. The rest is history, and they've been proved absolutely right.

'At the time there was a tiny ripple in the water. No one had really heard of Grampus Eight, the club that he'd come from, but the media were going, "This will be interesting". Imagine that same scenario now. There would be uproar, "Who is this wally? What has he done to earn the right?" That is how things have changed. It is a real in-a-nutshell moment for me.

'Appointing a manager used to be solely a board decision. Now there is a demand to include the fan base. Social media, and the fans' view, is so powerful. One of the biggest ironies is when the Premier League and the money came in they said, "The fans are going to go to sleep and nobody's going to care". Actually, clubs now care more than ever about fans' opinions. Fans do feel a connection to it, which can be good and bad, obviously.'

Sport in North America breeds a reverence for the coach; the culture of modern football elevates a manager because of his social prominence and assumed authority, yet disparages his professionalism since it is not merely permissible to second guess his decisions and standards, but almost obligatory.

Dyche uses a large television screen, mounted on the lounge's broad, central fireplace, as an allegorical prop. 'You're in my house, right, and we're looking at the TV. I'd be surprised if we couldn't actually guide a rocket into space from that TV. Do you know what I do? I turn it on and turn it off. But I guarantee in three years I'll get a new one because you just get bored. Football's gone a bit like that. It's "if it doesn't bring immediate gratification, let's change it".

'So, the idea of building, the idea of moving forward, the idea of using a bigger picture approach to remodelling a football club, is very rare. We've done it at Burnley but it would never have been possible without the successes, or relative successes, along the way. For us it has been about getting in the Premier League and staying there.

'The judgement on my work is "are you giving that instant hit of winning, or winning enough?" At other clubs it is more literal, in terms of winning silverware. If you are not supplying that hit, there's no growth period to allow things to evolve. It is "right, get rid, move on". People can become bored with managers.

'The priority is results, and by the way, I never hide from that. That's our job. We all get that, so let's take that as a given. But we've all seen it. Sometimes there's a change of ownership. There's a dislike taken, for no apparent reason. That happens in life, we're all guilty of it, but that can spread like wildfire: "He's not the right man. We never wanted him in the first place." All that sort of stuff. It has always been there, but today it's magnified, enhanced and rushed through very quickly.

'If you hold to the truth and core values, you can keep it as purely aligned as you possibly can. You have to look beyond outside forces at times. That's the thing that has changed, off the pitch. There's a lot of noise in and around football now; that can get into people's minds and change thinking.

'They love pragmatic people in business. In football, it's boring. So if you're a pragmatic manager, you're boring. That's not an opinion, it's almost a fact. The idea I stand by is that the board of directors, chief exec and manager, are there for a reason. They have been chosen for their skillset. Well, stand by your skillset then and deliver it because people will come as long as you get it right.

'If you're letting outside influences make those decisions, that's a below-par start point. It's not that those
influences are invalid, because a lot of fans actually give
you some real good sense, but don't align with others to
cajole them into a different opinion. You can drive
yourself mad, worrying what people think of you.
Remember the reality of what you are. Ask, how can we
grow what we are?'

Dyche is associating himself with two of the most
contentious words in the football lexicon, command
and control. They defy the modern game's manic
demand for a loose form of democracy, which so often
mutates into anarchy. He shares Wenger's spirit, as a
dynastic manager whose attention to detail borders
on the obsessive, and, having signed a new four and a
half year contract in early 2018, is now the last man
standing.

The contrasting nature of their clubs is inescapably
relevant. Burnley is the beating heart of a small town,
the most enduring connection to a community that has
lost the formative influence and economic nourishment
of the coal and cotton industries. Arsenal is a global
investment vehicle that has sold portions of its soul.
Wenger was hopelessly compromised and undermined
from within over the course of a year.

His departure from the club, confirmed on 20 April
2018, was received with the reverence devoted to the
death of a monarch. The sense of release was a gracious

reference to his gradual weakness, and the praise for his innovation and unrepeatable longevity rang true. He lay in state for the final eight matches of the season, as the hypocrites dabbed their eyes with suspiciously dry handkerchiefs. He had been neutralised, even José Mourinho paid his respects.

Homage due to Wenger for transformative work undertaken, once he walked through the symbolic splendour of Highbury's marble hall and into an introductory press conference on 22 September 1996, did not entirely silence the crude chorus of the mob, or the whisperings of self-serving courtiers. Internal critics gave him the disparaging nickname 'Mugabe', after the discredited Zimbabwean president.

Sadness, watching him enduring a consequent range of emotions from confusion to defiance and eventual resignation, was tangible. Mistakes had multiplied, reinforced by stubbornness. Collective mismanagement took its toll. Wenger's loyalty to his staff and his players was counter-productive; he lacked Sir Alex Ferguson's instinct for a surgical strike on those closest to him.

Bill Walsh, the great NFL coach, retired after ten years at San Francisco 49ers because he felt his players had stopped listening to him. He was burned out, physically and intellectually. Even after 22 autocratic years, and with his reputation stained by stasis, Wenger is worth hearing out; the tragedy is that too few ultimately had the faith and patience to do so.

He is taller than expected in the flesh, his keen intellect offset by quirky humour and the hint of a robust ego. He has an ascetic air; it is easy to imagine those eyes, underscored by the caterpillar tracks of time, staring out from a monk's cowl. Football may be his canvas but the broad brush strokes of his opinions give texture to societal problems way beyond his control.

As a manager, he defines himself as 'the carrier of the values'. Acidly, but accurately, he observes that 'five hundred years ago the target for people was to be a saint. Fifty years ago it was to be a hero in war. Today it is to be a billionaire or, even more, a celebrity.'

His 'basic belief in human beings' is tested by a constant search for substance 'in a society that is more demanding and opinionated'. His distaste for the narrow ideological impulse of Brexit is mirrored by his quiet despair at the lack of trust in professional expertise and a prevailing climate of intolerance and suspicion, where 'people can be selfish and mean'.

On this particular morning he arrived from a photo-shoot for the club's official suit supplier and a pre-breakfast press conference, at which he used the concerns of German Chancellor Angela Merkel to support his argument for reform of the transfer system.

Our pre-arranged subject, youth development, allowed him quickly to expand into the wider impact of the isolation and intensity inherent in the academy system. 'It is important to have the boys early enough to get them to learn technical aspects of the game, because traditionally you first have to make the ball your friend. The earlier you do that, the more chance you have to achieve that. But the perverse situation is that maybe we create too early a feeling that they will be professional football players. You make them think their future is only in football and that's not the case.

'It creates a problem for them to adapt to society. There is basically no contact any more with what passes as normal life. A boy of fifteen, sixteen, seventeen, even until nineteen, should go to a normal school and have multi-sport activities. He should meet people who are not in the game, people who play basketball or do theatre. I feel always it would release the pressure. The pressure on them is too early, too big to focus.

'The family many times stops work to take care of the boy, which is understandable looking at the amount of income. We have gone from a society where your father told you "if you don't work well at school, I will stop you playing football" to a system where the father asks the boy "how did you practise today? What did the coach say to you?" The pressure is on the whole family for the boy to be successful in sport.

'If we had a system where players would earn exactly the same until the age of seventeen, when they sign professional, they would choose the clubs only for sporting reasons. At the moment the financial factor is a huge influence on the decision. It's understandable because they get the money very early. In my opinion, that's where the system is very poor and very weak.

'Somewhere in some part of your life, you have to feel the strength of your dream, as long as it looks impossible to achieve. That is a test for you. How much do you want it? It doesn't come immediately. When things come too early, with too much money, it can create bad habits, the feeling you are already there. I don't believe it gives you the strength in your desire that is needed to make a big career.

'If you have a talented child in mathematics or literature you have to pay for their study. We are the only activity who pays students to learn. And today we have gone to the extreme, where we make millionaires of people who would never even be football players. We just speculate on their talent. There is a big investment in our industry on young prospects. The prices of transfers are spiralling.

'We pay early, so we don't have to pay one hundred or two hundred million later on. But we have to think deeply about the process because we know, in the last statistics, that sixty-seven per cent of the players who were in an academy between sixteen and twenty-one do not play any more football at all after the age of twenty-one. Sixty-seven per cent! Can you believe that?

'That means something is not right. Perhaps the disappointment is too big. Perhaps we make them believe too early they will be successful in football, and when that dream collapses we have not prepared them to deal with it. That's why we could give them exactly the same education and keep them in normal life.

'I do highly concentrate on the academy process, and what I have lost in the last ten, twelve years is I've had to dedicate much more time to the first team and the environment. The media demands for example are huge now, so I have a restricted availability. But I still follow up. One of the parts of my job that I enjoy the most is to give a chance to young people.'

He seemed eager to continue the debate, but we had long since exhausted our allotted time. His day, like that of a prime minister, was micro-managed in 20-minute blocks. It would be instructive for his most trenchant critics to shadow him, since his role is multi-faceted and requires constant mental agility, yet he is doomed to be judged in isolation.

I was struck, that day, by a sense of self-sacrifice. Wenger seemed to welcome abstract debate as a diversion from the latest revelation of conspirators, seeking to stab Caesar. His death scene would be played out not in Ancient Rome's Theatre of Pompey but in the modern arena of the Emirates Stadium. He would survive the Ides of March, but his fate had been sealed, with the apparent compliance of his chief executive. Et tu, Gazidis?

My mind went back to his tour de force at Arsenal's chaotic AGM in 2017, where he seized the floor with the following speech, in which his human touch exposed the patrician folly that had preceded his intervention. 'The only thing I can say is I dedicate ninety-nine per cent of my lifetime to try to make you happy,' he began. 'Looking at what happened today, it's not easy.

'I feel that a football club is about the past, the present, the future. On what we see now in the evolution of the game, football is ahead of society. And what is for sure, the weight of the past and the weight of the future has been kicked out of the game. The weight of the present has become heavier. It's the only one thing people want.

'That means for me it is here and now. Win or out. It is acceptable but I always guided this club with one idea, that a club is first about values that have been created by the past. When I look at photos of 1930s, 1950s and 1960s, they have not always won but there is pride, happiness in the mind of these people for the sense of belonging to this club.

'I think that is important. I have been guided all my life here by respecting these values and I serve this club with integrity, total commitment. I will never betray these people who have created these values. We have to be proud of them. Arsenal is a highly respected club not only because we won the last game but because we represent something that is exceptional.'

It was a paean to lost perspective and unattainable purity, which reinforced an unlikely affiliation with Dyche. The Burnley manager may identify more naturally with Eddie Howe, as an English coach who has organically developed a similarly small-scale club, Bournemouth, but he shares Wenger's sense of duty, emotional depth and commitment to modernity.

Dyche takes pride in the accessibility of his players, their unaffected response to strangers in public places. They have greater wealth because of recent success but are yet to require the erection of a security screen. They are profiled psychometrically, so he can best utilise their learning styles. Many are more comfortable in communicating through text messaging than speaking face to face.

'If they want more depth they go and speak to our psychologist, who chats on lifestyle and acts as a sounding board. One of my golden rules is that process is totally private. It's nothing to do with me. I just want to help them learn. Mental health and wellbeing is going to be a big part of the future. How can you get not just a player, but his people, his team, to buy in? I can foresee meetings with agent, parent, brother, whoever. Not daily but now and again, saying "this is where he's at". Management has gone full circle.

'When I was young, Brian Clough was held up as a great example of a man manager. Sir Alex, too. Then, ten, twelve years later, it became very tactical. We had the big technical debate about English players. Now, because of the academy system, where the one thing they are is technical, it has almost come round again, to how you manage the people. One of my big rules is, affect the person and you'll affect the performance. I believe in rapport-building; me, my staff, the connection amongst the group. This idea of team-ship is going to be big. People think it's a gimmick and it isn't.

'It makes me laugh when people say a new manager is going in to change the culture. Like that just happens overnight. It's difficult. It takes time to realign an environment. I go back to my first board meeting at Burnley. I think they were quite surprised but I said, "This is how I work. Tell me what kind of club you believe this is." I had five different answers.

'Someone then stood up and said, "We have to be solvent". So, we can start by driving towards that goal, and dealing with the ups and downs. Once we get there, where can we move it on to? It often links into recruitment. We had a good start to this season, and some of the press lads were saying, "Well, Sean, you seem to work only with good characters and only sign good characters".

'Who wouldn't? That's common sense. It's pragmatic, that old, untrendy word. But then I mentioned our friend Joey Barton. They looked at me and went schtum. I talked about the person I came to know, not the person in public view. A good character in a different way perhaps, a winner, wants to learn, wants to improve, wants professionalism, wants detail. What is underneath those layers?

'If one of the main start points is good character, you need depth of knowledge. Let's take Chris Wood. I knew him as an eighteen-year-old at West Brom. I knew players and coaches who were with him there, who I could speak to. "What is he like, what do you think, how has he done, where was he then and where is he now?" You can get so much more in-depth information, other than just through your eyes.

'A lot was made recently of recruitment models, and how everyone is poring over a computer screen full of stats. A start point, maybe. You get tipped off about a player and you think, let's have a look. There are so many systems now, I use Wyscout as an obvious one, so you go and get some clips. You think, OK, quite like the body language, that's what I want to see. Let's look at stats – yeah, decent. Right, now, let's get some eyes on him.

'Let's get eyes on the level he's playing at. Let's get eyes on where his club are. Let's get eyes on him away from home. Let's get our eyes on the player that's third from bottom, not third from top. How is he delivering performances in a struggling team? It all goes into the melting pot. Eventually your eyes don't lie, but don't just go on your eyes, because if you do, you're in trouble.

'"The look", they used to call it. Well, I've seen a million players come and go who looked easy on the eye. You get them in the room and you go, "oh dear". Tick as many boxes as possible, and then decide on the market you want to enter. The Premier League is like the

London house market. It's not about true value and worth, you pay or you don't. It's as simple as that.'

Burnley cannot afford the lapse in judgement that results in a £20 million signing being quietly ushered out of the back door for £8 million. Dyche's training philosophy is designed to maximise talent through repetition, the concept of automaticity. He cites the certainties of a golfer's practice regimen, from the stance, through visualisation to consistent execution of the perfect shot, as a telling example of the fusion between art and science.

'They know when the pressure's on, they need that seven-iron like their life depends on it. They will do it right because they have laid that down in the fibres that run through their brain. If you can get to that level of automaticity your body will just do it. Bang, I'm ready. And you will just keep going and going. The more you do it, the more natural it becomes, like catching a ball.

'In theory, it is not as easy when you bring a football match into it, because there are a million and one things that can happen, but when we train, we train properly all of the time. I stop warm-ups if I see something that's unacceptable. I talk a lot about high-level common sense. Trust is part of the alchemy. Players need to know they can trust you.

'I give them artistic licence to be the kid in the playground that they used to be, but we have to work. It's a profession. I still want them to be enthused by the daily work we offer, the thrill of training hard all of the time. It's a brilliant job, a fantastic job, there's no luck. I don't like that word. When a player says, "Oh, I've been really lucky", I say, no you haven't. You've worked really hard to be where you are.'

A modern manager must deal with exaggerated expectation, constant scrutiny and artful diversions from those with an agenda to pursue. Dyche's ambition is understated but underlined by his insistence on being the highest-paid individual at the club; his new contract is popularly assumed to involve an annual salary of £3.5 million.

He has no immediate wish to leave Burnley but accepts the theory that his next job, logically at a bigger club, is unlikely to be as all-encompassing. At the age of 46 he is entering a new phase in his career. Intriguingly, for such a viciously competitive profession, there is an obligation to mentor less experienced coaches, potential rivals in the medium term.

Dyche's advice is direct, and to the point: 'Learn how to deal with the media. Give it some real focus. Most are fair with me but learn not to get annoyed if you are mis-quoted, or served up as clickbait. Roll with the punches. Consider how you are handling things. Be careful, in my opinion, not to send out me, me, me messages. The team and club are way more important.

'Even when you're going well, you're going to get some stick. So try and depersonalise it. Try and understand the fact that fans just want to win. If the team aren't winning you're the man who has to front up. If you're not aware of that, then don't do it, don't become a manager. Get used to being in that lonely space where everyone is looking at you and saying "come on then".

'The best definition of leadership in football I've heard is "knowing what to do when you don't know what to do". That's not mine, I nicked it from an LMA course, but it encapsulates what we are talking about. Sometimes you've just literally got to go on instinct. Sharpen your instincts. Be aware of everything. I've learned every little thing counts in football. Every conversation counts.

'I've learned to be as detailed in my thinking as possible. What message did I send out and what came back to me? You improve at man management. Some have a natural aptitude, of course, but there's more detail in that, as a learned skill. I'm not talking about the arm-around-the-shoulder guy, "Hey, Mike, well done, you're doing great, just keep going". There's more depth to it than that.

'Learn not to get annoyed about the business side of it, particularly the agents. There are some very good ones, and there are some not so good ones, and they will annoy you with some of the practices involved in trying to get a deal, or shift a deal. Don't get too personal about it. It's business, simple as that.

'An agent ten years ago would be offering advice on a contract, more or less. He would want information on what you planned to do with his player. Now, depending on the level of the player, he is offering personal financial advice, legal support if and when needed, a car, PR, possibly a book, a stylist, other outside influences and interests. It gets to the point of supplying personal physiotherapy, sports science.

'Brand has become a big word in football, personal brand, individual brand. I can only imagine because I've never done it, but if you're managing one of those superpower clubs, it's like managing twenty-five CEOs, because in theory a player is like the CEO of a mini company. You've got to get a buy-in from the player who then has to get buy-in from other people, who all have an opinion.

'Some players surround themselves with very good people, who give very informed opinions, or reinforce the opinion of the manager or the coach or someone they trust. Some advisers will give an opinion that the player wants to hear, not the right opinion, just the opinion the player wants to hear. You've got to manage that situation, not just the player.'

A football manager lacks the anonymity of his industrial equivalent, whose most contentious decisions play out from the sanctuary of the boardroom. Privacy is unsustainable in the Premier League; public accountability, before an audience of millions, imposes such strain that even the trade's acknowledged master, Pep Guardiola, has spoken of getting out of the game as close to his 50th birthday as possible.

'The originals in my era had to keep working, not just because they loved it, but because they had to keep meat on the table at weekends, as my dad always said. That's changed. The sport is very wealthy and managers get paid well so they can make a choice. I don't think managers will go on until their seventies in the future. The demands are too great.

'I got into this because I had a feeling that things I learned as a player could offer someone else a chance. It's not about me. I'm done. It's about you. I want you to be ten times better than me and I'm going to offer you the things that I think will help. The hardship of management is that you've got to win because, if not, your chance to help them will be diminished.

'My be-all and end-all – sit back, glass of wine, thinking, that's good – is when the development of the players has allowed them to be successful. Seeing them grow, mature, improve and get their rewards along the way when they win. That's my nirvana of football management, and it's not changed since I was a youth team coach. I still believe in it now.

'The downside is that internal loneliness. Not missing your kids or your mates, but the sort of loneliness your friends and family won't understand. That's why, after the game, the managers gravitate towards each other, because they are the only two in that room who know how it feels. Everyone's got the biggest opinion until they sit in the chair. If you want to be a manager, get ready for it and learn how to cope with it.

'Learn that the only bit that's real are the people and the pitch. The rest is fake, plastic. As long as you can get your head around that, you'll be OK. But if you struggle to cope with the rest of it, you get swallowed up very quickly. I love it, and enjoy it, but football won't dominate my life completely. I look at my kids today and they are still the focus. You have to know where football lives.'

Occasionally, football has suitable symmetry. Dyche was the opposition manager in Wenger's last home game, a 5–0 win at the Emirates on a broiling Sunday afternoon in May. He formed part of the honour guard that set the tone for an elegiac occasion, which was given an idiosyncratic intimacy by Wenger's self-reflective response.

His speech to the crowd was received in reverential silence. 'Thank you for having me for such a long time. I know that it's not easy, but above all I am like you. I am an Arsenal fan. That means more than just watching football. It is a way of life. It is caring about the beautiful game, the values we cherish and something that goes through every cell of our body.'

His final press conference at the Emirates, a stadium 'that is part of myself', was equally affecting. 'I have managed eight hundred and forty games in the Premier League,' he said, his voice rising briefly, before falling, as if burdened by the weight of his words. 'Do you know how much that means? Do you know how many sleepless nights that means, before and after games?

'I have to think about all that. I have had to learn to disconnect. I have told myself, "Don't analyse how you feel any more. Forget about you. Just concentrate on problems you have to solve." This is a story that ends. I have to learn to reconnect with myself now ....'

CHAPTER EIGHT

Life Lessons

'I know where I am going to be in ten years. I will fight fucking hard, every single minute of every single day. You have to decide what you want to be. We all own our behaviours. Your career will flash before your eyes. If you want it, you have to grab it. No one wants to live with regret. Get out there and give it full Heavy Metal Harry.' – Team talk, Danny Cowley, manager, Lincoln City

There is no stigma in being sacked. Football managers look after their own, since they share secret scars and intimate memories of rejection. Pep Guardiola waived his preference for privacy out of respect and invited Paul Clement to study his training sessions; Sir Alex Ferguson, a discreet mentor for many, welcomed him as a weekend guest.

Lessons and insights were recorded in the journal Clement uses as a combination of textbook, diary and mind map. His cachet as a coach led to opportunities to expand his knowledge in the United States, where he visited franchises in the NFL and NBA. Networks needed to be replenished. He 'had the feelers out', watching games, visiting clubs, picking the brains of agents and making the rounds of TV studios.

This is the aspect of football management that no one really considers. Life goes on at a gentler pace without easing restlessness. Passions shift, persecutors seize other victims. Someone like Clement, discarded by Swansea a matter of months after being shortlisted as manager of the year for saving them from relegation from the Premier League, quickly becomes just another name on the tombstone.

The narrative of his decline and fall in South Wales, just before Christmas 2017, was set by the incredulity that froze his face when Renato Sanches, the Portuguese starlet whose season-long loan from Bayern Munich seemed such a coup, was so bereft of confidence and direction that he passed to an advertising hoarding at Stamford Bridge.

That was a hugely symbolic but ultimately deceptive image, since failure cannot be compressed into a single moment. It is a cumulative outcome, in Swansea's case from palsied recruitment, a by-product of a club wrestling with a new ownership structure and a disaffected fan base. Relegation from the Premier League was a collective failure.

The spring of 2018 was Clement's time for 'self-improvement'. It was an unwelcome but important opportunity to pause, re-evaluate and renew ambition. To do so, he needed to work through an acutely personal form of loss.

His tone, as he described the experience of coming to terms with dismissal, was characteristically earnest. 'The first phase is one of disappointment, almost a sense of relief. It has been hovering over you for a while. The pressure builds. You are in the middle of it. You know elements of the media are going after Premier League managers. I started badly and suddenly it was my turn. Then it was on to Mark Hughes at Stoke. They're just picking us off.

'You then move into the second phase. You feel raw, hard done by. You think of the stress on those around you. You learn from the nature of the calls or messages you get after you lose the job. Some, from people you expect, you get, some you don't. Some surprise you, in a good way and a bad way. They quickly fall away. Then you're checking your phone to see if it still works.

'There's no respect now. I had a fan sending me a message calling me a c-u-n-t. Unbelievable. It's not something that upsets me, and I know I am not going to change it, but it is not right. You are either wonderful or a disgrace. You try to say to yourself, well, that's the game these days, but is it? Should it be? You know you can't be bitter.

'You tell yourself, that's what happens, and go into a period of unemotional reflection. That's the third phase. You start to look at yourself. It can't have been everyone else's fault. You ask yourself what you might do differently if you had your time over. You start to challenge yourself. These were the things you couldn't do anything about, but these were some of the things you could have done.

'I should have been more insistent about recruitment at Swansea. I accept that, as a head coach, it is not under my control, but I should have been stronger in my approach, more focused. You go in with the idea of building behind the scenes – science, data, medicine, youth development – but you've just got to go for results. They are everything. Monday to Friday you plan and prepare. Saturday or Sunday you execute.

'Criticism will be there. Some of it will be deserved, and some will be undeserved. You've got to learn to not take too much notice of it either way. Things can change very quickly. A dark time can become a good time, and a good time can become a dark time. Just focus on preparing well, and work on the details.

'I have unbelievable respect for Arsène Wenger. We know there is no empathy for coaches and managers, but he has to have the thickest skin of any of us. How has anyone got the right to abuse him, to say he deserves to be sacked? Football is his life's work, and they are trying to bully him out of it.

'Sir Alex had a fantastic impact on a wide range of people over many years. I am sure there are owners out there who would like the idea of that at their club; certainly managers would love the chance. But in realistic terms, it won't happen again. I'm pretty typical. My two managerial jobs have lasted under a year. It is not about the long term any more. It is get results and see where that takes you.'

Clement is best known as an assistant, to Carlo Ancelotti at Chelsea, Paris Saint-Germain, Real Madrid and Bayern Munich. His task is to convince doubters that he can re-emerge as a figurehead at Reading, who appointed him to succeed Jaap Stam on 23 March. 'I didn't expect to be back in so quickly,' he admitted.

Judged objectively, his range of experience is a unique asset. 'I've coached at grass-roots level, youth level, international level, European level. I've been a teacher, a youth developer. I've worked in elite performance in England, France, Spain, Germany. I've managed in the Premier League and the Championship. I'm not an old manager. I'm 46. That's quite a lot when I think about it . . . .'

He laughs gently but his dilemma is summed up by a Premier League chief executive, who had done his homework on him in anticipation of a vacancy arising. 'Paul is an outstanding coach. His work on the training ground is exceptional. But is he the classic number two, who is not best suited to being a number one? Does he have the right man-management skills?'

Such questions hang heavily. Communication in the modern dressing room, between a figure of authority and a collection of multi-millionaire footballers with a lovingly cultivated sense of entitlement, must be subtle and multi-dimensional.

Intriguingly, Clement comes from an illustrious line of PE teachers who have become accomplished managers. Roy Hodgson taught at Alleyn's School in south London. Rinus Michels, the father of total football, taught at a school for deaf children before becoming head coach at Ajax and taking Holland to the 1974 World Cup final. Most pertinently, on a number of levels, Guus Hiddink, who Clement watched calm a fractious Chelsea dressing room after Luiz Felipe Scolari was sacked in 2009, spent a decade teaching disturbed children.

'That was my first experience of stepping up to senior level, seeing how a very experienced coach in his sixties, someone who had been round the block and won things in lots of countries, managed a volatile situation. Guus got everyone together so quickly. We pushed on in the league and won the FA Cup.

'He used all his skills, experience and charisma. He didn't come in with notebooks and presentations, but he had a really good smell for the dressing room. He understood the different personalities. He knew those he'd have to get close to him, those he'd have to be strong with, those he'd have to hover alongside.'

Teaching crystallised Clement's character and child-hood experience. His earliest football memory is from infancy, being propped up on a seat in a family room at Loftus Road. He would kick a ball around and collect conkers when was taken to training at the Bank of England ground by his father Dave, who moved from QPR, where he won five England caps, to Fulham.

He became the man of the house, at the age of ten, when his father, depressed after breaking his leg, committed suicide. Driven by a sense of responsibility beyond his years, he helped bring up his younger brother Neil, who went on to have a good career with West Bromwich Albion, in addition to pursuing his education.

He had 'a feeling inside that football would be important for me', though his playing career extended no further than non-League stints with Banstead Athletic and Corinthian Casuals. After acquiring teaching qualifications at St Mary's College in Twickenham, and what is now Brunel University, he coached at Chelsea's Centre of Excellence while working, for five years, at Glenthorne High School in south-west London.

'Looking back, that provided me with the building blocks, the right principles and fundamentals. I had an inkling that I might work in an elite environment with young players, but no idea I would end up being a manager. It taught me the importance of having good subject knowledge, and open communication.

'There are so many similar skills in teaching and coaching; understanding how people learn, organisation, the ability to plan in the short, medium and long term. You learn how to motivate. Ultimately, you're leading a variety of people. You're dealing with different personalities in any classroom environment and every football dressing room.

'You'll have self-managers, and those who require a lot of energy because they need extra attention. You'll have high-flyers that need pushing. Football is slightly different to school because you calculate how much the effort is worth. Players can be talented but if they have things missing you can spend a lot of time with them and they are still never going to be what you want them to be.'

His bookshelf is a miscellany of leadership statements, with a North American accent. It features the wisdom of Bill Walsh and the drive of Vince Lombardi, another Hall of Fame NFL coach. Basketball brings perspective through the mysticism of Phil Jackson, the compassion of Dean Smith and the obsession of Billy Knight.

Above all, Clement relates to John Wooden's altruism and sparsely expressed belief in the individual. The life story of the UCLA basketball coach, who died four months short of his hundredth birthday in June 2010, is a homily to lost American values. Born on a farm that lacked electricity, he shot a homemade ball through a tomato can that served as a hoop and was schooled in the values of community and service.

It was as an English teacher at the South Bend High School in Indiana that Wooden developed his Pyramid of Success, a summary of qualities, personal and professional, individual and collective, required to be not just a successful athlete, but a better human being.

Clement distilled those 25 behaviours into his own model, which has six basic tenets. 'First of all I like the idea of the pyramid structure. Establish firm foundations and build to a pinnacle. The base is formed of three mental aspects: unshakeable self-belief; determination and perseverance in the face of adversity; and the will not only to win but to prepare to win.

'The next level is more tactical. I want my team to build chances through having possession, and to have the tactical intelligence to change systems to gain an edge, either during a game or in preparation.

'Right at the pinnacle is team spirit. I work on that with the players, talk about it all the time. The pyramid model is very visual; at Swansea I gave the players little black cards with it on. That's the team identity.

'The next level down is how we work. Dean Smith's culture was play hard, play smart, play together. Mine is work hard, work smart, work together. The last element involves ten standards of performance, which I took from Bill Walsh. There are no rules or strict boundaries, but these are expectations of how we behave with each other, and how other people see us behaving. So there is our culture; the pyramid, the identity, how we play, work and behave.'

Clement does not follow the orthodoxy of the age, that short attention spans and a millennial fashion for brevity in all forms of communication means that modern footballers are limited in their capacity to engage with the coach, and respond to detailed demands. Again, he uses North American sport as his template: 'I challenge it because if you go to an American football team, you see athletes that are not necessarily academic, that have had tougher upbringings, economically and socially, in team meetings that might last for two or three hours a day. They're sitting there with massive ring binders of material; they've got their pens and their pencils and their coaches are taking them through hours and hours of film.

'Now, it might be mundane and a lot of our players might not like it, but it is not because they can't do it. I embrace the fact attention spans are shorter, because of how much information is available. We live in a world in which "I've got to look at my Instagram, my Twitter, play my video game", but if a player leaves a meeting he should be able to reel off some very pertinent information.

'Be clear and concise. Bang, bang. My meetings are little and often, rather than long, so I plan carefully, to try and get the information across right from the start of the week up to the end. I don't cram things in. You can't stand still. You've got to keep moving. I think that's one of my strengths.

'I always feel very guilty if I've not delivered a quality coaching session for the players. I feel terrible afterwards. I never want it to be a five-a-side culture. A few boxes, let's have a game, off we go. I could never be like that. Every session needs to have a purpose, a structure, an objective. It needs to maximise the amount of time available.'

Every manager begins with a clean canvas; colours are applied through those who engage the intellect and seize the imagination. Clement's role alongside Ancelotti moved him close to the seat of power. He balances personal experience of the titans of his profession with the need to express his individuality. 'All I try to do is be true to my beliefs and my personality. I don't try and be Carlo, or the other inspirational coaches of my generation that I look to, José, Sir Alex, Wenger and Guardiola. You can try to find out about their unique leadership qualities, but you have to be yourself. Carlo really taught me that. He was a master at work.

'People would often criticise him and say, "Oh, you're too laid back, you're too friendly with the players, your training's not intense enough". But he was comfortable with his personality. He had been very successful because of his way of doing things. I worked closely with him for seven years. I saw him at his best and his worst, in his high moments and his low moments. I was learning on a subconscious level. When I became a manager I found myself recalling situations that helped me.

'Sir Alex was very open with me, very kind. I was intrigued by José the moment he came to this country. There's nothing like seeing him work. I watched him run training. The intensity, the organisation, the demands he put on players and staff, mentally, really stressed people. Some find it difficult to keep up with his demanding mentality.

'I admire Wenger for his longevity, his stubbornness, his passion. What Guardiola did at Barcelona was really, really special. Not only did he win but he did it in a way that was unique at the time. He was a pathfinder, a bit like Arrigo Sacchi, Carlo's old coach at Milan. He took a team, a club, a philosophy of hard pressing and possession, and people followed.'

English football breeds timidity, a tired acceptance of convention. Clement's refusal to be imprisoned by an island mentality has underpinned his development. Dealing with the minutiae of daily life in a different culture may be challenging, but the rewards of being stretched, personally and professionally, compensate.

'Try doing things you take for granted in your own country, like getting your telephone connected or setting up the gas and electricity, in a foreign language that you don't know. When we went to Paris Saint-Germain, they were not the club they are now. The money and the investment had just gone in but the infrastructure was not there.

'I didn't know half the players' names, never mind coaching them in French. The kids are in a French school and they're coming home upset. Their mum's upset. It was a strain, initially, but you adapt. You get through it, no matter how uncomfortable it is. It makes you stronger for future challenges.

'Going to Real Madrid was easier. I didn't have to pretend that I was some great ex-player, because I wasn't. I was someone who was a PE teacher. That has never been thrown back at me. Not once. All the big players, Cristiano, Zlatan, Lampard, Terry, have been very respectful.

'I'm very clear about what defines players of that level. They have physical talent. They're hard working and professional. Mentally, they can cope with pressure. But the difference in the real elite, for me, is that they are never satisfied with the moment.

'The memory of winning the Champions League with Real Madrid, when it looked like we were going to lose it, sums it up. We're in the dressing room. The cup is being passed around. All the photos are being taken. Euphoria. Then I look around and I hear players saying "we've got to do it again next year". I was like, Jesus Christ. I know the journey, what we've gone through, the fine lines and the effort. It was unbelievable. And that's what the best – Ramos, Ronaldo, Zlatan – are like.

'Stories about Ronaldo coming back from European trips at four in the morning and going straight into an ice bath are absolutely true. We had one at the training ground, but he had the full recovery set-up, including a pool with a treadmill, installed in his house. We'd get off the plane and he'd be on to Pepe, "Come on, we're going to do ice baths". It's a buzz being around people like that, amazing.'

Despite the Gothic splendour of a backlit Lincoln Cathedral on the hill, Danny Cowley works in less salubrious, more straitened circumstances at Sincil Bank. The office he shares with Nicky, his brother and assistant, is infused with a musty smell traced to a plastic bag containing training gear and a muddy pair of Adidas Mundials by the side of his desk.

The brothers, former teachers, are responsible for an edifying Everyman tale. They took Concord Rangers from playing in front of 50 people in the Essex Senior League through three promotions to the National League South, and rejuvenated part-timers Braintree Town in similar fashion. In their first season at Lincoln City, they returned the club to the Football League and reached the quarter-finals of the FA Cup.

They bring impulsive energy, resourcefulness and a gnawing need for enlightenment to their work. Their players were unable to shower at the ground on the day I spent with them because the club was staging a police international between England and France, but after training on a bare school pitch they were at least able to recover in a borrowed mobile cryotherapy unit.

A chance observation, sparked by my conversation with Paul Clement the previous day, piqued Danny's attention. He spoke eagerly of studying YouTube clips of Clement's training sessions and seeking out examples of his methodology. It quickly became clear his enthusiasm extended beyond his affinity with a fellow coach; he recognised a fellow teacher's search for validation in his pupils: 'Paul's manner is like he's almost looking from the outside in. He's calm, always in control. The teacher comes across. Actually, I don't like to say this in football because it gets around, but teaching is about ten years in front of coaching. It makes me laugh when I go to FA seminars and they talk about independent learning as if they are reinventing it.

'They're so far behind. I'm not talking about PE teaching because I was disappointed, if I'm honest, by the PE profession, but top teachers in science, maths and English have some unbelievably novel ideas. I taught for nearly twenty years; now my job is to make my players good learners. I try to teach them to be curious.

'To be a good learner you have to be open-minded. You've got to be a good listener and want to learn. The best thing education taught me is that nothing comes easily. One of the oldest sayings in football is "I wish I knew that". When you finally work out the game everyone gives up on you, because your body has worn out.'

The bloodlines are clear. His father was an accountant whose work ethic was shared with his mother, who became a senior executive at JP Morgan in the City of London after initially supplementing the family income by serving at McDonald's. Danny professes not to be academic but he willed himself to earn a first-class honours degree at the University of Greenwich.

He spent five years as head of PE at FitzWimarc School in Rayleigh, Essex, where he taught the son of Millwall manager Neil Harris, before entering management on a full-time basis when he joined Lincoln in the summer of 2016. His philosophy overlaps twin professions because it is based upon a commitment to the individual.

'Set three, year nine, period five, bottom set kids, Friday afternoon. I'd always try and teach them the same as set one, Monday, period one. That's because a child only has one education. It doesn't matter how tired I am. I've got to make sure that the lesson is planned, the equipment is ready, and I know exactly where I'm going with it so that their learning is completely catered for.

'That was always really important to me in education. In these types of roles, you can have a real influence on a lot of people's journeys. You've just got to try and do the very best you can for them, to give them the best chance to make something of themselves. Making people better, seeing the light go on as they improve, is a buzz.

'A lot of kids hate everything about PE, so you are learning how to deal with different personalities. I look at academies appointing ex-footballers as coaches, but they don't have the people skills. They know football at a really high level, but they don't know how to convey that knowledge. They don't know how to get into the mind of a ten-year-old.'

The sacrifices of nine years' part-time management were formative. Going straight to school, to do a full day's work after arriving back from a midweek away match at Barrow at 5.50 a.m., taught him the importance of managing his time and compartmentalising his tasks. He found mental dexterity a natural antidote to pressures that are so often self-inflicted.

'I had quite a senior role at the school, so I was dealing with child protection issues, kids with real problems. There can be some really horrific things going on, even at a good middle-class comprehensive like the one we were in. I'd come in and focus only on teaching, but as soon as I got to the bottom of the school steps I'd just close it off and open up my football world again.

'It worked the other way around. If we had lost on the Saturday I would walk back up those steps on Monday morning and forget it. Leave it. Box it up. It's only work. And work is only work if you don't like it. If you love your job you don't mind the long days and the difficult decisions.'

We met on a relatively gentle 17-hour working day, announced by a 5 a.m. alarm call and curtailed by a

9 p.m. interview for a new kit man. When I turned up, at 8 a.m., Danny had already watched an Irish League match on his computer. Nicky, the younger brother who doubled as his captain in the early days, absent-mindedly buttered a slice of toast as he confirmed the day's session on his iPad.

Perhaps naturally, their office had the feel of a school staff room. The door was usually open and the formation of the weekend's game plan was collegiate. It began with a free-form discussion that also involved, at various points, player-coach Jamie McCombe, chief scout Dean West and goalkeeping coach Jimmy Walker.

Mike Hine, officially known as Lincoln's Head of Sports Science and Medicine, but introduced as 'Bucket Boy' by his manager, graphically underlined the stamina-sapping nature of a League Two season. Only six of Cowley's 19-man squad were fully fit, rated green on his colour-coded ratings system; 11 had an amber warning, signalling their workload needed to be handled sensitively.

One of them, captain and talisman Michael Bostwick, pulled up sharply towards the end of training, and sank to his haunches in obvious pain. Hine rushed to his side from the school car park, where he was collecting a stray ball. 'Back's gone,' Bostwick confirmed, in a gravelly whisper; it took him several minutes to take off his boots before he was taken to the ground for treatment by conditioning coach Luke Jelly.

Danny was solicitous, respectful to his most senior pro. 'He's a warrior,' he murmured, admiringly. Remarkably, Bostwick played, and scored, 48 hours later in a 4–1 win over Crewe Alexandra. He had been spared the week's other ritual, individual self-assessment meetings with the Cowleys.

Players' performances are analysed by a bespoke statistical system devised by Matthew Page and Toby Ellis, University of Lincoln graduates who have developed an online data assessment tool for teachers. The Cowleys concentrate on creating from 'Quality Street', 40-yard areas on either flank; they calculate 26 crosses will lead to one goal. Eighty-four per cent of goals are scored with one or two touches in a centralised 12-yard box in the penalty area.

'I'm trying to make it a science. And the only reason I'm trying to make it a science is because I want the definitive answer.' Danny laughs ruminatively, pauses, and is suddenly reflective. 'I'm not proud of this, but it is the truth. My life is better when we win. I want to make winning a science, black and white, so I get to the stage where I know exactly what to do. Football isn't art; that's too airy-fairy a concept.

'I just can't get it out of my head. I'm obsessed with it. I think about it every single minute. It's the first and last thing I think about every day. Sometimes I forget to phone my kids, and my wife can't get her head around that. That's on my conscience. I miss them, like now. I'm talking about them and I feel emotional, but as soon as I'm working, I'm working. I've got this football fog.

'That's why, wherever we are, I always go home on Tuesday night. At seven forty-five on a Wednesday morning I take about sixty kids on my daughter's cross-country. I love it, but sometimes I've only had two hours' sleep. Kids give you so much energy, because they've got so much enthusiasm for life. That contact time, half an hour, forty-five minutes with them, gives me more energy than eight hours' sleep.'

He summons images from that fog: a wooden target set up in the park, where he and his brother, under supervision from their father, tried to get height on their kicks; a scan showing the reality of an apparently innocuous hamstring injury – the tendon had come off the bone – ending his playing career at the age of 28; the mental rehearsal of difficult conversations he knows will impact on families and livelihoods.

The psychology of brothers working together is equally complex, given the balance between sibling rivalry and natural empathy. It was expressed in a team meeting, where the squad studied a video annotated with 56 points from the previous match. Danny, who led the discussions, was largely understated, urgent when required; Nicky shifted nervously from foot to foot, his interventions sharper in tone without being threatening.

Once again, Danny laughed at the implication of the observation. 'It's an interesting dynamic. We live in each other's pockets so we kind of know where the other one is going. Trust is quite hard to find in football and obviously we have got that. When you've come from our level we have lived most of the jobs and know what we want.

'Nicky's a bit more brutal than me but he thinks I am harder on them. I remember my grandad saying to my wife and I, "Don't both have the hump with the kids at the same time. Just one of you tell them off. The other one needs to be there for them to go to." It's the same with players, but if you're always good cop and bad cop that can become a bit too predictable.

'When I told a child off at school, I was never angry. I might have been disappointed in their behaviour but it was always just for effect. Maybe earlier in my football career I was more caught up in the emotion of it all, but though I can appear to have lost it, I'm in control and always know what I am doing.

'I've never seen the red mist. You need to be really careful not to overuse anger because I think otherwise where do you go with it? I've played for managers who have kept me in the dressing room for an hour and a half, effing and blinding, throwing tea cups, and you can feel players going, here we go again.'

His career remains on an upward trajectory. In excess of 28,000 Lincoln supporters saw them win the much-maligned Checkatrade Trophy in April 2018, beating League One Shrewsbury Town 1–0 in the club's first Wembley appearance. Lincoln lost to Exeter City in the League Two play-offs. He turned down approaches from Nottingham Forest and Barnsley, clubs seeking stability in the Championship. His next move will be definitive.

'The message I try to get across to my players is that you've got to know your path. What and who do you want to be by the end of it? You have to be self-aware. I just want to end up as high as I can. There will be certain limitations, prejudices: school teacher; didn't play at the top level. Those will be the barriers but find a way. If you can't go over, go under, and if you can't go under, go around it. If you can't do that, go through it. It won't stop me.

'I've got a belief in my skillset and my work ethic. I've got to keep improving. I've got to keep adding to my skillsets and improving my tactical knowledge, my recruitment. I've got to keep working on my eye, my ability to identify talent, because I think I've got the management skills. I think I can lead people, get the best out of them on a daily basis.'

Our two-hour conversation had reached a natural conclusion, but in a move worthy of his original ambition to become a journalist, he produced what Fleet Street veterans will identify as the 'reverse ferret'. 'Go on,' he said. 'You be critical of me ....'

I wondered about the limits of idealism, his ability to inspire cynical, inordinately wealthy players as he moves up the football food chain. Could he acquire greater tactical flexibility, manage upwards, to foreign owners and clinical investors? Above all, could he deal with the unspoken subtext of his professional life?

'You will get sacked one day. Everyone does.'

'Maybe.'

'You know what they say. You're not a manager until you've been sacked.'

'Yeah, of course, but that would really hurt me, that failure. Not having the opportunity to turn it round, because I know with time I could.'

'But there's no time in modern football is there?'

'No. That's what you've got to try and do, buy time. I think you buy time by winning. I know this sounds weird, like I'm exaggerating, but that is an out-of-body experience . . . .'

CHAPTER NINE

Suffragette City

'I'm not a gender warrior. I'm one of you. I want to talk through the prickly things, honestly. The first thing I say to any man that works for me is my first job is to make him a better husband. If I can do that he'll be a better coach. People want perspective, balance and conversation. They don't want to be faced with the facade.' – Emma Hayes, head coach, Chelsea Ladies

The amygdala, an almond-shaped set of neurons in the medial temporal lobe of the brain, is responsible for processing such basic emotions as anger, fear, pleasure, sadness and sexual attraction. It changes in size and shape, depending on gender, hormonal activity and age. It is associated with male aggression and female compassion.

At the risk of offending the neuroscience community with such a shamelessly simplistic summary, it might also be football's missing link. It highlights why Emma Hayes, in the process of outgrowing the women's game as head coach of Chelsea Ladies, has the potential to be a pioneer in an age where empathy is regarded as the basis of effective leadership.

Women are increasingly familiar figures in modern support teams in the men's game. They work as physiotherapists, conditioning coaches, doctors and psychologists. Coaching is the final frontier; someone with Hayes's professionalism, philosophy and experience needs a fundamental shift in mindset to challenge successfully the patronising assumptions of old-school sexists.

She is sitting, flicking counters around a small-scale tactics board, in the canteen in hub number two, a functional example of dated local authority architecture in a far-flung corner of Chelsea's training ground in the Surrey village of Stoke D'Abernon. Rooks nest in nearby trees that mark the boundaries of a 140-acre site that contains 30 pitches, six prepared to Premier League standard.

Though her sessions are watched by Eden Hazard and David Luiz, the setting, divorced from the environmentally friendly, technologically advanced facilities used by the men's teams, is suggestive of institutionalised inequality. Hayes is carrying twins, due to be born in June 2018. Well into her second trimester when we meet, she has overcome severe morning sickness that literally left her on her knees in the dressing room, retching before going out to oversee training.

Any type of vulnerability is feared in the men's game, a closed environment that stunts emotional growth. Hayes is, by turns, frank, funny, thoughtful and subtly provocative. She is no Emily Davison, willing to sacrifice herself by throwing herself beneath the hooves of Proper Football Men, but the suffragette spirit is strong.

'A woman coaching in the men's game is not going to be easily achieved, but the interesting thing about it, for me, is that it is absolutely needed. Can you imagine what you could do with the right females on the technical side? We are nurturers. I've spoken to enough male professionals who struggle with the lack of clarity in their own position.

'The most important thing for women, given the circulatory system of our brains, is relationships between each other. We need to be social. It's critical. So we have a natural propensity to engage our amygdala. Women communicate a little bit better, but I also know when they are all over the place. There might be no eye contact. It might be the body language. It might be noticing someone didn't eat at breakfast. It's intuitive.

'Most of us have been massively influenced by a female in our lives, whether that's our mother, a sibling, whoever. For the most part, sons have experienced that dynamic, and yet they are faced, on a daily basis in football, with fear of being different, of showing weakness. The only way that splinters out is in a situation in which they can talk to a woman.

'I can think of players in this football club who have asked the cooks, the dining staff, "how do you think I should manage that, then?". A member of staff might have said to me, "It's so tough in here. I get called a gay boy day in, day out because I love my wife an awful lot and I don't want to talk about women the way they talk about women." It's male stuff. I get that.

'Give them an outlet and it pours out. Then you sit there and think, well, no wonder we've got so many mental health issues, because not every man is the same. They're in an environment where you have to show toughness all the time. I call it caveman behaviour, and if you don't join in, you are stigmatised, even marginalised.

'Coaching courses make me giggle because I am always the only female. I can think of one guy, a former Premier League footballer. His session was horrendous. It finishes, he's having a one-to-one with the coach in the middle, and I'm thinking, "how fucking awful". He comes straight back into the circle of lads, and goes "yeah, I smashed it".

'All the lads walked off and he went, quietly, "what did you think, Em?". I asked whether he wanted feedback. I always do. I don't just want to solicit and give you my opinion. "OK, I think you lost control there. I like your manner but I thought you went on too much." It stands out so much because, until that point, the bravado was laughable.

'Putting balance into a room, through gender or diversity, is not going to change things instantly, but it is going to take pressure off people. Because you know what? Others have to be conscious of their behaviours, their words, their actions. That's the starting point. With time, they can be educated to see things differently, to recognise injustice or imbalance.'

She is 41, broad faced, and carries authority easily. She honed her coaching philosophy in the United States for the best part of a decade, apart from a brief spell at Arsenal, before taking over as Chelsea's head coach in 2012. They have won the Women's Super League twice in the last three seasons and completed the domestic double in 2018 by beating Arsenal 3–1 in the FA Cup final before a record Wembley crowd of 45,423. The ultimate aim, after being knocked out by Wolfsburg in the semi-finals, is to win the Champions League.

It is a convincing CV. Her training methods are intense and inclusive, and her skills are transferable. Yet she accepts it may take another generation for a woman to be judged on her own merits in the men's game. The dangers of tokenism, and a chairman or owner with a penchant for the reflected glory of appointing a female manager, are obvious and omnipresent.

'One of my good friends is Chris Ramsey at QPR. An absolute legend. We talk about this a lot. Obviously with the Rooney Rule coming into play, he is passionate about opportunity for BAME coaches. I said, "You talk about it like you're the shit on the shoe. What do you think it's like for female coaches? There's a bar lower than you."

'John Herdman, the manager of Canada women's team, has just got the job as men's coach. I'm never going to be the men's coach here at Chelsea, yet I'm probably the only pro-licence coach on this site. I'm not bitter about that. It's not something that prevents me from going to work or feeling hampered or hamstrung.

'If I'm ever going to go into the men's game, I've got to be a thousand per cent, a million per cent, more ably qualified than a male candidate. I've got to develop confidence, knowledge and wisdom to put myself into the position where I can have football conversations with the right people. It will take a brave board to make the breakthrough decision.

'Do I think it will come in my time? There's a generation of female coaches coming into the game now that might work in academies. I don't think Chris will have any issues with me saying this, but if I was out of work and rang him and said will you give me one of your teams, I know he would. But it is not about doing things at all costs.

'I am at a great club and have everything I need. I don't think I'm going to be moving to Grimsby, just to get into the men's game. I'm being realistic. I've journeyed a lot in football. It is the only thing I have ever wanted to do, in my heart. Am I going to leave for a ninety-grand contract somewhere, with an average shelf life of six months? I'm not going to rush.'

Her role models are diverse. She aspires to the tenacity and creativity of her earliest PE teacher, Debbie Ramm-Harpley, who works extensively in inner-city areas, and is following the progress of Becky Hammon, who, flourishing in the inclusive culture created by Gregg Popovich at San Antonio Spurs, is tipped to become the first female head coach in the NBA.

She identifies with Eddie Jones, England's rugby union coach, because of his willingness to empower his players. Yet the biggest influence on her stems from a chance conversation on military tactics with a stranger at a coaching conference. Anson Dorrance, a former lawyer, won the first women's World Cup with the US in 1991, and has led North Carolina Tar Heels to 22 national titles.

'Here was this guy, who had English parents and travelled around the world while his dad was in the Navy. I had no clue who he was until, at a regional camp, he handed out a manual about how he did everything. And I thought, oh my God. He's told you how to beat him. But he's so confident, you won't. He doesn't care.

'He's one of the most brilliant men I've ever met. He captured my mind. Football has always been about whispering behind your hand, "don't tell anyone this", and here he was, doing exactly the opposite. That was massively influential because I'm not afraid of being open. The game will evolve tomorrow and we will all have to find another solution.'

The personal relevance of Dorrance's philosophy of 'transcending ordinary effort' is telling. Hayes kicked a ball around as a toddler but the lack of cartilage in an ankle, possibly the result of an impact injury at the age of 12, effectively ended her playing career before it began. Coaching has become an extension of her personality, an expression of formative adversity.

'This was back in the day when they didn't have micro-fracture surgeries like they do now. I'm left-footed, so every time my foot slammed on the floor, it felt like my bone hitting the ground. I grew up con-stantly thinking about being in pain, but playing was something I loved doing. I wrestled with it, but there was no future with it.

'I had to get my head down, get an education. I had a beautiful upbringing, but I aspired to something more. My background is as working-class as hell. My dad's always been self-employed. We had no brothers – he had three girls – and we've all had to work in the family foreign exchange business. We still do.

'Family comes first, always. My two sisters run the business on a daily basis and I still do the strategic ele-ment. I've built websites, back-end content management systems, learned by working with geeky project managers. I like the combination of technology and process. Without a framework, opinions fly all over the place. It's the death of an organisation.

'I treat everything like I was flying a plane or about to cut your kidney out of your body. That's not done without following a certain set of procedures. Football, for me, is the only industry in which you go through an education process where you are never really taught why you are doing what you are doing on a daily basis.

'In this country we love to hire people – strength and conditioning coaches, scientists – and leave them to it. Why? What the fuck are we doing as coaches? It's important to be knowledgeable, holistically, so that you know exactly how to load a player appropriately. One, so they recover, to be fresh on game day, and secondly, so that you've got continual development. I've had to go to Holland and Germany to learn that methodology.

'I have to credit my dad for this. While he's always been ambitious and driven, he's chaotic. I was always going, "Dad, you've got to put some order into this, some logical thinking". It is the same in football. Some coaches just make it up as they go along. "We're doing four vs four today." Well why? What's our purpose? "Well, we do it because I did it as a player."'

Women's football has survived scarcely credible ignorance; it was banned by the FA for 50 years, until 1971. Fifa's veneer of inclusivity was exposed by president

Gianni Infantino, who welcomed delegates to a conference in Zurich in March 2018 on the theme of 'Making Equality a Reality' less than 24 hours after attending the Tehran derby, from which female spectators were banned.

Such depressing double standards are unsurprising, since the women's game is accustomed to the betrayal of lofty intentions. Only three years into the professional era in England, it has yet to complete its evolution. The biggest study of women's football, a survey of 3,500 players from five leading leagues by FIFPro, the global players' trade union, in December 2017, underlined the lack of plausible career progression.

Only 12 per cent of players in England's top tier earn in excess of £18,000 a year; 87 per cent do not have a retirement fund; 26 per cent do not have their expenses covered; and 11 per cent lack even a written contract. Little wonder 58 per cent are considering quitting for financial reasons. Just 1 per cent are mothers; crèche facilities are provided by only 3 per cent of clubs, worldwide.

The FA's authority in such matters was fundamentally undermined by an admission, in March 2018, that their female staff earned 23.2 per cent less than their male workers. Their commercialisation of coaching courses militates against female coaches, who cannot afford the fees involved in personal progression through the licensing system. Tottenham Hotspur Ladies advertised for an academy manager, to oversee eight age-group teams on a voluntary basis.

Such disparity reflects the disproportion of modern sport. According to *Forbes* magazine, there was not a single woman among the world's top 100 best-paid athletes in 2017. The Champions League is the most valued prize in club football, regardless of gender, yet Uefa paid the 2017 winners of the women's version €250,000, and the men's version €57.2 million.

Hayes is a realist. 'We have to see women's football as still in its infancy. It doesn't mean your first cohort of professionals is the best. There's a period of time needed to sift through those that are going to stay on a level, and those who are going to be world class. You've got to teach what being a professional is, because it's not a washbag and a Mercedes-Benz.

'When I first started turning a lot of the girls pro, I was like, "Yeah, you look the part, but you don't live the part". That's the holistic part of being an athlete. Is your nutrition right, is your psychology right, is your recovery right? Are you doing the extra work on the training pitch, the analysis that needs to happen? That's cumulative development.

'We need more clubs. There are probably only two others in this country, Manchester City and Arsenal, developing players at our level. To be honest, in sixty per cent of games you are not really tested. Yet for a club like Chelsea to compete in Europe we've had to recruit worldwide. Champions League teams are very diverse, very multi-cultural, very worldly, but domestically, the gap from top to bottom has grown. That gap needs to be bridged.'

Manchester United's belated decision to form a women's team, and establish it in the second tier of the Super League in the 2018–19 season under the management of former England captain Casey Stoney, was a timely, if revealingly reticent, statement of faith.

Broadcaster Jacqui Oatley, the most pertinent observer and progressive contributor to the women's game, is optimistic. 'I think we're heading in the right direction, but the problem is, and it's a historical one, that the default setting for sport is men's sport. That's what you experience, what you see on the TV, what you read about in the paper. If we pay these senior professional full-time women the respect they deserve, hopefully that could seep through to the rest of the game.

'Women's football was banned because it was unladylike. A lot of people don't realise that was an official FA stance. In the US they don't differentiate between the men and women's game because they don't have the history of prejudice we have in this country. You can't just undo that unconscious bias, which is an expression I've picked up recently, overnight.

'It is going to be a generational thing. It's going to be my three-year-old son Max growing up with my six-year-old daughter Phoebe, who loves football, puts on Sky Plus in the morning, and watches any game, men's, women's, she doesn't care. Max is not going to have that innate bias and misconception that women can't or shouldn't play football, because he'll be surrounded by girls and women with an influence that say we love football too and we play it.

'You've got to showcase the top talent, get people engaged, buying tickets and merchandise, going to games, and encouraging their girls to play, whilst actually building from the grass roots up. The FA are going into primary schools and trying to strengthen coaching. To give one example, a lot of female goalkeepers haven't had any specialist coaching, until about sixteen, seventeen. People who laugh at female goalkeepers chucking one in do not appreciate that it's not a level playing field. It's lazy criticism. Show me Peter Schmeichel if he'd never had any goalkeeping coaching until he was sixteen or seventeen. Would he have still been that iconic goalkeeper we saw? No, of course he wouldn't. At that age it is almost too late to teach good habits.'

Growing pains are intermittently acute. The BBC's Vicky Sparks endured sexist trolling when she became the first female TV play-by-play commentator at a live World Cup match, between Portugal and Morocco in Moscow. Women in Football, a catalytic group that has done so much to reinforce the female presence in the game, are understandably impatient for greater equality of opportunity.

Senior FA figures were eviscerated in a Commons committee hearing by Chelsea striker Eni Aluko, a revealingly turbulent figure who moved to Juventus in the summer after impressing as an ITV pundit at the World Cup. While many applauded her exposure of the governing body's incompetence and incoherence in her racially charged case, several England teammates were privately scathing about her role in the downfall of national manager Mark Sampson.

Hayes had no interest in succeeding him, even though she fitted perfectly the job description of 'an outstanding football coach with a track record of consistent and successful management and development of elite players and coaches to high-performance levels'. The FA's choice to lead England into the 2019 World Cup, Phil Neville, seemed blatantly populist, faintly condescending and failed to meet advertised criteria.

The appointment, accompanied by the confected controversy of Neville's failure to delete historic, allegedly sexist tweets, was yet another reputational calamity. Unwisely, he indulged in needy protestations of professionalism, which veered into paranoia when he complained 'people want me to fail, one hundred per cent'. Such posturing glossed over the fact the women's game is a distinct entity, with additional physiological and psychological dimensions.

Since it is played on a full-size men's pitch, there are unavoidable physiological and tactical limitations. Goalkeepers are, on average, between three and five inches smaller than their male counterparts, but goal frames have the same dimensions. Profitable goal kicks into an attacking channel, a feature of the men's game, cannot be reproduced because a female's range tends to extend no further than the halfway line.

The lack of susceptibility to long diagonal passes allows Hayes to narrow her defence, with wing backs augmenting two traditional centre halves and a sweeper. Her research of senior international football suggests 70 per cent of goals in the women's game stem from a central corridor. They are scored either from a centralised through ball, a cut-back into the penalty area, or a square pass across the box.

In the year since she made her tactical tweaks, Chelsea have scored more goals, and conceded fewer, than in recent memory. Space has been truncated, giving the flow of the match an aura of urgency despite players' relative lack of speed. The ball is in play more often, and there is much more interplay through the phases.

Culturally, women's football has an endearing innocence. 'There's less cynicism,' Hayes confirms with a chuckle. 'Do you think I can get my goalkeeper to fucking fall over and get the physio on the pitch so that I can get some information out there? She can't do it. She's too honest. Players do dive, but they're not brilliant at it.

'Players who do so are stigmatised. Women try and drive it out of the opposition. They'll shake someone's hand at the end of the game and say, "Listen, you're a cracking player but you need to stamp that part of your game out". There's a moralistic edge to it that always makes me laugh. Women don't go over as much, when they get the chance.'

The periodic intervention of Mother Nature is another under-considered factor. 'A woman can jump higher during her period than the rest of the month, but her reaction times are slower, because she has to deal with a massive physiological event. It's a fact. We've measured it. It's fascinating.

'Equally, women can do mental things on their period; they can get their best strength gains and, though it's an absolute contradiction, they are more vulnerable to a ligament injury. Men don't have to deal with that.

'During at least a ten-day spell every month, our serotonin levels are depleted by fifty per cent. We just suffer. Our bodies have expanded. We've got eight per cent more blood plasma, and need to be more hydrated. Diets have to change. Women, when they recover during their period, mobilise carbs, not fat. Men do it the other way around. So we gain weight, by doing nothing.

'Because we are so left-right-side dominant with our brain, rather than front and back like a man, we need certain things. And one of them, I always tell the guys in here, is a hug. Physiologically, we absolutely need it. You've got issues with dopamine. It decreases, and we've got to be able to compensate. They often say the best way to do that naturally is with a hug.

'People often ask me, do you think women shouldn't train during their period? No, but they might have to ingest different food, along with certain things like evening primrose oil and vitamin D. Pre-menstrual tension is an issue. A woman can be short-term at that time; she cries more easily, craves chocolate, but as soon as the period comes she's like, OK, that's what it was.'

My experience, in helping set up Olympic support programmes for the English Institute of Sport, was that women had softer skills. They defused aggression, diluted the testosterone levels of the alpha males that elite competition tends to attract. But the counter-balance to their natural empathy was the toxicity of intra-female hostility.

'Women can be more venomous. Things fester a lot longer. Men equally can be catty, but are less confrontational, verbally. They might square up on the pitch, but they're wary of delicate situations. They can skirt around things. To give you a recent example, my strength and conditioning coach came to me about one of our squad players. Her body fat composition was too high.

'I just told him to tell her, but he was reluctant because he felt it was such a sensitive area. Why? She's not going to break, she's not glass. I told her if she wanted to kick on and be a regular in the first team she had to see the nutritionist because these marginal gains will make a difference. And she went, "thanks very much". It's not always that easy to manage.

'I'll never forget being away at Sunderland. It gets to half-time, we're two-nil down, and there's a row in the changing room. But we don't really know what it's about. One's crying, the other one's upset. I turn round, no joke, and said, "Listen, I don't know what the fuck's going on here, but the game's going to be lost today, while this shit is going on. Sort your crap out."

'We went out and got beat four-nil. That evening, my staff went out for dinner and I spent about six hours in the hotel getting to the heart of the matter, because if you don't solve it, it will fester. I'm going, I think there's an issue here. I'm not sure if the two of them are in a relationship, but something's happened in here, or on a night out.

'You've got to be prepared to deal with all that comes with that. If you go to a woman and say, "what the fuck's going on?", first you've got tears, then you've got emotion, then you've got to calm her down. Then you've got to go to the other party, go through the same process, and try to find a resolution.'

These are delicate issues for a male observer to address, since they invite accusations of prurience and ignorance. Yet Hayes's willingness to expand upon the complications of diverse sexual orientation within women's sport is a sign of substantive progress. It can be contextualised for collective understanding without recourse to Chinese whispers, or the sacrifice of privacy and dignity.

As Professor Jonathan Zimmerman, a leading US commentator on socio-sexual issues, observes: 'Across our society, the taboo on male homosexuality remains far greater than the one on lesbianism. That makes it more difficult for male athletes to come out as gay, but it also extends the historic burden on sportswomen to prove they're not. And it makes it harder for all of us to be what we should be: ourselves.'

Hayes is unequivocal: 'We're getting the elephant out of the room. I always educate to listen, to empathise first. And you've got to be prepared to do that. It's risky, there's no doubt, and you will have multiple situations throughout the course of the season where you know, intuitively, that something doesn't feel right. You can either turn your back to it or acknowledge it.

'The make-up of the dressing room, in terms of play-ers being heterosexual, bisexual, gay, is much more even than it used to be. I've coached teams where there have been couples in relationships; sometimes it's been hor-rendous, sometimes they are very professional, and sometimes, if there is a break-up, it can be problematic.

'Ultimately they are here as individuals. They are paid to do a job and if it's compromised there are conse-quences. But I think it has to be spoken about because otherwise you get the unwritten stuff, you know, "she's not passing the ball to her partner because they've broken up". I deal with it straight up. Don't get me wrong, it's not ideal, but it happens.

'You have to be in a position to make sure there is a very clear understanding of boundaries, otherwise it will impact negatively on the team. There has to be confrontation if the environment is compromised. If it is being spoken about amongst the rest of the team, because they've seen a couple isolating themselves, it has to be addressed. To ignore it is to your team's detriment.

'Remember these are young people. They're high achievers, mollycoddled, in an environment where everything is done for them. It isn't until they reach the back end of their twenties, the early part of their thirties, that they are much more conscious of somebody other than themselves. That's where the mentoring comes in.

'What I have found is that by doing workshops around perception, how it looks internally and externally if you're in a couple in a team, it is possible to develop a culture of balance. Without the conversation, you have a risk of your dressing room being massively splintered. There has to be diversity in there, for you to cope. If it goes too far one way, phew ....'

Society sees women's sport through a long lens; marketing teams, with the complicity of the media, veer between celebration of femininity and creation of hypersexualised imagery. The success of Sport England's 'This Girl Can' campaign was a convincing response to the fear of judgement deemed to be the primary barrier preventing female participation.

As someone effectively holding down two demanding jobs, while going through what is officially termed a geriatric pregnancy, Hayes was conversely vulnerable to the Wonder Woman syndrome. According to a study undertaken by Umea University in northern Sweden, the pressure to have it all means that twice as many females are at risk of burnout, compared to 25 years ago.

'When a child comes out of me, it will change me. But it is a change that I feel readied for. There's trust in my relationships with my staff and players. They've been an important part of my journey, too. I've asked for their support, asked them to be patient with me. I struggled in my first trimester, but they understand this is a big event in my life.

'When you create the right environment, where there is the right structure and process if you are not present, you are less controlling. You know individuals won't take decisions at the expense of the collective. As I am evolving as a leader I find myself more comfortable with shared decision-making down the food chain.'

A glance around the canteen confirmed the concept. Swedish goalkeeper Hedvig Lindahl was pondering Chelsea's defensive shape, moving counters around a tactics board with quiet deliberation. Hayes had shared lunch around a circular table with five players, sent away to work through a tactical dilemma before reporting back to the group.

'This is a great example,' Hayes murmured, with evident pride. 'They will look at some ideas, but if the way we set up doesn't work, I'll leave it to them to solve the problem in the flow of the game. I very much believe in empowering people, rather than me making decisions, which was probably the situation in the early days. I feel less stressed about it.

'My whole motto is, "no excuses". What does that look like for us as coaches? We won't José Mourinho them to death, with sixty-seven slides. I've seen how he works. No, no, no. We're going to engage their critical thinking. We're going to shine a torch on them at different points. So they do it in here, and then they go out there, on to the pitch, and repeat the process.'

The rhythm of a football week is similar across the sexes. Chelsea Ladies play on Sunday, undergo a recovery session on Monday while Hayes oversees match analysis, and are given Tuesday off. Wednesday is what the head coach calls 'our start-up day. We get the cold car out of the garage. Muscles are still fatigued so there's no short-loading. I'll get the right rest-to-work ratio.'

Thursday is an overload day, where players are subjected to their hardest volume of training. Friday is given over to defensive strategy work, 'eleven v eleven, no fucking about'. Saturday is devoted to attacking play, and a collective reaffirmation of the game plan. The pre-match team talk is increasingly visual, either through stills or moving images.

Sleep tends to be elusive on Sunday night, when Hayes purges herself of the patterns and peculiarities of the match by watching it two or three times on her laptop. Before she was pregnant she craved a glass of wine immediately the game ended. Her deepest enjoyment, beyond the fix of the result, is the tactical component, watching players make decisions and solve problems.

Like many of the best coaches, Hayes is an enabler. She is involved on the board of Chelsea's charitable foundation, and makes a point of involving herself in HR policy, budgetary planning and marketing strategy. She has also aligned herself with the women in leadership movement.

Her future, beyond motherhood, is fluid. 'I wouldn't be averse to becoming the head of women's football here, helping us to become a huge global player as the game grows. I could manage a fashionable European club somewhere, provided I was settled through my early parenting years. I could take on a different capacity in the men's game, but if I'm the one that opens that particular door for a female coach to walk through, that would make me perfectly happy.'

Emma Hayes gave birth to a healthy baby boy, Harry, on 17 May 2018, 48 hours after watching her team become champions on TV as a medical precaution. Sadly, a statement released by the club confirmed she had lost the other twin during her third trimester. Chelsea asked for her privacy to be respected while she summoned a mother's strength and compassion.

CHAPTER TEN

Sleeping with the Enemy

'How well does he embed new players? How deeply does he involve himself in the recruitment process? Can he maximise squad value? How much does he improve performance relative to resources? What is his favoured percentage of peak-age players? Are there other underlying traits which give a potential employer greater confidence in the fit? The context of the club will dictate the recommendation.' Ben Marlow, head of football, 21st Club.

The call came from yet another traffic jam on the M25 at the end of a long, freezing February day. Karl Robinson had planned and conducted training, finalised the game plan, overseen a team meeting, discussed summer recruitment, held a press conference, met his chairman, assessed academy graduates and staged a coaching session for Charlton Invicta, an affiliated LGBT-friendly amateur club, as part of an anti-homophobia campaign championed by the Community Trust.

'I think I'm gone,' he said.

It took a month for the consequences of those words to become apparent. Robinson meant everything he said in an effusive statement confirming his departure from Charlton Athletic, a club with impassioned support, proud traditions, a productive youth policy and a viable chance of promotion. He left by mutual consent; unusually, this was not a euphemism designed to soften the blow or soothe the ego.

Managerial reigns rarely end with table-banging, nostril-flaring anger. This one was tinged with sadness, and reached its natural conclusion after a conversation between two friends. Lee Bowyer, Robinson's assistant and eventual successor, had asked Harry Kewell, his former Leeds United teammate, about rumours that an Australian consortium, leading candidates to buy Charlton, intended to install Kewell as manager.

Football works through such networks. Kewell was content at Crawley Town but once he confirmed was aware of interest in him the cards began to fall. Managers are not isolated from the mundanities and responsibilities of everyday life. They have families to protect, bills to be paid, relationships to sustain. A career path is far from straight, and has deep, damaging potholes.

Sumrith Thanakarnjanasuth, Oxford United's new owner, had waited 59 days to appoint someone who fitted his preferred profile. At 37, Robinson was young but hugely experienced. A progressive coach, a developer rather than a dictator.

At a time of transition, he remembered a conversation over breakfast with Steven Gerrard, when he was an emerging coach in Liverpool's academy. 'I asked him why anybody would leave Liverpool, and he just stopped. "We all leave," he said. "Concentrate on the effect you have on a club while you're there. The only thing that stays for ever is the badge and the fans, who are there for a lifetime. Understand that concept and cherish every moment that you are in that club."

'That resonated with me. We're passing ships, in some ways, managers and players. Two, three, four years, in a hundred-odd-year history. The club will be around for two, three hundred years hopefully. We're all in a portal. We're in, we're out. But whilst you're there, you have to manage the owner's money, make money if possible. Win. Keep the fans happy. Keep the players motivated.

'At different stages of the week, all those things become of differing importance. Theoretically, managing up is the hardest job. At six o'clock on a Saturday the owner's going, "come on, meeting in the office". He's emotionally driven. Fans booing, players being rubbish, you pick the wrong team, he storms in the door. It's almost like the Wild West – you drop your gun and hold your hands up.

'These are key moments. No pro licence teaches you that. You've just picked the wrong team, you've just been beat, the owner's fuming. You've just had an injury so for your next game you won't have one of your best players, who could be out for the next three weeks. You're stood there naked, basically.'

He laughed at the image he had created. 'We all make plans for someone else to take on, when we're gone. And here's another weird one that everyone comes up with: if the chairman gives you ten pounds, spend the ten. If you only spend five, the next man will have fifteen. I've never been like that. I've never tried to run faster than my legs can take me.

'Sometimes we look at things and think money is going to solve everything. Theoretically, that's understandable. But if you look at the table of finance to finishing positions, it's rarely the case. My job is not to grab more money, to worry about getting sacked in a week, or a month. My job is to worry about the long-term goal.

'A manager can ruin a football club very, very quickly, if he is so self-absorbed he concentrates entirely on winning. I'm not naive; I know we're judged on results. I've got a win ratio of around forty per cent so I've done my fair share, but at no stage has it ever been my daily job. I worry about the now in the morning; the rest of my job, working with the kids, being seen with the academy players, is about the future.

'Clubs get in trouble when the manager looks for the quick fix, bringing in players in their thirties. What happens next year when you've spent all that money on senior players just to keep you up, to push on towards the back end of the season? Then you're left with a wage bill that's flooded with thirty-three-, thirty-four-, thirty-five-year-olds that you can't get out on loan anywhere.

'That can have a long-term effect on a football club. Why not play some of the young players, have a look at the development group? Maybe you'll lose a game here or there, but you do so knowing that next year, one, they're on less money; two, they are only going to get better; and three, the end game is you're going to be a better team.'

He put such principles into practice at Charlton over three transfer windows, in which he spent less than £100,000 and realised in excess of £10 million in the transfer market while reducing the annual playing budget by £2 million. He trusted in League One specialists and used his contacts to bring in good loan players from leading Premier League academies.

A healthy balance sheet and honeyed words go only so far. A manager must read his owner's personality before he can respond to his priorities. It will take time for Robinson to build a relationship with Thanakarnja-nasuth, who mercifully answers to the nickname 'Tiger'.

The Thai's background, as a businessman who made his fortune in property and clothing manufacture, offers certain clues.

He ran Reading until May 2017 as part of a consortium involving his sister, Lady Sasima Srivikorn, and majority owner Narin Niruttinanon. They sold a 75 per cent stake to Chinese brother and sister Dai Yongge and Dai Xiu Li, but retained ownership of land around the Madejski Stadium and its hotel, earmarked for future development.

Robinson will not have to deal with the rancour that defined his time at Charlton, where he was the longest-serving manager under the reviled Belgian owner Roland Duchâtelet, who got through ten managers in little more than four years.

He never attended a match during Robinson's 16-month tenure; they spoke on the telephone six times, and the manager visited him twice. The caution of eight confidants, who warned Robinson that taking the role represented 'employment suicide', seemed to be justified by a surreal introduction to a club at war with itself.

When he took his parents and daughter to a home game against Sheffield United two days before he officially took charge, protesting fans bombarded the pitch with plastic pigs and taxis. In his first match, ironically against former club MK Dons, he glanced at his watch when he heard a fan yell 'Robinson. This is useless.

What are you doing here?' Precisely two minutes, 44 seconds had elapsed.

'I had to prove to myself that I could go into adversity, with foreign players, foreign ownership, high expectation levels, and under-achievement. I experienced that a little at Blackburn with Sam [Allardyce], but realistically everything has always been quite smooth. If I want to have a long run at this I've got to learn how to deal with an owner who doesn't live in this country.

'I took over a team created by six or seven managers over the previous two and a half years. They had all signed their "type". The fans slaughtered the owner, but fundamentally it was only through their love for their football club. A manager has to disconnect himself from external turmoil, while trying to incorporate passion and desire from the terraces to form a unified group.'

Football is so often shaped by love and loss. Duchâtelet's dislocation was predictable, since he clearly had no understanding of the tightness of emotional bonds formed in seven years of exile from the Valley, playing at Selhurst Park and Upton Park. His was a disrespectful, contemptuous form of investment.

'When I came into the club I was told it was only 1 per cent of his life. His concept was, "I've got millions in this business, and millions in that business. I've got so many other things to take care of." That's immediately translated as "you don't really matter". So you've an owner that has basically said "you're nothing to my life". All fans want you to do is love their club.'

Robinson must build that trust at Oxford through his actions, and the authenticity of his personality. His initial goal, reaching the promotion play-offs in his first full season, is complemented by a longer-term vision that matches the ambitions of owner and club. Clarity is of fundamental importance, since managerial appointments are like marriages, made in haste and repented at leisure.

Recruitment has become more strategic and sophisticated, just as managers, through masterclasses organised proactively by the League Managers' Association (LMA), are given lifestyle advice, financial training and guidance in relationship building. Health checks and peer testimonies help them to cope with the inevitable stresses of the job.

Blake Wooster formed 21st Club in August 2013, on the premise that 'if we were the 21st club in the league, how would we achieve an edge?'. He created a software application to aid recruitment, aligning the distillation of performance data with softer, more intuitive skills through a partnership with a more traditional head-hunting organisation.

Occasionally clubs ask for their own shortlists to be analysed, but more generally the process begins with a questionnaire, completed by owner, chief executive and director of football, if one is in place. They are asked to gauge, independently, the importance of aspects of managerial expectation on a sliding scale.

Potential recruits, drawn from a database of around 1,000 managers and head coaches, are assessed or identified by six criteria: performance, experience, playing style, recruitment principles, youth development and preferred profile of the first-team squad. The context of the request is taken into account; a club in danger of relegation, for example, logically prioritises short-term stabilisation over long-term growth.

'We'll see questionnaire responses where the owner is looking for one thing, but the chief executive and the director of football are looking for something totally different, and so before you even do any work, you say, right, guys, you've got to get some alignment here, because it's pretty clear you don't even know what you are looking for.

'When we feel we've got a decent view from the club on what is important to their strategy and philosophy we go through the database. That is as easy as pressing a button. We give them a list of twenty managers they should be looking at, and I guarantee that the uniqueness of that list is that they will never have heard of fifty per cent of the names.

'Then it becomes a question of bravery, to see how open-minded they really are to hiring someone that can move a needle or whether they will revert to what they feel is a bit safer. We're not saying there are no good

British managers out there, by the way. If, for example, Eddie Howe appears on a list that acts as validation, so they may look at other guys working in Germany, Finland and Sweden.'

Wooster is sitting in a ground-floor meeting room in the heart of London's jewellery quarter, Hatton Garden. The walls are lined with examples of statistical probabilities (Manchester City have a 98.7 per cent chance of winning the Premier League at the time, a statement of the obvious); analysts work from an adjoining office, narrow and slightly claustrophobic.

He is joined by Ben Marlow, his head of football, who refers regularly to the ubiquitous laptop. He embodies the company's challenge to the status quo, since he comes with the perspective of having been a consultant in the financial services industry for PwC, the global auditing and professional services firm.

'There is a lot of noise around football,' says Marlow. 'It's a really emotional industry, so you want your decisions to be defensible. If you make a call, you're going to get judged by thousands and thousands of people, very, very quickly, on Twitter, in the press, whatever. And therefore it's quite hard to do something a bit different, a bit left-field. So you find a lot of clubs resorting to hiring known quantities.

'You would never find another business hiring an employee of equivalent influence to a manager in the way that clubs have historically done it, which is, "Who has recently failed enough to be sacked and available? Let's go and get them because we know them and they are a name." Manager hire has traditionally been behind player recruitment in football.

'Huge amounts of time and money are put into hiring a managing director or head of department, who probably has a smaller influence on another type of business than a manager would have in a football context. Football is now starting to appreciate that. I get a sense the industry is beginning to change.

'We're obviously focused on the analytical side but it's important to bolster hard-nosed subjective performance analysis with softer, human aspects. There is openness to technology and data to drive decisions. People know this information is out there and it can now be used in a really useful context.'

Most projects focus on immediate recruitment and can involve the provision of specially tailored interview questions. A significant proportion of clubs, however, are starting to seek guidance on succession planning. Some, in the Premier League and Championship, are framing contingency plans in the event of their manager being poached.

Marlow drills down into the details: 'We're saying, "Here are the candidates across Europe who have demonstrated the type of capability you want as a club". So if performance is the key driver we look at how they improve the team, relative to the resources they have at their disposal. We also look at how they performed against their predecessors and successors, because sometimes managers can do well because a club is really well set up, so you need to add context.

'Squad profile is another element. That can vary; are they used to working with big names, young squads, mixed squads with a high turnover? How proven are they in getting young players into the first team? Is the manager open-minded in taking what is perceived to be a risk in that area? How reliant on recruitment has he been?'

Wooster professes to being 'amazed by how emotive decisions seem to be when a manager gets fired'. A time lag in appointing a successor, which can stretch up to eight or ten games at a critical stage of the season, is an avoidable inefficiency. Immediate action, which inevitably involves a degree of covert planning, is seen as petty betrayal rather than pragmatic business principle.

'That's actually a good signal of a decent process. They've been doing their succession planning in the background, have made the decision to move the current head coach or manager along, and they've already found a replacement. Often the process doesn't begin until the day after. It is almost like they emotionally fire the manager and go "right, who's available, what are we going to do?".

'They are often too scared to start the process because football is quite a small cottage industry. They are too afraid of upsetting the incumbent if they try and embark on some form of long-term succession planning process. They feel like they are going behind the manager or the coach's back in doing that, but actually it's pretty normal in any industry.

'I wouldn't be safeguarding the future of this business if we didn't have some kind of risk plan in place if I was to get hit by a bus or one of the key guys in the business was to leave, for whatever reason. That doesn't seem to happen in football because they are too frightened that word will get out.'

Their service depends on early surveillance of emerging talent. That represents another cultural challenge to those influenced by the supposed security of conventional wisdom, often a shallow misnomer. Old-school articles of faith are a bulwark against meaningful change; when their limitations are exposed, Wooster accepts a push-back is inevitable.

'When you're looking at numbers, Premier League experience, or even Championship experience, is hugely overrated. The first thing a club will often say to us is, "We want someone that knows the league". That's the first thing we have to challenge. We're not saying it is a bad thing, but research shows it is overvalued.

'Whenever you launch a new, disruptive business that has essentially been established because you feel there is a better way of doing things, you're always going to face some resistance. That's the same in any industry: look at the resistance that Steve Jobs got at Apple, or the resistance that most entrepreneurial tech start-ups face.

'One of the biggest assumptions people in the football industry make about us is that they think we are only about data, or only about analytics. It's kind of a defence mechanism, their default position. And, of course, that's not what we're saying. The personality of a manager that's going to come into your culture is deeply important.

'There is absolutely a place for objective decisions making life easier through data and analytics, but there are also people, not necessarily from that world, who have unbelievable natural talent for people-driven, emotionally intelligent work that captures culture and fit. We are not here to threaten anyone's job. We're here to exploit inefficiencies in the market.

'The Football Man will not become obsolete, but technology moves so quickly. The future? We're looking at the potential of artificial intelligence, machine learning. A new sub-group of people is emerging in football from different industries. It is not just a generational shift but an intellectual shift. Clubs, driven by new ownership from the US and China, are becoming smarter.'

Wooster cites Southampton's Les Reed as a pioneering figure, yet the margins of influence are terrifyingly thin and worryingly relative. The threat of relegation from the Premier League, narrowly avoided in May 2018, cast into doubt the philosophy on which Southampton was run. Trust in a system that evokes a strange mixture of admiration and cynicism was stretched as never before.

Flaws were exposed in successive managers, Claude Puel and Mauricio Pellegrino, whose arid personalities and cautious philosophies alienated players and supporters. Recruitment faltered and the quality of academy graduates declined. The wage bill rose 32 per cent in the 2017–18 season to £108.7 million, a figure exceeded only by the top six.

Relegation prompted an executive bloodbath at West Bromwich Albion, the only other Chinese-controlled club in the Premier League. All eyes were on the understated figure of Gao Jisheng, whose family purchased an 80 per cent stake in Southampton from Katharina Liebherr for £210 million the previous summer.

Gao, whose Lander Sports company is primarily involved in power generation and property dealing, had invested in a distinctive football business model, based on shrewd buying, regular selling and talent development, without showing his hand. An ideal was at stake and Reed, who as vice-chairman ran football operations at a strategic level, was vulnerable.

Reed oversaw the appointment of Mark Hughes, on a three-year contract, following the club's survival. Though faith had wavered in the 'Southampton Way', its five constituent values – respect, unity, creativity, accountability and aspiration – were as relevant as ever. The strapline 'turning potential into excellence' continued to have a practical dimension.

Six full-time teachers oversee the educational needs of academy players. A cohort of 30 coaches and analysts are undertaking a three-year BSc honours course in elite coaching for football. Every member of the support staff joins a multi-disciplinary international study group, assigned to week-long visits to leading European clubs and other sports.

Anyone who attends an international tournament is expected to submit a technical report on lessons drawn from a different culture or playing philosophy. Sports science and medical staff have published ground-breaking research on hip and groin injuries in conjunction with Oxford University. Reciprocal programmes have been undertaken with the Rugby Football Union, British Cycling, the Lawn Tennis Association and the Royal Ballet.

Collective standards are set and reviewed by a biannual meeting of the club's 400 employees, distributed into a series of workshop groups to ensure buy-in to Southampton's broader belief system.

Reed, who led a restructure after initially joining as a consultant in the aftermath of emergence from administration in 2009, may be 65, but he has a millennial's comfort with innovation. 'It is critical to remind people of our culture, especially in times of adversity. We have these values because it's the right way to behave. Why would we change that when things aren't going so well? And we've gone through that process a number of times, certainly on the football side, where we've stuck to our guns, worked our way through it, remained calm, and then come out the other end.

'It can be on-trend to have a mission statement, to put it on the wall or in a manual, and then forget about it and just get on with the day job. Our idea was to derive a set of standards and values that we all agree to live by, rather than the more traditional top-down approach, which dictates how the staff should behave.'

His philosophy was shaped by three spells at the FA, where he rose to become technical director and ushered in the era of academy football. He foresaw the potential of St George's Park when it was a random parcel of agricultural land. A secondment programme with British Aerospace in Africa and the Caribbean, advising on coach education and player development, proved pivotal.

Working with the Ghanaian FA, in an abandoned school in the southern coastal town of Winneba that served as a training base for the national and Olympic teams, gave football a human dimension beyond the clinical geometry of tactical planning or the dogma of technical development. There was a yearning for knowledge, a reverence for betterment.

'It was an unbelievable experience. It shows that if you can ignite someone's passion, if they have a real hunger to learn, and you put the infrastructure in place to help them, you can make big strides. Coaches had been specially selected, but one guy turned up two days late. With my FA hat on I said "see you later", and then he explained he'd been walking for two days to get there.

'That was the enthusiasm they had. In the evening the national coaches were in my bedroom, going through videos of the team, and asking for advice on the sort of sessions they should be putting on. It was a fantastic grounding in just what can be achieved in a short period of time when everybody is really motivated.

'Africa has a long tradition of football, but their countries are beleaguered with politics. It is a bit like Brazil; they are born into football, born into poverty, and are desperate to try and get out. We've seen with individual players just what they can produce, but the biggest problem is the enormity of getting organised, having a really good structure that is designed to deliver, without being interfered with by everything that goes on in the background.'

Premier League clubs were slow to pick up on the significance of player pathways, which initially led from Africa to France, Belgium and Portugal. At international level Nigeria and Cameroon have come close to fulfilling latent potential without neutralising anarchic elements of administration. Southampton's long-term opportunity, through its new ownership structure, lies in becoming a proactive partner in the development of the game in China.

'Over 18 months to two years before they came in, it became clear they were looking to invest in stability and consistency. They weren't looking for a fire rescue investment, an opportunity to take a club that was on its uppers and build it up and sell it on. There was a marriage of ideas. They never intended to buy a club and change it, run it, revolutionise it.

'One of the things they have invested in is the South-ampton Way. They like our principles of player development and think we can be a leading light in helping develop football in China. If that opens lots of doors and we can generate bigger commercial revenue that gets ploughed back into what we do, then great.

'We might spend a little bit more on players as time goes on, but I'm not overly concerned by having a big treasure chest of money to spend in the transfer window because that will change our culture. We would be a different club. We might get a worldwide fan base throughout China, but your fan base that turns out on a Saturday is as big as your city can provide.

'So unless Southampton doubles in size it's not like being in London. We have 30,000 seats, not 60,000. When I was at Charlton we put 15,000 extra seats in. We went up to the Premier League and they were filled. But there are 15,000 empty seats there now because they are down in League One.'

Idealism dies quickly, and painfully, in modern football. Reed's overview, informed by his access to the inner sanctum of the Premier League and wider roles as an FA councillor and membership of the Professional Game Board, combines bleak reality with dogged optimism. It is a difficult balance to strike in a world that blurs the boundary between opportunism and impropriety.

'The level of strategic involvement I have obviously gives me a lot of insight into how things are changing in the world, but we feel as a board, as a club, that it is really important to defend your beliefs. A favourite saying of mine is, "What makes you one of the big six is not the money you afford to spend, it's the money you can afford to waste".

'Once you start to abandon your principles, you go into the murky world of multi-disciplinary transactions, which involve different people, fees going here, there and everywhere. Once you're in it, you can't come back out of it. You've sold your soul. We're not big enough financially to sell our soul, gamble and waste money. We have to keep everything right and tight.

'The only way you can do that is by keeping your principles. That means sometimes you might lose out if you're not prepared to enter into a business transaction which involves changing your culture, changing your values. We feel it's worth losing out in order to stay like that. Over a period of time you get a feel for the people in your network.

'There isn't much in football I haven't done. I've been a player, a coach, a manager, a technical director. I've worked for a federation, been around the world. You get to know who you can trust, who will tell you the truth, the ones who are a little on the edge and the ones who are definitely dodgy. You know who, and what, to avoid.

'Sometimes you can get far down the line with some-one you're not sure about, and you realise, no, I'm getting a bad feeling here. If it doesn't feel right, walk away, don't get yourself hooked into a situation that gets to a point where it's very difficult to do so. Generally your instincts are proved right.

'It is the same when you are talking about young play-ers. I'm not going to mention any names, but maybe you'll get someone at twenty. He's been at one of the big clubs, done a loan here, a loan there, another loan there. And you think, now they'll let him go, we can get him. Then the agent or other collaborators, and sometimes even the parents, are looking for a little bit extra. They tell you "we did this with another club", all that kind of thing.

'Walk away. Generally they'll come back, bite the bul-let, and say no, we didn't mean all that, because they see Southampton as a fantastic showcase. But my view is if we scrub all that, and take him, that problem is coming back in a year, two years, three years. We've been proved right on a number of occasions.

'There are plenty of prospects who have gone to big clubs for big fees and big money, and now they're not in the team. They desperately want to leave but they are paid too much so they can't advance their careers because nobody around them is going to let them take a pay cut. If we stick to our principles, and recruit on our terms, we'll get more right than we get wrong.

'Keeping the pipeline going has always got to be part of what we do, and to enable us to do that we need to remain pure. It's not going to be easy, but we have to work hard or change our culture completely. We have to do it on the basis that we don't get ourselves into a position where the way to get out of trouble is to buy our way out of it. When you get to that point, you have to invite in all the things you've been trying to keep at bay.'

Reed's is a voice of reason, in an unreasonable environment. He cannot control football's capricious nature, and its fondness for a short-cut. Invariably owners are too preoccupied with grandiose schemes, and attendant self-promotion, to care too deeply about the inner being, or the most precious doctrines.

PART THREE

The Club

CHAPTER ELEVEN

McDons

'There have been horrible moments. My thirteen-year-old daughter, as she was then, was abused on the telephone at two o'clock in the morning. To get rid of them she reminded them it was paedophilic and the police were listening in to the conversation. I can't be proud that happened because of something her dad did.' Pete Winkelman, owner, MK Dons

Pete Winkelman, the man who supposedly stole a football club, invokes fear and loathing on a grand scale. To summon the spirit of many of his critics, who have the obsessional devotion of Harry Potter followers, he is football's Dark Lord, a malign, murderous presence whose mutilated soul deserves to linger in limbo for eternity.

Meet him in the flesh, in the black granite edifice of Stadium MK, and he has the distracted air of an assistant spells master at Hogwarts, rather than the menace of Voldemort, the evil wizard. The shoulder-length bird's nest hair, rumpled dark suit and open-necked shirt have become a personal motif.

His walk, a stiff-shouldered scurry, is that of a man in a hurry. His talk, often a stream of consciousness delivered at speed in surprisingly soft tones, suggests the neurons are careering around his brain like dodgems driven by hyperactive children. Ideas, opinions, theories and conclusions collide, yet he rarely conducts major interviews and is careful to the point of pedantry.

When, understandably enough, he asked for the context of this book, he waited almost a month, until he had read its inspiration, Arthur Hopcraft's *The Football Man*, before confirming our conversation. He took me to the fourth floor of the stadium's integral 304-room Hilton hotel, greeting maids along the way, to give the optimal view of the pitch before descending to a deserted third-floor bar, where he sipped Ribena and had to be nudged from a series of monologues.

His instinct is to look forward, to a future in which MK Dons match the growth of the new city they represent and develop into a Premier League club within the type of global framework pioneered by Manchester City. His problem is his inability to escape the magnetic field of the past, and the debilitating reality of the present.

MK Dons' relegation to League Two for the first time in a decade in May 2018, aligned to AFC Wimbledon's survival in League One, was celebrated like the Relief of Mafeking by his many critics. The pustule of bitterness generated by the transplantation of a football club precisely 67.8 miles from the south-west London borough of Merton exploded messily.

Many have stopped listening but, as Winkelman tells it, in June 2003 he received a call from administrators, who intended to liquidate Wimbledon FC the next morning. They informed him of FA approval for a move to Milton Keynes, but needed 'half a bar', half a million pounds, to keep the 'hopelessly insolvent' original club, which had debts in excess of £20 million, alive.

It took a year 'with many false twists and turns', including a late challenge from the tax authorities, to emerge from administration. It took Winkelman, who had supplied initial interim loans of £1.5 million, three further years to renounce the claim on the intellectual property rights of the extinct club, principally the FA Cup-winning exploits of the Crazy Gang era.

By that time MK Dons, aka Franchise FC, were in their new stadium. AFC Wimbledon, the supporter-owned club launched in the ninth tier of the English game in 2002, were on their way to being the first club formed in the 21st century to reach the Football League. In December 2017, when they were both in League One, AFC received permission to build a new stadium on the site of the old Wimbledon Greyhound Stadium, 300 metres from Plough Lane, the phoenix club's spiritual home.

Rivalry was toxic. Board members mutually refused hospitality at respective away games. The Football League initially reflected the pettiness of the situation, taking disciplinary action against AFC for refusing to mention MK Dons by name on the cover of their match programme, and for referring to their opponents as simply 'MK' on the scoreboard. Eventually, they saw sense and brokered an uneasy peace.

This will expose me to the wrath of the cyber warriors, but I'm broadly sympathetic to the view English football now has two viable clubs, different in character, aspiration and instinct, where it once had a moribund institution, whose relatively small group of loyalists was betrayed by its Norwegian owners.

The abuse Winkelman receives, more than a decade on from his heretical opportunism, remains visceral. 'I think I can take it on the chin. I don't mind taking it personally because you don't move English football clubs around. I completely get that. Would I be horrified if MK Dons went somewhere? I'd be absolutely gutted. It would be the end of my life. What I don't get is, one, why I had the opportunity; and two, why it affects my players, or our supporters. That's the impact that upsets me.

'Whilst we may have got here in a very strange way, when we've been here we've tried to do the right thing.

We've some brilliant supporters that travel all over the country and get extra stick. That's the bit that's most unfair. AFC have created a brilliant history of their own, yet they harp back to a history that isn't their own. And I don't understand how football doesn't see the difference.

'Maybe it's because we didn't get our message out strongly enough, maybe we've never been able to present the facts in the right way, and maybe it's because inherently I do feel guilty. For the first couple of years after the move, I was absolutely destroyed by the media, destroyed by football supporters in general. I'd brought condemnation on my home town. That wasn't actually what I meant to do at all.

'It has been a rollercoaster experience, and much of what I did, I did out of naivety. Now I've run a football club for a fair time, longer than a lot of people, I understand the circumstances we were in at the time were unique and exceptional. I don't think those circumstances should ever have happened, but what I can be very proud of is what we've done with that opportunity, through the way we operate our football club.

'It has an inclusive nature. There is female representation in our business, at every level. Our disability facilities are the best in English football. We are involved in seventeen disability teams. Our Sport and Education Trust deals with around fifty thousand people a year. We have an FA girls' Centre of Excellence and an academy that has produced fantastic players like Dele Alli.

'Time will be our judge. When I've gone, when the personal politics of the situation have died down, I want people to see an exciting, dynamic, well-resourced club with a brilliant infrastructure that reflects the values of the new city. For all the controversy, I'm actually a throwback because I'm a local businessman running the local football club, the custodian. It's quite ironic in that the great tradition of football, how it is centred in its community, is very, very relevant to us.

'To be honest, I've learnt to value and respect and almost adore the traditions of English football. As chairman of a football club, there is a huge onus of responsibility. We support so many people across the city in so many different ways, whether it's providing a facility for a charity function, or programmes for disadvantaged people. We are making a difference and I really value that.

'That puts me on the right wavelength with most people in football, from managers to players to other owners, who don't see us in the way that maybe the general public do. They understand what we are doing and how difficult some of it has been. We have to be holier than thou, whiter than white. We've had all the controversy that the club can stand in its infancy. We want to make our own history, our own traditions.'

His critics will accuse him of hypocrisy, in taking a short-cut instead of organically growing an existing local club, and until recently had a skeleton to produce as evidence of murderous intent. The low-ceilinged stand of Milton Keynes City FC's 4,000 capacity ground, where the so-called Gladiators played until folding in 1985, following a brief, opportunistic takeover by Ron Noades, the then Wimbledon chairman, fell into disrepair.

Its corrugated iron roof, mottled by time, was visible through a curtain of poplars from the main arterial road. The pitch became scrubland, overgrown and bramble-infested, until the land was cleared and used for housing. A reincarnation of the club, which played ten miles away in the north of the city between 1998 and 2003, has been supplanted by a vibrant new MK City FC, an amateur club that runs youth teams from under-sevens for both boys and girls.

In modern Britain progress comes at a price in all areas of civic life. Football's growing pains reflect those of the new city, founded in 1967. Picturesque villages, with traceable history to Roman settlements, have been swallowed. Twenty million trees might have been planted, but Milton Keynes' infamous concrete cows symbolise the contradiction of what planners envisaged as a 'forest city'.

Winkelman was a typical migrant; he had two children under the age of five, an entrepreneurial spirit, and sought a better quality of life. In 1993 he sold recording studios in Fulham and Birmingham and converted a manor house in one of the original villages, Great

Linford, in conjunction with the late Harry Maloney, former manager of Manfred Mann.

A 'coulda, woulda, shoulda' footballer in his youth, he formed a new social circle through sport. Coincidentally, our sons played together at Northampton Town's academy. Bobby Winkelman's dream of becoming a professional footballer ended when he sustained an anterior cruciate ligament injury, which required five unsuccessful knee operations. His father preferred to watch training in the shadows, but rarely missed a session.

The Dons' football philosophy is based on youth development. There is a common thread from the academy to the first team; possession is cherished, teams play through the thirds, and calculated risks are encouraged. In January 2018, when the club dropped into the League One relegation zone, Winkelman sacked his manager, Robbie Neilson, and went back, briefly, to the future.

Old-school football men reached for the popcorn and a pint. Dan Micciche, Neilson's successor, did not fit their blueprint; at 38, the former England Under-16s coach had never taken charge of a team in senior football. He carried the hopes of a generation of emerging, imaginative, English coaches, knowing failure would reinforce the forces of fear and conservatism.

Winkelman's faith was founded on Micciche's underpinning work at the Dons' academy, before he spent four and a half years at the FA. The new manager, of Italian descent, embodied the new city's modernity and sense of adventure. His formative influences included Brian Ashton, the former England rugby coach, and his late cousin, who forged a successful career as an artist, painting with his mouth, after sudden illness as a 16-year-old paralysed him from the neck down. Each informed the slogan with which he confronted his new players, 'No limits'.

A manager's introductory team talk forms lasting impressions. Micciche, small, olive-skinned, stubble-chinned and casually dressed, did not conform to the outdated authoritarian stereotype. Factual yet emotionally engaging, he had the air of a college lecturer as he spoke of being expressive in possession and disciplined out of it. His twin targets had a timescale: five months and five years.

The former inevitably referred to survival. Statistically, that would require a minimum of 52 points. A top-half finish required a further nine. Though, wisely, he would not invite scorn by speaking publicly about the possibility of stealing into the promotion play-offs, he privately spoke of reaching the 73 points he estimated would be needed to do so. They ended with 45.

'In five years I want us to be in the Premier League,' he told his players. 'Don't look at me like you think I'm mad. Bournemouth did it. That team, on minus seventeen points in League Two, was made up of Arter, Pugh,

Cook, Francis, Ritchie. They were the bedrock of their success. If they can do it why can't we?'

To reinforce his point he played a clip from his computer library, of a Tottenham goal against Southampton the previous month. His commentary was succinct: 'The ball is played into Dele in the pocket. Son's on the shoulder of the full back and makes a diagonal run. Dele rolls him in. He squares it, Harry taps it in. Two of those players, Harry and Dele, were playing in League One five years ago. It is doable.'

Micciche has mentors in the field of psychology and child development. His experience at Tottenham brought him into contact with two of the most understated but highly respected men in youth football, John McDermott and Chris Ramsey. His most direct role model, in his new job, was Eddie Howe, rather than Pep Guardiola. 'Of course, Guardiola is a genius. He consumes himself in the game plan, and delegates training planning. That's an important lesson for me. I have realised there is no need to micro-manage your staff if you ensure they feel supported. Hopefully it sends out the message that I'm not a control freak. We adopted a similar philosophy with England.

'Eddie is a young English manager who has done it with his local club. He has got them up the leagues playing in a certain way. That is the sort of model this club can adopt and I think the potential is huge. We are in the middle of the country, accessible for players. We have a history of developing players, a brilliant stadium. It is all set up. It is down to somebody, and I think that person is me, to take this club forward.

'I understand entirely why some think I represent a risk. But if you look more deeply, I have had fifteen years coaching. I have studied. I don't believe playing expressive football is a risk if you understand basic movement patterns and you have the capacity to provide solutions to immediate problems. Eight out of twenty managers in the Bundesliga are in their thirties. We haven't got their balance of young and old yet.

'I understand the massive responsibility I have got. As well as paying my own mortgage, and my reputation being at stake, there are a thousand people that work here who are dependent on me, my staff and eighteen players. I'm the type who surrounds himself with good people. On top of that I understand what this football club is about. It is a distinctive club.'

Just how distinctive became apparent as we chatted, with his assistant Keith Millen, in the tunnel at Stadium MK before their official unveiling. Winkelman was abuzz, an electrical charge in human form; comically, he couldn't open the double doors leading to the pitch, to ensure a grand entrance for the cameras. He waited beneath a sign that read 'Welcome to the Jungle' as appropriate bolts were slipped.

It is at such moments Winkelman can appear ignorant, or at best semi-detached. His thought processes have the serenity of a mountain bike ride down a ski-slope. His attention wavers, as though he has an unconscious, child-like inability to concentrate on current matters or relationships. Once outside and confronted by an inter-viewer from a local TV station, he veered spectacularly off message in bemoaning 'an absolutely horrible year'. He spoke of 'going backwards' and evidently amplified an impatient internal monologue by mentioning 'the unwrit-ten story' of 'not being investment ready'.

The custodian's mask had slipped. The shrewd prop-erty developer who has positioned a football club at the heart of a retail and leisure park that features fashion brands, family restaurants, a cinema, superstore, hotel and multi-purpose arena emerged. Winkelman may define football as 'the emotional driver' of his project, but it is a means to an end. He wants to franchise the franchise.

'We're living through a technological age and there is disruption all the time,' he rationalised, when chal-lenged. 'You can't over-worry about it because if you do, you're not going to be powerful enough in your own position to actually have an influence. You'll just be fol-lowing events. Whereas if we concentrate on ourselves, try to do the things that we do well, we get our culture, our values. We set ourselves out to be what we're going to be, like it or hate it.

'I'm getting eighty per cent of it right, but the most important twenty per cent is having success with the football. Not for ever. Not always. Not every year. But you've got to have enough success to establish the club as a top twenty club, because we're already a top twenty city. We'll be a top ten city in the next twenty years. And that's why imagining Milton Keynes as a top ten football club in England is not an outrageous thought. It's just a stretch from where we are at the moment.'

At that moment, relegation seemed unthinkable. It was confirmed soon after he sacked Micciche, who won only three of his 16 matches in charge, on 22 April. At the risk of mixing motorised metaphors, he spoke of a 'car crash' and threw the young coach under the bus. 'I took a risk,' he acknowledged. 'I thought it was a good gamble, but it was not to be. It's either going to happen or it is not. With hindsight I probably would have made a different decision.

'Dan had a plan. I liked the plan. I wanted to give him a go. Maybe I was naive. This is not what I expected or wanted. Having that final conversation with him was one of the most difficult things I have had to do. Football has a knack of reminding you that things can get worse, and this is absolutely horrendous, the worst thing that could have happened.'

His choice of Paul Tisdale as Micciche's successor was impressively logical and characteristically distinctive. Tisdale, only 45, had supplanted Arsène Wenger as England's longest-serving manager at Exeter City, where his intelligence and unorthodoxy sustained a small club for twelve years before he seized the chance to 'build a unique environment and culture' at Milton Keynes.

The human chemistry is intriguingly unpredictable. Winkelman estimates the club has cost him between £2 million and £3 million annually, over 13 years ('do the maths') and admires the achievement of Dean Hoyle, the Huddersfield Town owner, in reaching the Premier League on a lower quartile budget, far-sighted recruitment and an inspirational left-field choice of manager in David Wagner.

'The Premier League is the dream I hold on to. It keeps me going every day, spending more money. The reality is that we'll probably need some big partner, some saint or billionaire that understands how economically important it is going to be for Milton Keynes, and potentially our investors, to be in the Premier League. I'm very aware that might mean the end of me.

'To say I've been a reluctant club owner is probably the wrong phrase, but I never meant to own a football club. Really, you need to be a billionaire. We knew that was the way it was going ten years ago. I've met lots of people that have said, "I can help you with this, I can help you with that, and look at what we can do here, or do there". But I've not believed in anybody enough to take that risk.

'I will not take my eye off the infrastructure, because I've seen other clubs fail to take note of that, only for it to end in tears. Today or tomorrow, if the right opportunity came, one that our city and supporters could believe in, I'd take it. But unless the deal sang of that possibility, I'm probably better keeping going whilst I've still got a job to do.

'We only finished the stadium a couple of years ago; we're now on to the training ground, which is still probably another five years off finishing, so I've got time to find the right person, whether they be foreign, whether they be individuals, whether they be a state. There are so many things involved in football that you have to have your eyes wide open.'

Winkelman's focus has settled on the transformative potential of the City Football Group (CFG), a global conglomerate that is likely to double its current network of six clubs across five continents by the end of this decade by expanding into China, India and Africa. The parent club's saunter to the Premier League title in 2018, under Pep Guardiola's guidance, was a game-changer.

As an expression of soft political power, wielded by Abu Dhabi, and entrepreneurial vision, incorporating their Chinese co-owners, CFG is unprecedented. Franchises are designed to enshrine a common corporate culture; they will eventually all play in the same colour, primarily light blue, conform to a progressive pattern of play and have 'City' in their title.

Two deals, on the penultimate day of the January transfer window of 2018, summarised aspects of their supplementary advantage. The holding company model allows players to be recruited for, or developed at, various levels, locations and ages around the world and sold between constituent clubs within the network. In that sense, Jack Harrison and Mix Diskerud were the future, made flesh.

Harrison, a former Manchester United trainee who moved to the US at the age of 14 and developed into an England Under-21 international at the New York City franchise, was loaned to Middlesbrough in the Championship immediately after signing a three and a half year contract with Manchester City. CFG were in a no-lose situation; even if he fails to progress into City's Premier League squad, he will doubtless be sold on for a profit. The fee paid to the US franchise remained in a collective pot.

City's signing of Diskerud to a four and a half year contract was rather less logical. At 27, he had been on loan at IFK Gothenburg from New York City. Though capped 38 times by the US, he was named as the 'most overrated player' in MLS in a 2017 poll of his peers. Scouts of my acquaintance suggested he would struggle even in England's second tier. That news of his transfer was broken by the Twitter feed of Umbro, distant rivals of City's suppliers Nike, hardly helped.

'I'm very eager to be a part of people and organizations that constantly strive to bring our sport, values and gear to new levels,' Diskerud trilled in a press release that dripped with corporate pretension. 'Man City is probably the best football club in the world, and Umbro design the best cleats, and not only for me. Both are historic brands looking to shape the future of our sport.'

This clumsiness went against the underpinning principle of so-called 'glocalisation', a concept in which global brands are seamlessly adapted to local markets. It was adopted by City after being popularised in the late 1990s by British sociologist Roland Robertson. The most visible practical example is provided by McDonald's, whose menus are customised to suit local tastes and cultures.

McDons? Winkelman rather likes the sound of it, or something similar. 'I have to admit, the City Group model is the one I most like. Football, talent recruitment and development are a global business these days. To be part of something bigger than us, in a pan-global opportunity, would be the most realistic end scenario for me. Who knows? I am trying to think as outside of the box as I can, or at least take as much notice as I can of developments in international football to see how they could best play out for the future of Milton Keynes.

'We have a unique advantage in the economic power and growth potential of a new city. So you could certainly imagine MK Galaxy or the Detroit Dons. They are not unrealistic things to think about. But, again, it's very much a question of right time, right place and right grouping to put together people that share that vision and that dream.

'I have had conversations over the years, involving different scenarios. The one I come back to is the global alliance. I've been watching what City do, and I'm hugely interested. Everyone can criticise foreign ownership but if you see what has been done to east Manchester it has been incredible. I went there when they built the Commonwealth Games stadium, and it was in a desolate city.

'Go there now and it is the most vibey, happening place, because they have spent hundreds of millions of pounds regenerating it. I love the economic effect that international sport can have. This is the power of sport, the power of football. It can change communities. We have changed Milton Keynes, in putting football and the stadium here. That's the legacy we've already created.'

Winkelman was one of nine commissioners in the MK Futures 2050 project, drawn from politics, business and the arts. Assigned to define civic progress over three decades, they identified six areas of growth, including the area's accessibility, land options and a skilled, educated workforce. Optimism was based on an existing influx of more than 20 advanced technology, knowledge-driven firms.

Synergy with such multi-national companies, expressed in their report as 'brain gain rather than brain drain', has an inevitable sporting relevance. At a club where 35 per cent of season ticket holders are under 18, planning requires foresight beyond the limitations of an average home crowd of 8,948 in the first half of the ill-fated 2017–18 season.

Mercedes-Benz has its head offices in Milton Keynes. It is not difficult to envisage the Dons being reinvented as a company-oriented football club, in the way that Wolfsburg, in the Bundesliga, is a wholly owned subsidiary of Volkswagen. Red Bull, which has an expansionist international network of football clubs and operates its Formula One team from Milton Keynes, is another obvious potential partner.

He has spoken to the company, whose Leipzig franchise employs Paul Mitchell, the former MK Dons captain, as head of recruitment. Wisely, at a delicate stage of development, Winkleman cautions that he does not consider that relevant 'in the here and now'. Yet he appreciates the logic of feeder clubs being introduced by stealth, through strategic recruitment and marketing.

'That might be how some of the lower league clubs might be able to survive. I'm not going to sit here and say it's definitely a bad thing. It just depends on how it plays out. What we have to do is make sure that we're in a good place as an individual football club, with the new Oxford-Milton Keynes-Cambridge national infrastructure, brain belt, Silicon Valley of the UK vibe going on.

'We have got an enormous opportunity, whether it involves partnering with international clubs or selling out to somebody because they've got an amazing plan. Just to say that I believed in it wouldn't be enough. It would have to be obvious that it was the right thing to do, because you're going to take a whole city with you.

'Football is our national game, the sport that engages more people than anything else, and for that reason, we've got to treat it with specialness. We run a massive professional game, much, much bigger than probably it should be, so there are some big choices to be made. There are so many politics playing out, so many disparate people and so many vested interests. It is a moment in time, and I try to look beyond all sense of the moment.'

So where will his brainchild, or stolen child, according to taste, be in another 50 years? Since he is 60, with the obvious proviso of his own mortality, he allows himself to dream.

'By that time we'll probably be number eight city in the UK so the football club could replicate that. We'd be on the edge of Europe, regularly getting into international competitions, possibly part of a larger group, possibly Dons playing all over the world. Do I think we'll be important and powerful? Yes, I think we are already. In terms of what we do, we punch above our weight.

'I would like to see more money go into our grass roots, where I started as a parent with a kid who was quite good at football. Can I even get close to the joy that I had watching that? The tournaments we'd win, well, it led to all this. That's how much joy I had doing it. I want to make sure that's very relevant in the future.

'My boy reminds me of how important football was to me as a kid. All we did back then was play football, every time we got together. Sometimes the kids were four, five years older and you loved it even more when they kicked you off the pitch. We've lost that now everything has to be more organised and everyone has to have a strip on and follow health and safety guidelines.

'That's the world we live in and we can't change that, so we have to support the game in a slightly different way. If we lose sport, lose real competitiveness, and it all becomes robots playing on our screens, then really the human condition is all over at that point. What makes us human is our physicality, our living, breathing body, and sport represents the pinnacle of what we can do in that.'

For a moment there he almost had me. Then I remembered another self-styled 'tie-loathing adventurer, philanthropist & troublemaker', Richard Branson. He, too, has an answer for everything, and a knack of confusing personal interest with popular philosophising. Pete Winkelman isn't the ogre some make him out to be, but his benevolence should not be taken at face value.

CHAPTER TWELVE

Back to the Future

'I have never changed my opinion that football is a game for the people. During my career, I tried not to lose sight of the fact that we were striving to be successful for the supporters as well as for ourselves. Yes, we could all carry on playing the game without them, but there wouldn't be anything like the sense of enjoyment and satisfaction when things go well. Those memories cannot be forgotten.' – Graham Taylor

A single piano chord and a synthesised drum beat set the tempo. String instruments swoop, pursued by flautists and the heavy artillery of the brass section. A choir helps to underlay a series of still photographs from another time, where boyhood heroes are captured in excelsis. As the soundtrack reaches a crescendo, a caption silently celebrates 'The Impossible Dream'.

I am watching the 94-second video, a Raining In My Heart production, on a giant screen to the right of the stand at Vicarage Road that bears Graham Taylor's name. It is a frigid, slate-grey Saturday afternoon and memories, already stimulated by the walk to the ground, past overgrown allotments that will one day form the Watford Health Campus with the adjoining hospital, merge.

Elton John's song 'Are You Ready for Love?' plays over the public address system. It accompanies another montage, of crowd invasions, goals struck through sandy penalty areas, and fans trying to kiss Taylor's hand as he walks down from the Royal Box at the old Wembley Stadium. Another caption stands sentinel: 'Our Greatest Manager'.

This is 13 January 2018, Graham Taylor Day. He passed away, aged 72, 366 days previously. The choreography is impeccable; scarves from different eras are raised above the heads of a crowd that has never lost its Home Counties homeliness. Southampton supporters curtail a signature chorus of 'When the Saints go marching in' to join in as a mark of respect.

It is only later, when I study photographs of the occasion, that I notice that not a single scarf is raised in the directors' box. Crusty convention dictates against such demonstrations of allegiance in the posh seats, but it is hard not to use the image as a corollary for a change of emphasis at the club that I grew up with.

This would be Marco Silva's last home game as Watford manager. His team were abject, fortunate to trail by only two goals at half-time, yet secured a point when Abdoulaye Doucouré used his hand to steer in a 90th-minute equaliser. The Portuguese coach was a distant, distracted figure, idly twirling a microphone as he excused such unapologetic gamesmanship.

His unbridled ambition and destructive disaffection at being denied the opportunity to join Everton reached its inevitable conclusion when he was sacked. Within hours Javi Gracia, an itinerant Spanish coach on the rebound from Rubin Kazan in Russia, was installed as the tenth manager at the club since it was acquired by the Pozzo family in 2012. It was Gracia's tenth job in as many years.

Taylor was the first manager with whom I worked, as a grammar school refugee let loose on the sports pages of the local newspaper. He engaged and energised an entire community in the six years it took him to transform Watford from a moribund Fourth Division football club into runners-up, behind Liverpool, in the old First Division in 1983.

His illuminating honesty and arresting directness, which Elton John would later cite as an enabling influence in his battle against substance abuse, were summarised by his advice at our first meeting. I was awestruck; he spoke as a journalist's son: 'If you want to be anything in your business, remember you've only got one reputation.'

Our career paths overlapped, occasionally uneasily. Although he became a popular figure in press rooms through his radio commentary commitments in later life, he bore the scars of his failure as England manager. My most personal and painful vision of him is of him acting as host in the chairman's suite at Watford in late autumn, 2011.

He had a melancholic air, as if he was conscious he was legitimising the then owner, a glib, graceless man who had changed his name from Laurence Bazini to Bassini when he was made bankrupt in 2007. 'I just couldn't work him out,' Taylor admitted in his posthumous autobiography. 'Any attempts to ask him about his background quickly became confused.'

Taylor resigned as chairman when Bassini was bought out the following year. He had done his duty by the club and became living history for a tragically brief period. He observed, wryly, that the average age of those supporters who approached him for an autograph or photograph had soared. The town stopped for his funeral, where his daughter Joanne expressed his credo: 'Family first, except on match days.'

My values were shaped by adolescent experience, long before I acquired professional perspective. I grew so distant from the club I had only a peripheral interest in its fortunes. In retrospect I wanted to preserve it in a personal portal, a link to a different land, where I was thrilled by the intimacy of being a ballboy and travelled to my first away game, at Oxford United, in a neighbour's sidecar.

I returned in an attempt to answer nagging questions. Does the mind play tricks, recreate football as a Norman Rockwell painting, a stylised image of domestic harmony? What has our national game sacrificed in its development into a shiny, flat-packed product? Is societal change, and the fast-buck, instant indulgence of the Premier League, irreversible? Can constant upheaval fairly be portrayed as the new stability?

Terms of reference were set over an informal introductory lunch in central London. Scott Duxbury, Watford's chairman and chief executive, knew of my scepticism but was prepared to offer rare insight into an undeniably proficient business model, based upon a global scouting system. As befits his background as a lawyer, once seconded to Manchester United, he presented his case clearly and concisely.

Giampaolo Pozzo has owned Udinese, the Serie A club, since July 1986. He is accepted as the eminence grise of Italian football, despite a suspension imposed when he was implicated in allegations related to match-fixing in the early 1990s. He owned Granada, the Spanish club, for seven years before selling it to Chinese businessman Jiang Lizhang in June 2016.

Watford is owned by his son Gino. He was introduced to Duxbury a decade ago by Gianluca Nani, the former technical director of West Ham, where Duxbury was chief executive until the takeover by David Gold and David Sullivan in 2010. The Pozzo family's unconventional leadership style was reinforced when we reconvened at Watford's training ground in London Colney.

Gino, a formally dressed figure with a mane of dark hair, greying at the temples, worked from a large circular table in front of a picture window on the right-hand edge of the canteen. He was a study of quiet diligence in an unlikely setting; his suit jacket hung over the back of a plastic chair as he switched focus between his laptop, a sheaf of papers and two mobile phones. Though he acknowledges visitors, interview requests are routinely denied.

'Gino is here every day. Every single day,' said Duxbury, with emphasis. 'He is fiercely ambitious and absolutely loves football. It is his whole focus. He's moved his family to London and dedicates his entire life to the football club. He is passionate when it comes to player recruitment. The transfer window is when he comes alive; he's already thinking two steps ahead.

'This was a club with three stands, and a previous owner of questionable reputation. Gino came in as a footballing man. He doesn't have any other business other than the business of football. He makes great pains to stress the separation of ownership, and that the local community is integral to the club's development. He doesn't come here and make this club Udinese. It's Watford.'

What is a football club? Is it best expressed as a clinical distillation of financial efficiency, or as a living, breathing organism? Is it a product of art or science, a rich man's indulgence or a working man's inheritance? Can its local heroes come from diverse countries and cultures? Does it have enduring characteristics, or must it move with the times?

Duxbury had pierced the heart of the issue. 'That's exactly what we're talking about. You have to deal with the reality. Graham Taylor is an interesting analysis, because he and Elton were the focal point in growing the football club. In the modern Watford Football Club you have myself and Gino. We are the stability.

'We've moved away from the ideal of Graham's era, that a young home-grown player is pivotal to supporter engagement. If you're going to unlock those huge resources that the centralised TV deal gives you, you have to create the most competitive team, which doesn't necessarily include young Johnny from the academy.

'Yes, you do lose romanticism, the Roy of the Rovers stuff, because quite frankly the Premier League makes it more and more difficult for that scenario to occur. Many supporters, and certainly our fan base, are pragmatic enough to understand that is payback for a four-sided stadium and the growth that money unlocks.

'Romanticism has a huge place in football, but it doesn't equate to longevity. It's nice when it happens, but that's a different story. Rather than accept the media myth that it's an emotional journey, and that manager and players should be here for ten years, accept that that isn't true, and what we are being is professional.

'We are using our resources correctly to grow a stable football club with the full knowledge that you don't build your entire infrastructure around its most short-term, vulnerable aspect, the players and the coaches. We're in the fortunate position that from day one our supporters have understood that.

'Our ethos is to create a stable club that is able to prosper and deliver success over a long period of time. We take a pragmatic view of who we are; we're relatively small compared to some of the teams in the Premier League so we've got to use our resources wisely. The best way is to make those resources club-owned, through investment in the infrastructure.

'We take the view that coaches have a two-year life-cycle. They're either going to be phenomenally successful and move on to a bigger club, or it won't work out. We don't want that person to be in charge of the whole development of the football club, so those resources leave with him, or a new guy comes in with a completely different ideology, and you have to duplicate costs and spend.

'It's not as limiting as perhaps the media would like to portray it, because we will engage with that head coach with regards to what style of player he wants, and indeed discuss specific names. But when it comes to actually sourcing those players, that's what we do. We allow the coaches to focus on the grass, the training and tactics.

'We have an unfair reputation when it comes to coaches, because they will all say we are very support-ive. If we're happy with the work he's putting in, and we can see the tactical preparation he's doing but results aren't happening, then we know it's not the coach's fault. We know it's the players' fault, and we haven't got recruitment right for him.'

Three of Watford's 35 full-time scouts monitor head coaches and assistant coaches. A database contains con-tractual details of those in work, and statistical summaries of those 'resting'. When a vacancy arises, video evidence from at least ten games and, if possible, subsidiary coaching sessions are studied for tactical preferences, flaws and philosophies.

One of the three, Frenchman Romain Poirot, works for both Watford and Udinese. He describes his exper-tise as 'developing relationships with clubs to remain fully aware of emerging talent and contract situations'. He speaks four languages, including Serbian (five if you include the robo-prattle of LinkedIn), and spent seven years at Manchester City, initially in a youth recruit-ment capacity.

'The research process is as thorough as our player scouting network,' Duxbury confirmed. 'Reports are constantly being fed back to us, so we know how poten-tial coaches operate. We have a particular interest in young coaches that are up-and-coming, that perhaps aren't on people's radar.

'As I say, we take the philosophical view that we know a coach is going to have a short shelf-life. So we need to be prepared. You'd be surprised how accommodating a lot of clubs are, particularly in Europe. They are proud of the work they are doing. Our scouts will be invited to see training sessions. They will watch the coaches in action.

'The key to success is what happens on the training ground. We have an idea, first of all, of how we want to work. We don't like having numerous days off. The training ground is a place of work, where you've got to get ideas and strategy across to the players. You can only do that by having a certain intensity of work ethic. Working hard when you don't have the ball, pressing, high tempo, to get the ball back, is how we like to play football.

'Football is a game of mistakes and the fewer mistakes you make, the more chance you have of winning. So, we need a coach who shares that philosophy. You'd be surprised how many people, when they look at recruiting a coach, are looking at a name. They have no idea how that person actually works.

'We watch videos to see how he sets up, how he operates during a match, how he responds to tactical changes. If we can't, for a variety of reasons, see his training sessions, then we'll speak to the coach to get a true understanding of how he likes to organise. Then we can see if our philosophies are compatible. It's just trying to take a little bit of the risk out of what is an important position, the person training the assets that we're purchasing.'

So, coaches can be for Christmas, and not for life. Duxbury is sensitive when I refer to Watford's 'churn rate' in terms of players and management, and in fairness they are not an isolated example. Watford were one of ten Premier League clubs to change managers in the 2017–18 season. His strident defence of creative tension will strike a chord in many boardrooms.

'Long term is a myth. You only have a season in football. Every player, every coach, everybody in the game will accept that. If you have a poor season and you're relegated, then all bets are off. Put the emotion and the romanticism to one side, and have a conscious, professional, objective evaluation that necessitates decisions.

'At the end of every season we evaluate everyone, from the tea lady to the star striker. It is incumbent on any business – and we are a business – to evaluate what was good, what was bad, what was wrong, what are we facing in the future, and whether we have the required resources to face that challenge.

'Ideally you get to a point where you've built your squad, you're happy with it, and there is very little tinkering required. If the coach is performing then, absolutely, we will go into the next campaign with nothing changing. But as I said, if he is successful with this club for successive seasons the chances are he will move to a bigger club.

'We have no problem with that. We tell coaches and players that all our goals are mutually aligned. If you deliver success, this club will improve in the league and will grow. If that means that you then move on as a player to Real Madrid, or as a coach to Paris Saint-Germain, then fantastic. Football's short-termism is not something we shy away from, it's something we fully embrace.

'Players understand that playing regularly at a proactive, ambitious football club is their best opportunity to further their career. So, it's almost psychological profiling. Our ambitions are mutually compatible. We want to grow, be successful in the Premier League, and push, in time, for those European places.

'The players we attract inevitably have hunger and desire. We don't get those who just want the shiny badge. We get players who don't want to be in the development squad. We tell them, come and play now, in one of the best leagues in the world. Then, on your terms, move to one of the best teams in Europe, or indeed the Premier League, as a starter. Do not be just one of the numbers.'

Head coaches are provided with a choice of ten players of suitable style and potential in each position they request to be strengthened. Scouts are co-ordinated by technical director Filippo Giraldi, who moved from Brescia to spend six months evaluating Watford prior to the Pozzos' purchase of what was then a Championship club.

Giraldi plays up to the mysteries of their recruitment process, joking that 'it's like a spy story'. Duxbury is rather more prosaic. He confirms the primary importance of South America as a market and admits to 'having one eye on' emerging nations like India and China. Watford's streamlined senior management structure means they can move swiftly when opportunities arise.

'We're looking all over the world, literally everywhere. If there's an international tournament we will send one of our scouts. Europe is becoming less and less interesting because names are known and clubs are more established. There are some real gems in South America, but you can't limit yourself.'

They have at least four internal scouting forums each season; recommendations do not have to be unanimous but must be supported by at least two of the most senior scouts, outside the triumvirate of Gino Pozzo, Duxbury and Giraldi. Though there has been a strategic shift in the recruitment of emerging English talents like Nathaniel Chalobah, Will Hughes and Ben Wilmot, an 18-year-old defender signed from Stevenage, Watford loan out 15 young players, on five-year contracts, who cannot play in the UK because of visa requirements.

'We have to move to sign them before they are known. The hope is that they will either play in another league where they will get European citizenship or their international career will develop so they can get a work permit here. If those scenarios don't occur, we still have faith they will develop a commercial value. It's our secondary thought but at least our investment won't be lost.'

The Pozzos are considering purchasing a Spanish Second Division club. It is a physically demanding league, with a compatible culture for South American players. It is also a convenient place to park those of African origin, who are not included in legislation limiting clubs to two non-EU players. Football, as a whole, doesn't like to think too deeply about the morality of such human Jenga.

The incestuous nature of the Pozzo football family is underlined by the development of Venezuelan international Adalberto Peñaranda who, at 20, was brought back to Watford in the summer of 2018 in anticipation of his Premier League debut. He was discovered playing for Deportivo La Guaira, 30 kilometres from Caracas, and signed by Udinese in June 2015.

He was immediately loaned to Granada, where he became their youngest ever La Liga player in a 2–0 home win over Athletic Bilbao. He signed for Watford in February 2016 and was loaned to Granada and Udinese. Following successive failures to secure a work permit, he gained intermittent La Liga experience with Malaga over 16 months from January 2017.

Similarly, Malian left winger Aly Mallé was signed from Black Stars in Bamako by Watford in July 2016, and immediately loaned to Granada. Following their relegation from La Liga in the summer of 2017, he signed a five-year contract with Udinese, who loaned him to Lorca in the Segunda Division for the second half of the season without giving him a first-team debut.

Gambian international Sulayman Marreh is another seeking to emerge from a twilight world, at the age of 22. The defensive midfield player made a solitary La Liga appearance for Granada before he joined Watford on the expiry of his contract in the summer of 2017. He played four matches for Valladolid in the Copa del Rey before being sent to Almería, another Segunda Division club, for the second half of the season.

Watford's most promising sleeper, Colombian striker Cucho Hernández, is earmarked for integration into the Premier League squad in 2019, unless market forces impose their will. Watford turned down €15 million for him in early 2018, when he was 18, and, with Duxbury describing him as 'the new Agüero' Barcelona's subsequent interest has doubled his nominal worth.

Hernández made his debut for Deportivo Pereira in Colombia's Categoría Primera B before moving to Granada in September 2016. He was loaned to America de Cali until the summer of 2017, when his international rights were assigned to Watford. He spent the 2017–18 season honing goal-scoring and decision-making skills at SD Huesca, who were promoted to La Liga.

Richarlison is one step further along the pathway, but not immune to growing pains. The Brazilian winger, signed for €12 million from Fluminense in August 2017 when he was on the verge of joining Ajax, was the break-out star of the first half of Watford's third season back in the Premier League, but struggled for consistency after he was linked to Chelsea, Tottenham Hotspur and Paris Saint-Germain.

His fluctuation in form conformed to internal scouting reports, which dated back to 2015, and his original club, América Mineiro. The risk was deemed manageable, though a change in tactical emphasis by the new coach, Javi Gracia, left him in tears when he was substituted against Chelsea. They reached a rap-prochement in a meeting conducted in *portuñol*, a mixture of Portuguese and Spanish favoured by South Americans.

A broader explanation for his discomfort was teased out by football's Brazilian diaspora, including Chelsea defender David Luiz and Watford goalkeeper Heurelho Gomes. Richarlison lost five kilos living in a hotel because he struggled with its British menu; Gomes found him a house close to the training ground, and introduced him to a Brazilian supermarket, where he could buy his staple diet of rice, meat and beans.

His motivation is understandable and shaped by childhood poverty. 'Look, everybody wants financial security for their family,' he told *FourFourTwo*. 'When a player says otherwise, he's lying.'

Duxbury praises his character, but accepts that personal faults are occasionally excused or overridden because of the urgency of the recruitment procedure. 'Since we are looking at such a young age, seventeen or eighteen, the primary focus is on technical ability. We're trying to find a player that can play in the top four teams in the Premier League. If we believe he has that growth potential, we will invest. We try to do background checks, but they are not perhaps as sophisticated as some clubs, who use private investigators.

'We will start to invest more in profiling because, without naming names, we signed some technically very, very gifted players, but when it came to their attitude to training, to London nightlife and other distractions, it was a huge barrier to making it as a professional footballer let alone in the Premier League.

'Perhaps some pre-profiling would have revealed that. But I'm honest. Sometimes you are blinded by technical ability. If, for example, you have a Messi at a young age but someone says, "well, he likes to go out, he likes the girls", it is very difficult to turn away, and believe you can't adapt, you can't make him something special.'

Only Liverpool, Chelsea and the two Manchester clubs spent more on agents in the year to 31 January 2018 than Watford. They contributed £13.4 million to fees totalling £221 million, which fed the frenzy. The transfer market has its murky corners, where multiple agents attach themselves to promising players on the most dubious of pretences. Third party ownership problems are common.

'There are certain players we can't sign, because they have that entourage, the financial add-ons. When we locate a player, particularly at that younger age, it has to be commercially advantageous, because we're taking a huge risk. First of all, most of them can't actually play for the football club; there has to be a period of X years developing them, in order to get a work permit or citizenship.

'With certain South American players the financial demands can be quite challenging. If so, we walk away. There is always another player, another prospect. We don't get hung up on one particular individual. Players don't understand sometimes that they price themselves out of a particular opportunity because of all the add-ons, the additional people that need to be compensated. There's always another solution, always.'

Unsurprisingly, Duxbury is prepared to argue for Premier League B teams to be incorporated into the domestic pyramid. He recognises that 'politically it would be very difficult to achieve' but has sanctioned the introduction of a B team, which will operate outside the Premier League's futile and featureless under-23 system from the 2018–19 season.

This will incorporate fringe first teamers, young professionals and aspiring scholars. Recruitment is overseen by former Brentford manager Andy Scott, who is seeking to align home-grown talent with 'players from abroad, who can come in at seventeen, eighteen or nineteen and fit into how we want to do things'.

It is another who-killed-Bambi's-mother moment, and a smoking gun hangs by Duxbury's side. 'Developing a nine-year-old kid over a nine-year period to be your superstar is a wonderful idea, but I don't think football clubs have that time. A coach needs a player right now. It is becoming harder and harder for a kid to come through.

'Our academy is important for a number of reasons. It is part of the club's DNA and, together with the Football in the Community programme, enables kids to engage with the club. Now and again that academy will produce a player, but it's becoming more and more difficult for clubs like Watford to believe that will happen.'

Pro contracts, of the type offered to Lewis Gordon and Ryan Cassidy, local boys associated with the club since the age of seven, in the spring of 2018, keep the link open and the dream alive, but this is a stripped-down business model that prioritises success over sentiment. Watford reported a pre-tax profit of £4 million, from a record turnover of £124 million, for the 2016–17 season.

Gross debt, at £50 million, and the wage bill, £76 million, are relatively low. The Pozzos are committed to expanding stadium capacity from 21,577 to a maximum of 30,000, but typically insightful analysis of the accounts by financial expert Kieron O'Connor, who posts on social media as Swiss Ramble, notes the high level of interest charged for the club's parent company loans, principally £40 million at 6 per cent above base rate. That generated £4.1 million, a gesture considering the wealth of the ownership.

Football is a sexier way of turning a profit than toolmaking, the basis of the Pozzo family fortune, and rival clubs regard their progress with wry detachment. In the words of one executive: 'The Pozzos love football and they want to make money. If you had a shitload of money anyway, what better way would there be to spend your time, working the way they do?'

Gino Pozzo has not moved in the 90 minutes or so in which Duxbury has outlined their vision. He is clearly absorbed by the minutiae of his model. It might be a little simplistic to portray this as a glorified game of real-life Football Manager, but several suitors have been rejected and there is a resistance to the assumption that everyone in the modern game has their price.

'We have had people come here and offer a lot of money to buy the club, but what would be the point?

Gino's passion is to be successful in the Premier League with Watford, so if he sells it, what's he going to do then? There's no financial reason to sell, and we have a point of difference that allows us to be competitive and successful.

'This is where your romanticism comes in: the beauty of football is, there is no end game. Who knows where this can take us? If you'd have asked Leicester five years ago where their end game was, I'm sure they wouldn't have said they were going to win the Premier League. Keep growing, evaluate, re-evaluate, change, and let's see where it can take us.

'There's nothing sinister about it, you know. We are here for the long term. Initially, this was a very difficult concept for people to understand but after six years of delivering on all our promises, in terms of stadium development and promotion to the Premier League, I think they can see it is a sensible way to run a football club. The inconvenient truth is we are the very model of stability.'

Graham Taylor is still listed as the club's honorary life president, as a timeless mark of respect. I went in search of his spirit on that cold January day, and found it in a converted executive box, built close to the site of the old wooden supporters' club, where I once played darts with Elton John, a fetching figure in pink satin suit and feather boa.

Watford's Sensory Room hosts a maximum of six children on the autistic spectrum, with their parents.

Some come in buggies, others in wheelchairs. Many carry their own toys for comfort. They are attended by Sara Lavender and Collette Sturgess, specialist carers who were season ticket holders before they joined the club's match-day staff. This was the expression of football as a celebration of community I had sought.

Autistic children, generally boys, tend to be self-obsessed. They struggle to make eye contact and are protective of personal space. Some watch the game from yellow beanbags placed in front of a picture window. Others prefer the distraction of a calming area, featuring a bubble tube, fibre-optic carpet, a glitter-ball with a colour wheel and a Bluetooth speaker system, which offers a selection of soothing music if a child becomes distressed.

Many communicate through magnetised strips, featuring such explanatory words as 'noise', 'quiet', 'hungry', 'thirsty' and 'toilet'. Doors are double-locked for safety but when Harry the Hornet, the club's mascot, arrives at half-time its actions are mirrored by enraptured children. The sense of wonder, of unlikely release, is captured by a father who confides, 'I never thought I would come to football with my son.'

Outside, lost in the crowd, is a nine-year-old boy named Jacob. Designated as a high-functioning autistic child, he was 'very, very anxious' on his first visit to the Sensory Room. Sara remembers, 'he just sat there, terrified'. Yet from leaving after half an hour, he learned to love the experience. He now turns up with his father five minutes before kick-off to ease potential tension and sits in the main stand.

No price can be put on that boy's discovery of pleasure in a simple game, shared by thousands on site, and unseen millions from a world he struggles to comprehend. Be careful, lest you tread on his, and our, dreams.

CHAPTER THIRTEEN

Dreamers

'Sport in this country is being taken over by rich people who take the piss. Football is a gambling den. It's not an industry. It is just a casino. It's awful. Some clubs are like Formula One cars, allowed to fit rocket boosters. I'm still pedalling this little bike like mad.' – Andy Holt, owner, Accrington Stanley

The stranger was in his early forties, with black hair greying at the temples. A man of small stature but urgent intent, he bustled through the celebratory scrum to find Andy Holt sitting contemplatively with a friend, Ian Liddle, in the main stand at the Wham Stadium. Once he gained his attention, by shouting from the bottom step, his lower lip quivered and he burst into tears.

'Andy. Thank you, thank you so much,' he blurted out, before pausing. It appeared as if he wanted to say more but he melted into the crowd, as if embarrassed by the audacity of his emotion. Five minutes earlier, Accrington Stanley had been promoted to League One for the first time, 130 years to the day after the club, in its original form, became founder members of the Football League.

On the pitch, players and supporters mingled deliriously. It would be a long night; midfield player Scott Brown eventually woke in his kit, with no recollection of how he got home. He had lost his phone and the keys to his car and front door. Manager John Coleman, an 18-year veteran, danced on the concourse and conducted a drummer as he led a chorus of 'We're Stanley through and through'.

Holt, the local boy made good, inherited ownership of the club from a 15-strong board of directors against his better judgement in October 2015. An affable, bespectacled figure in a grey flat cap, it took him an hour, nursing pints in a plastic cup, to 'catch on to myself'. As he did so, his thoughts were dominated not by memories of great goals or famous results, but by names and faces: Bill Holden, the supporter who, at 75, acts as an odd-job man around the ground, fixing leaky toilets, damaged roofs and gates; Naz Ali, the local solicitor who volunteers as kit man and works from a tiny room filled with washing and drying machines behind the Clayton End, home to the self-styled Stanley Ultras; Martyn Cook, the groundsman who, God willing, will celebrate five years of sobriety on 23 September 2018.

There was something karmic about promotion night. Billy Kee scored both goals in the 2–0 win over Yeovil Town to mark his installation as League Two player of the year. Yet his greatest achievement in a career-defining season had been the searing honesty with which he articulated his fight against depression, 'the rat in my head that won't stop'.

His interview with BBC reporter Juliette Ferrington went viral. He spoke of suicidal thoughts, of driving his car into a wall. He described 'sitting on my bed, head in hands, rocking, crying, not wanting to go to work'. Holt and Coleman gave Kee a month off when he intended to retire; he laboured for his father on a building site for three weeks before he missed football's competitive frenzy.

'Why is someone with the best job in the world going to kill themselves?' he asked rhetorically. 'It doesn't make sense.' He is on medication, having been diagnosed with bipolar disorder Holt has become almost a surrogate father. Like Martyn Cook, the recovering alcoholic, Kee seeks to repay the intimacy of the support he receives by sharing his problems, to engender greater understanding. 'I can come in in the morning and say, I'm really struggling today. They'll put an arm round you and they'll give you a cuddle. You don't get that in football. It's a lot of fronts but with our team, there are no fronts. They're so honest. It is all about education. Everybody needs to understand a little bit. It could help someone thinking, I do that regularly. Oh, have I got that? They could just have a little look into it, they might have nothing but if it helps them in some way, brilliant.'

When Holt spoke of Accrington Stanley as a 'time capsule' he was referring to the sense of identity and community he believes football has lost. Yet, as Winners' Hour, where pints are sold for £1, stretched into the early hours, he began to appreciate its personal significance, in the value it placed on his family.

He saw the joy expressed in his son Joe's eyes and realised he had missed too much of his childhood, because he was building his business. 'There's more to life than money,' he rationalised. 'Another lesson learnt.'

In a natural progression, he summoned the spirit of his father, who died just before his 16th birthday. 'Dad would have been proud. I have missed him more than anything else. Mum won't go to the games. She's getting on a bit now, and just sits at home listening to the radio. This will probably never happen to me again, so I want to take it all in. I'm humbled and drained right now, mate. It is a blur. All I have done is put a floor under the place, made sure people got paid on time.

'I fancied we'd do it. Sometimes in life things don't work whatever you do. Sometimes it just seems to go your way. I'm a council estate kid, and none of us had owt. We made do. We might not have money at the club but we have togetherness. Players and staff go through walls for each other. That's a really good feeling.'

A sign at the corner of the ground referred to 'the club that wouldn't die'. Accrington went bust, with tax debts, and resigned from the Football League in 1962. It reformed in the Second Division of the Cheshire County League six years later and returned as Conference champions in 2006 before living hand-to-mouth for a decade.

Holt was a Burnley supporter as a boy. His family did not own a television, so on FA Cup final day he walked three miles to the centre of town from the Stoops Estate, to watch the match through the windows of a Rediffusion store that closed in the mid-1980s. Now 54, he has made 'a few million, nothing fancy' from What More UK, his plastics company.

On only his second visit to what was then called the Crown Ground, he was asked to be a sponsor at a preseason friendly against Burnley in July 2015. The club couldn't afford to pay the brewery, so the bar quickly ran out of beer. It sold advertising space in return for pies, which remained largely unsold because of the summer warmth. If the sprinklers came on at half-time, the toilets wouldn't flush.

He was told 'the game is up'. Bankruptcy loomed but he agreed to look at the books, with a promise that, if he walked away, he would donate £100,000 as a gift so that wages could be paid until September. His decision to take over, settling a £1.2 million debt and providing initial working capital of £600,000, was dependent on a private meeting with the local council and MP. 'I told them if they didn't support me I would walk away, without telling a soul. No one trusted me. They thought I was just another shyster. This wasn't in my life plan, but I care about this town, this community. This club belongs to everyone. I have no ulterior motives. This is not an up-your-arse experience. We are doing a job for the town.

'There is nothing else in Accrington. The town centre is dead. Everything is going backwards. There is a symbiotic relationship between us and the community: we each need each other. Our Community Trust touches 10,000 people in a town of 35,000. We reach the disabled, autistic kids. We provide social inclusion programmes, health and drugs education.

'Stanley is a crucial community asset. This club will never be mine. When they tell me my job's done I'm not hanging around. I believe we have to compete aggressively as a nation and as a borough, the spoils of which have to be wisely distributed. For me we fail on all points. Social mobility is dead. The whole set-up is against kids doing what I was lucky enough to manage. Both main parties are shit.'

Like many, I first became aware of Holt in May 2017, when his stridency hit a nerve with the Premier League, whom he accused of 'destroying the game' by treating the Football League 'like a starving peasant begging for scraps off your table'. An unnamed official responded with feudal disdain, issuing a thinly veiled threat to withdraw so-called Solidarity funding for lower league clubs.

For Stanley that represents £430,000 out of a budget of £990,000. Holt was in a wine bar when first contacted for comment. 'I didn't want to respond immediately, but I woke up at four o'clock the next morning thinking, I'm just not fucking having this. They have opened themselves up for a kicking, and I am going to give it to them.

'Being straight in business is a major disadvantage in football. I detest the way the game has no basic core values. The Prem call the shots. They block proper debate. Everyone is too scared to say publicly what they say privately. I'm too daft to fall into line. My time in football may be limited. They may stop me being chairman of a Football League club but they can't stop me owning one unless they find someone with enough money to buy it.'

A pattern had been set. He challenged the EFL about following the Premier League line in supporting the imposition of an early closure of the summer transfer window, arguing that lower league clubs should have dispensation to trade all year round since 'player sales are a vital part of the jigsaw that keeps us solvent'.

He highlighted the institutionalised unfairness of the funding strategy, which allocates 90 per cent of income to the Championship, compared to 6 and 4 per cent respectively to League One and Two. The inevitable consequence of such inequality, he argued, was the destruction of the traditional 92 club model, due to the eventual introduction of an elitist, two-tier Premier League.

He found an ally in Darragh MacAnthony, the garrulous chairman of Peterborough. They quietly gathered support in an attempt to force the EFL leadership, specifically its chairman, Ian Lenagan, and its chief executive, Shaun Harvey, 'to act in all stakeholders' interests, not least the many thousands that pay to watch us in the pissing down rain'.

Holt's populism involves the transfer of a basic business principle that the customer is king. 'Fans are the only stakeholders in the game. We had nine hundred-odd in against Hartlepool. We had been up to three thousand but suddenly the average halved. You didn't have to look far to find out why. The authorities took flags off the fans. They wouldn't let them have a beer. They drifted away.

'That's why I go in the away end before the game, to give the kids a badge, and invite their dads to join us in the bar afterwards. Many places they go they're treated like dirt. They can't have a drink and can't get to a toilet. I treat them as our guests. Their terrace is uncovered but if it starts raining and there's room I invite them in under our stands. That model can work wherever we are in the League.'

Holt, seeking sustainability, is building a small new stand and community sports hub. One League Two club, thought to be Luton Town, operated on more than treble Stanley's budget. Seven, monitored between September 2017 and March 2018, had a budget in excess of £2 million. Even at the lowest level, he believes 'reckless owners are sowing seeds of discontent'.

His use of Twitter as a communication platform to allow fans 'into your inner thoughts and rationale' led to a surreal exchange with the authorities, triggered by two posts on 1 April, in which he explained that 'sometimes, when we win' he gave captain Sean McConville '£200, less the £21.37 I get back in change, to get the lads McDonald's or the like'.

The EFL, in a self-parodic response the following day, enquired whether the fast food was included in the club's 'bonus schedule' at the start of the season, as required under regulation 61.6. Holt initially kept his counsel, confiding 'I'm refusing all press interviews because it's mad.' On 6 April he was informed he would be allowed to continue such largesse, providing it was also offered when Stanley lost.

We had remained in contact after meeting at Accrington's opening pre-season friendly, a 1–1 draw against Huddersfield Town that, bizarrely, was watched by one man and his dog, a black Labrador, from the roof of a house behind the Whinney Hill Terrace, known locally as the Cowshed. On 8 April he sent the following message, revealing the method in the madness: 'I've kept this burger story going to deflect pressure from the lads. They know we are in a good position, but managing tension and stress is crucial. They're laughing at me instead of getting too worked up. We couldn't do this were it not for the EFL. As usual they never miss an opportunity to be on the wrong side of a story.

'Why didn't the EFL embrace us as a positive? Their PR must know that in a David and Goliath battle of budgets, David will always get supported. Britain likes underdogs and supports them. The EFL should be highlighting that a level of success can be achieved without massive losses. What we are doing is a positive for them. Their lack of basic common sense is helping me bang the drum. This is the only time they've helped us and they don't even know they're doing it. It's laughable really.'

The resulting ridicule prompted Harvey, somewhat self-consciously, to deliver a Big Mac and fries to Holt's table during the EFL's annual dinner, 72 hours before the Yeovil match. Four photographs of the handover were immediately uploaded on to the League's Twitter account, suggesting a much-needed human touch had been incorporated into the crisis management strategy.

'A lot of people in football support me but they choose not to be as daft as I am, and won't say so. Most of the owners don't attend meetings. Me and Darragh apart, they're not the guys paying the bills. They don't get involved in the arguments because they are afraid of losing their jobs. The tension in the meetings isn't healthy.

'But I think I am getting somewhere with the EFL. They're backing safe standing and reaching out to supporters in the debate. They seem to be listening, but still get involved in the little things, challenging me on burgers when they shy away from the big issues, like Blackpool being owned by a former sex offender, with a thirty-million-pound court judgement against them. If they can't be strong on that they can't be strong on anything.'

Owning a club often involves hoping against hope. In the case of another unlikely owner, Mark Deveney, it required a blind leap of faith. When he took control at Erith Town in May 2017, the club had no players, no ground and no fans. His first act was to discard his only inheritance, manager Ian Jenkins. He sent me a heart-felt message: 'I need my head testing.'

The club, formed in 1959, had been kept alive at an annual cost of £30,000 by Albert Putnam, whose 50-year association as player, manager and chairman was immediately recognised by his installation as life president. Deveney paid entry fees for the FA Cup, Vase and Youth Cup as a gesture of faith, and invested an initial £10,000.

'Why? If I am honest I don't like seeing clubs go under, because that is the way things are going, especially in London and the South-East, where green space is at a premium. I was a Charlton fan way back, from the days of the Valley party, and fell out with the Duchâtelet regime about six months before anyone else.

'I suppose I saw how badly some clubs are run. I have a blank canvas. It would be easy for me to be the sort of owner who wants to pick the team, but I'm not that guy. A lot of it is crazy, especially the way the players behave. I am not naive. There will be problems but when you can only afford to pay them enough for a couple of pints, and not even cover their petrol money, you have to think they love football.'

His insistence on structure and accountability challenges convention in non-League football, where many players expect to have half their earnings put through the books and half paid cash in hand. Erith have a budget of £300 a week, including players and coaches, in a tier five competition, the Premier Division of the Southern Counties East League, where top teams spend £2,000.

Deveney interviewed nine managerial candidates over 18 days, including a young Scottish academy manager from Spain's Segunda Division, before choosing someone with an existing network of contacts at that level. Adam Woodward promptly enticed nine players from his former club, Glebe. The crowd for one of his first matches consisted of six parents and five referee assessors.

The restructure was completed in 'six weeks of craziness'. Deveney calculated he needed to attract £29,000 in sponsorship to make things work, but was ambushed by the time-consuming complexity of official funding streams, 'where you have to create this Subbuteo-like stadium to get grants. It can easily take you over.'

He agreed to pay £15,000 for a season sharing the Oakwood ground in Crayford with VCD Athletic, a club formed during the First World War by workers from the defunct Vickers armaments factory. This gave him breathing room to negotiate a return to a council-owned athletics stadium in Erith in July 2018.

In the circumstances, Deveney's invitation to 'bandit country' for an FA Cup preliminary round replay against Whyteleafe in late August was irresistible, and immediately educational. 'Today has been a bollock-ache,' he announced, with feeling, on my arrival, two hours before kick-off. Running his carpet business had almost become an incidental indulgence.

His day had begun at 8 a.m., pushing a trolley around the aisles of his local Morrisons supermarket, searching in vain for mini muffins to augment the spread in the boardroom, a white-walled Portakabin that sits on a rise overlooking the pitch. By mid-afternoon he had helped his wife by making egg mayonnaise sandwiches for his guests.

He then negotiated premature rush-hour traffic to pick up the 24-page match programme from the printer. He produced the artwork, sourced advertising copy, prepared a column on their opponents and oversaw editorials by Woodward and Ian Birrell, the chairman, who, on cue, gunned through the car park on his Harley-Davidson, to the evident disgust of a bowls team on an adjoining green.

A strange evening began to unfold. In the circumstances, it seemed perfectly natural to spend the half-time break discussing rugby with John Sutton, owner of a decommissioned Russian 'Black Widow' nuclear submarine moored on the River Medway in Kent. 'Do you think Roman Abramovich would be interested?' he asked, with an arched eyebrow that suggested it was not a new line.

Anything seemed possible because, at that moment, Erith led 3–2 following a bizarre seven-minute sequence at the end of the first half, when four penalties were awarded and attention focused on linesman Fabien Le Houezec, a diminutive figure pilloried as 'a dirty little snake' by a young mum with a red baby buggy, who stood less than three feet from him.

The sun was setting behind pebble-dashed semi-detached houses at the far end of the ground, lending a violet haze to the skyline. Birrell, Erith's Easy Rider, offered me a cup of slightly stewed tea. 'We are just non-League anoraks and I'm just a sixty-six-year-old boy,' he explained, swiping two chocolate teacakes for consumption during a second half that became distinctly tetchy.

Deveney, though encouraged by an attendance of 94, radiated tension and chose to stand alone on a terrace that contained five spectators. Twelve travelling members of the Whyteleafe Massive, three in business suits, stood behind the goal and changed ends at the interval. Their guttural chant of 'Leaf, Leaf, Leaf' sounded suspiciously like a souvenir from a visit to Elland Road.

They were in a jaunty mood when their team, from a league above, equalised with ten minutes remaining and gleeful three minutes later, when Le Houezec ruled out a goal after the ball appeared to have crossed the line, following goalkeeper Matte Pierson's fumble of a free kick by former QPR trainee Andreas Felipe Losada Tobon.

One of the beauties of non-League football is its brutal intimacy. There was no escape for the linesman, who would have been forgiven for regretting his decision to replace the original appointee, who pulled out at 2.30 p.m. owing to his son's illness. 'Fucking joke, lino ... Show some bollocks, man ... You bastard ... Small Man Syndrome ... .'

Similarly, it was possible to eavesdrop on Woodward's team talk before the penalty shoot-out: 'We've got more in us, believe in it. This is the FA Cup, you've got to believe.' His players held their nerve, scoring all their penalties and securing victory when full back Dan Palfrey placed his attempt high, into the top left-hand corner of the net.

Reaching the first qualifying round for the first time in six years proved a highpoint of the season. As

Deveney predicted, four of his players, including long throw specialist Myles Keizer-Burrows, were poached by teams of higher status. Erith survived with relative comfort, despite a seven-match losing sequence in the run-in.

There were additional compensations. Joe, the owner's 14-year-old son, found his vocation as the club photographer. A youth section began to take shape. The compassionate response to striker Danny Gannon's double leg break, which involved 29 supporters donating £2,225 to ease financial worries since he was unable to work, proved the club had a beating heart.

'Every single person I have introduced to the club absolutely loves it,' Deveney summed up. 'There's an old-fashioned family feel. Everyone has a smile on their face. Local pride, in a local team: that's something to be associated with. We'll be having a good go next season, aiming for the top six. We need to – this is nearly killing me.

'I've learned that there's a lot more hurt than people realise. Administration is over-officious. I come from a business in which you have to be quick-witted, quick thinking. That sort of drive is what clubs like this need, but the system is nuts. Part of it, the ninety minutes, is fun but the rest is a bloody nightmare.'

Tony McCool would concur. He unnecessarily risked his reputation, as a respected scout and development coach, to manage Dunstable Town in the Southern

Premier League, a tier three competition that would be won, in front of a crowd of 4,556, by Hereford, the phoenix club whose manager Pete Beale was reputed to be earning £70,000 a year.

Hereford's weekly budget was in the region of £10,000, allowing them to pay goal bonuses of £400. Dunstable had no playing budget and fretted about paying £28 for a new ball. They trained once a week, on one third of a 3G pitch. McCool, like young players recruited from open trials that attracted 200 hopefuls in pre-season, was unpaid, apart from a £15 Amazon voucher given to squad members as a Christmas present. They were not even refunded petrol costs.

'Not a penny,' he chuckled, as if abashed by his idealism. 'The club is fan-owned and was going to the wall last season. This is just firefighting, but as a coach you can't help but respond when you see these young lads looking at you like puppy dogs, with eyes that say "please help me". My chest goes out a yard when I speak to people in the game. They know how hard this is. Honestly, it's so emotional.'

The story of his Everyman adventure was crystallised by three matches as his season built to a cruel climax. The first, a 400-mile round trip to play Merthyr Town in a rearranged fixture on a freezing mid-February night, involved him driving 14 players in a minibus borrowed from a local school. Their pre-match meal, pasta cooked by Nikki, wife of development squad manager

Colin Lauder, was served on paper plates in a Starbucks car park.

'It looked like we were on a camping holiday,' McCool remembered. It had already been a trying day; both he and Gareth Jackson, his assistant manager, had been in hospital, accompanying their respective wives, that morning. He ate beans on toast on the run, and picked up the kit, which had been washed by Katrina, wife of club treasurer Dudley Peacham.

Dunstable had a half-time lead through Ethan Lamptey, but conceded three times in the second half. Momentary lapses of concentration were critical, though they could be rationalised by fatigue and a journey that, to use McCool's graphic phrase, involved 'being crammed up in a phone box on wheels for four hours'.

The minibus arrived back in Dunstable just after 3 a.m. One of the players had to kick the door of McCool's car open from the inside, because it had frozen solid. The manager was in bed an hour later, unable to sleep due to the cans of Red Bull he had consumed to stay awake on the drive home. When he returned the mini-bus to the school later that morning he was 'so mentally and physically exhausted I could barely raise a conversation'.

It became obvious the one relegation place would be filled either by Dunstable, who contracted George Best and Jeff Astle in their glory days in the 1970s, or Gosport Borough, who increased their weekly budget beyond

£3,500 in a spasm of desperation. McCool targeted a home fixture against Hitchin Town, a mid-table team managed by a former teammate, Mark Burke, for a big push.

When it arrived he was on his ninth goalkeeper of the season. Nathan Harness arrived on loan from Stevenage to find his purple shorts, slightly too big around the waist, were the least of his worries. At 18, his first taste of senior football was visibly daunting. 'Look after him,' McCool instructed his captain, Gedeon Okito. 'Make sure he gets an early touch. He's terrified.'

McCool admitted he was 'running out of ways to try and motivate' a team that changed from week to week. He distributed a copy of one of his old scouting forms, asking his players to judge themselves against criteria listed for their respective positions. He referred them to a newly hung motivational poster featuring Muhammad Ali: 'You don't lose if you get knocked down. You lose if you stay down.'

Finally, he ordered them to read and sign another entreaty: 'Can you guarantee you won't make a mistake, won't misplace a pass or shot? Ronaldo or Messi can't guarantee that. No one can. Can you guarantee to work your hardest, guarantee that if you make a mistake you'll try to fix it? Can you guarantee you will be mentally and physically prepared, guarantee you will leave nothing on the pitch? YES. 100%.'

The rituals were familiar; players huddled around set-piece charts, shaking hands or sitting, eyes closed, nodding their head to urban music from a boom box that radiated yellow and blue light on the beat. Dunstable were without their best player, right back Peter Kioso, suspended after prompting a brawl the previous week by pushing away an opponent with the line 'you only come up to my nipples, bruv'.

McCool and Jackson embraced and gave themselves a minute's grace after the players filed out. 'If they concede early they are likely to capitulate immediately,' the manager confided. His fears were realised, quickly and decisively. Harness, ill at ease during a truncated warm-up, was responsible for two goals in the opening 21 minutes, missing a punch at a corner and mishandling a routine shot.

One of five flags hung over barriers by home fans proved prescient: 'The future is uncertain and the end is always near.' By half-time, Dunstable were 4–0 down and defending in a blind panic, lunging into unrealistic tackles and marking shoddily. Normally, McCool would play music to mask his team talk, since the wall between dressing rooms consists of a single breeze block, painted light blue.

Not this time. He began with quiet menace and gradually increased the volume. 'Have you been out on the piss? That's the most soft-arsed performance I've seen from any group of players in twenty years in a professional dressing room. You can't make excuses. It took forty-one minutes for you to have a go. Their keeper hasn't got a speck of mud on his fucking shirt.

'Lads, I hate coming in here like this. There's a lack of fight, a lack of bravery. Is it my fault you are freezing when you're needed? Yes, you are young. Yes, you are learning. But do you honestly want to be pros? How can I help you when you perform like that? It's disgraceful. Your concentration and focus on the ball is non-existent. It is a shambles.

'Can you hear that next door? It's like a fucking tea party in there. They're laughing and joking, talking about what bird they're pulling tonight, where they're going out. They are taking the piss out of you. Does that mean anything to you? If it doesn't, you can fuck off. What are you going to do about it? You've got to get out there and restore a bit of pride.'

The game dropped in intensity, as it usually does in such circumstances. There were no more goals. McCool chipped away at a poor referee but his heart wasn't in it. His thoughts turned to the task of picking up the pieces. 'My heart goes out to him,' he said from the touchline, as Harness made a good low save. He made a point of addressing him directly, in the dressing room debrief.

'Look around, left and right,' he told him. 'You've heard them say they all made a mistake. It is what it is. You are all learning. You're no different to the rest. You have things to work on, your starting position, your handling, but you will be better for us. You will have a career in the game. Lads, you are good people. We have to find a couple of wins to stay up.'

The young goalkeeper proved himself as the season ended in a blur of four matches in eight games. He kept successive clean sheets and made a series of brave saves. Defender Daniel Trif, whose wife Ella was fighting an aggressive form of breast cancer, released his pent-up emotion by leaping into McCool's arms when he scored the winning goal that sent them into an all-or-nothing home game against Gosport with a three-point advantage.

The Hampshire club had given themselves hope by winning their first game of the year, 7–0, in strange circumstances against Frome Town, who could raise only ten men and did not have a regular goalkeeper. They had spent heavily on four experienced players: James Harper, who played two seasons for Reading in the Premier League, stiffened midfield; Rowan Vine, a journeyman striker for 13 league clubs in England and Scotland, was quickly promoted to player-manager.

'One day my lot will realise how far they have come,' McCool rationalised. 'We've tried to do things honestly, with hard work and integrity. This year has tested me to the full. I didn't expect the depth I would have to dig. This is when we find out whether the pain and pride, joy and stress, has been worth it.'

The difference in resources stood out in a car park that quickly filled to capacity. Gosport arrived in a luxury coach that would not have been out of place in the Premier League; a more humble version contained supporters who swelled the crowd to 352, nearly treble the seasonal average. Someone in the small, low-roofed stand rang a bell just after kick-off; it tolled for Dunstable.

Aware a win was sufficient to secure survival, they shaded the first half, but succumbed to exhaustion. Failure to clear a long throw enabled Ben Wright, a physically imposing veteran of 22 clubs, to bundle Gosport into the lead with 18 minutes remaining. When another spring signing, player-coach Craig McAllister, squeezed a second under Harness players dropped to the ground in despair.

McCool gathered them around him at the final whistle, ten feet or so in front of the dugout. He gestured at the celebrating Gosport players, and his voice grew in intensity. 'Don't you dare act defeated,' he said. 'Not after everything we've been through all fucking year. All year. I know you are gutted, but just look at their faces and remember what this feels like.'

There was no fairytale ending. Dunstable lost 3–0 on the final day against Frome Town, who found the money from somewhere to fund a full team and regular goalkeeper. On the same afternoon Erith lost 2–1 at home to champions Sevenoaks in a match staged for the benefit of For Jimmy, an anti-knife crime charity run by the Mizen family.

Stanley became champions, beating Lincoln City 1–0 in front of a record crowd of 4,753. In the build-up, Andy

Holt revealed his biggest secret, that he had been appointed MBE for his services to manufacturing and the community.

He sent a photograph of the medal, in its presentation case, to Kee, with the following message, which referred to the striker's son: 'Billy. You're not playing for money, or bonuses. You're playing for something that will be Brady's for the rest of his life. You lads have the opportunity to pull off the greatest achievement in football EVER. Fuck Leicester. This is bigger. One last push from you lads, now. That's my medal, and when I'm gone it's all that will be left.'

Ella Trif passed away on June 2, four weeks after the end of the season. 'Sadness beyond words' reflected Tony McCool, who pledged to stay on as Dunstable manager. Their new season began with a game played in her honour, with all proceeds going to Breast Cancer Care and Thrombosis UK, which supported the manager's wife through life-saving treatment.

'Puts it all into perspective, doesn't it?'

CHAPTER FOURTEEN

Tale of Two Cities

'Players
Supporters
United we are strong.
We've achieved much over the years
We've shouted many goals
And we have shown, we have shown
That no one can ever break us
Blue and claret blowing in the wind
One valiant cry
We've got a name that everyone knows
Barça, Barça, Baaarça!'
(Second verse, 'El Cant del Barça' – FC Barcelona anthem)

Headlines dripped with poison and implicit promises of retribution. 'A Historic Humiliation … Suicide … A Failure with No Excuses … No Tears Left

... Fall of The Barcelona Empire ... Disgrace ... Disaster.' Columnists spread fear and self-loathing, raging at the 'forgers' responsible for the unexpected calamity of elimination from the Champions League in Rome.

The symmetry of Manchester City's simultaneous departure from the quarter-finals on a breathless April evening in 2018 prompted *Marca*, the newspaper that acts as Real Madrid's unofficial house journal, to frame the anguished face of Pep Guardiola at the foot of an exultant front page. No chance to ridicule an iconic coach, or the Catalan culture he represents, is wasted.

Ultimately, the hysteria abated. Both clubs realised a domestic league and cup double. A Barcelona team in transition had a record 13-month run without defeat in La Liga. City played with thrilling panache to reach another record, 100 Premier League points in a season. Their ambitions coincide but their rivalry is destined to fester, because they are products of a broken home.

Football, history and politics are entwined at Barcelona, the club described as the 'symbolic unarmed army of Catalonia' by Marxist writer Manuel Vázquez Montalbán. They have a different tone and additional complexity at City, because Guardiola's latest project uses the wealth and soft power of a sovereign state to underpin a project of limitless ambition.

By the time Ferran Soriano became City's chief executive in September 2012, they had won their first Premier

League title under the ownership of Sheikh Mansour bin Zayed al-Nahyan, the multi-billionaire deputy prime minister of the United Arab Emirates and member of the Abu Dhabi royal family.

He believed he had an edge in an industry that had a corner shop mentality and a multi-national corporation's capability, and was determined to purge himself of the frustration of five faction-fighting years as Barcelona's vice-president. Freed from the restrictions of its membership-controlled structure, he had a global vision to maximise City's brand recognition and revenue generation.

Since his approach was conditioned by the mercilessness of management consultancy and the backhanded compliment of imitation, friction was inevitable. Soriano angered Barcelona by immediately returning to the club to hire Txiki Begiristain, its director of football, to oversee recruitment. He oversaw the internal promotion of Omar Berrada, who spent seven years as head of sponsorship at the Camp Nou, to become City's chief operating officer.

When Rodolfo Borrell joined City, initially as international technical director in March 2014, he utilised an exhaustive summary of lessons drawn from his 13 years as a youth coach at Barcelona. He provided the finishing touches to a blueprint designed to transplant the principles of La Masia across countries and continents in clubs aligned to the City Football Group model.

Borrell's insight incorporated tactical touchstones, developmental philosophies, training ground infrastructure and recruitment strategies. His missionary work for Soriano accomplished, he transferred across the club to another Catalan enclave, as one of Guardiola's four assistant coaches.

Domenec Torrent, grandson of a former Barcelona player, was the most senior until he left in June 2018 to become head coach of New York City FC. Borrell was promoted along with Mikel Arteta, who is portrayed as Pep's potential successor, following a sustained flirtation with Arsenal. Performance analyst Carles Planchart has worked with Guardiola since 2007, a year longer than fitness coach Lorenzo Buenaventura. Manel Estiarte, an Olympic gold medallist in water polo, has a broader role, analysing trends in elite sport.

Borrell had spent four years at Liverpool, as head of academy coaching under Pep Segura, who was also recruited by Rafa Benítez in 2009, after winning the Greek league title as Olympiacos manager. Their transformation of the club's youth system led to Segura returning to Barcelona, where he had been a youth coach from 1997 to 2005, in 2015.

He revitalised Barcelona's academy, strengthening scouting systems and reinforcing coaching philosophies. He restructured the B team to prepare for the formative rigours of Spain's Segunda Division. In July 2017, he was promoted, as the club's new sport manager for football.

The bureaucratic mundanity of the title is deceptive; in effect, only president Josep Bartomeu wields greater power.

Barcelona won their seventh La Liga title in ten years in 2018, but Segura is judged by Guardiola's Champions League-winning team of 2011, which included seven La Masia graduates. He must square a circle of barbed wire, restoring pathways from the academy while restocking an ageing first team with those who possess growth potential, like Philippe Coutinho and Ousmane Dembélé.

Confidence that Antoine Griezmann would sign after the World Cup was misplaced. Barcelona refused to make the French striker their second-highest paid player behind Lionel Messi, as demanded by Maud Griezmann, his sister and agent. He signed a new contract with Atlético Madrid, announcing his decision in an artful TV documentary made, indiscreetly, by Gerard Piqué's production company.

Segura could have done without such theatrics, and the subsequent political fallout. He is attempting to reaffirm philosophical faith in home-grown players in the wake of a 14-month transfer ban, imposed before his arrival, and the transformative €222 million sale of Neymar to Paris Saint-Germain. He is appraised in association with Ernesto Valverde, a naturally cautious coach selected from a similar political and philosophical environment at Athletic Bilbao.

Segura rarely gives interviews, and his thoughts are carefully modulated, painstakingly expressed. His reverence for order and instruction, established through his training as a PE teacher, was immediately apparent as he settled on a two-seat black leather sofa in the trophy room at Barcelona's Mini Estadi, across the road from the Camp Nou.

He insisted on speaking in English, as an act of courtesy, and though he occasionally sought reassurance his point had not been lost in translation by lightly touching my arm, the only sign of stress was the metallic Morse code of messages being received constantly on his mobile phone. His club has reached a crossroads, and he must contend with countless back seat drivers.

'It is very difficult but it is not a pressure for me, because you have to know what you want. No one in the world wants to win more than me, but in this moment I know I have to recognise the way, the plan. The most important thing is a player's evolution, and you cannot know that in one game. The game is a test, an evaluation, and the work is done in the week.

'Bringing through a player is difficult because of the level of the first team. Imagine we are a group of friends, walking in the Pyrenees. We enjoy, fantastic, but afterwards one of us says, come to climb Mont Blanc. Some of us do, but then one of us wants to go to Everest. This team, Barcelona, now is Everest, the highest and hardest to climb.

'Evolution is constant. In the economy of the first team, the big players, inflation is massive. To look outside, in other countries, is very expensive. The second team is where I can introduce young players to our idea, our style, our home, over one or two years. They will cost less. With my position in the club I need to think about both.'

We had watched the B team lose to Cultural Leonesa, a typically streetwise side from the second tier, who stole an early goal and survived thanks to their swarming defence. A collective lack of invention was compensated by individual promise; the two youngest players, left-sided centre back Jorge Cuenca and Ramón Rodríguez, a central midfield player known as Monchu, were outstanding.

A Zen proverb, 'when the student is ready the teacher will appear', seemed apposite. At 18, the pair had been promoted, regardless of the result and despite the threat of relegation. In modern football, that requires moral certainty, unwavering foresight and a thick skin. Segura's job is paradoxical, since he must combine the higher calling of an emeritus professor with the reward-driven ruthlessness of a cold-calling salesman.

'Today you should remember the youngest,' he remarked. 'Why? We play the same way from ten years old until the first team. We wait for individual talent to learn their job, our job. Everyone understands their responsibility and function on the pitch. You have seen

Iniesta, Piqué, Busquets. Each one is completely different. But when they play, they play with the same idea.

'When I spoke with the owner of Liverpool I told
him to put one young player into the first team is very
easy. If I have a lot of money I will buy the best and
some will arrive to the first team. The more difficult
thing is to produce one, two or three with the same
idea of how to play. This is the value of the one club
policy. I see players who can make the first team soon.
I tell the coach not to worry when he needs them
because they know the way.'

Reserve team matches in England, or more precisely
their under-23 equivalents, are afterthoughts. Their
meaning, here, was reinforced by the stature of those
around us. José Mari Bakero, captain of Johan Cruyff's
Dream Team, has succeeded Segura as academy director. Unlike other former players of similar eminence,
he doesn't filter advice through his achievements; he
is an understated uncle, rather than a brash elder
brother.

Former teammate Guillermo Amor, who spent ten
years in Barcelona's midfield from 1988, is equally quiet
and calm. He was promoted to the club board in October 2017, with an additional brief as director of
institutional and sporting relations for the first team.
Slim and enduringly athletic, he once lived in the old La
Masia, a former country house beside the Camp Nou,
built in 1702 and used as a dormitory until June 2011.

Segura insists egos are left at the door. 'You have to have a certain type of person to coach in Barcelona. Until the second team they are all young coaches, usually teachers from physical education. We don't want a big coach at twelve or fourteen years old. We have pedagogy, a system. We develop the same idea. It is not I, I, I; me, me, me. We develop the same job.

'If a coach thinks only of win, win, win, OK, I say you are a fantastic coach, but find another club. We need to win, but we need to know how to win. We prefer coaches who are not here to grow their career. We prefer them to be educators. They work to develop players, not themselves. When you have a coach who uses his team to progress, uses the players for his interests, it is a mistake.'

Scouts must also be wedded to the system. Most, in club football, do not follow a philosophical template; they make conventional judgements of talent, technique and temperament on an individual basis. Barcelona's scouts are looking for players with precocious game intelligence; they must understand their role and fit a pre-assigned need.

At 18, Marcus McGuane faced a familiar dilemma. He made a brief first-team debut for Arsenal in the Europa League in the autumn of 2017 but, with his contract winding down, was conscious of being trapped by 'fake' development squad football. Juventus were monitoring his form and Sassuolo promised an immediate transition into Serie A, but Barcelona's interest, piqued by England Under-17 coach Steve Cooper, who worked with Segura at Liverpool, was enticing.

Barcelona looked to augment existing building blocks, knowing McGuane had been schooled from the age of seven as a defensive midfield player, who performed well as a right-sided central defender or wing back. They were prepared to invest in the potential of his durability, athleticism, vision and movement. Physiological assessments were impressive, and his decision to hire a private coach to improve his shooting, with both feet, signalled a willing pupil.

He signed a three and a half year contract in January 2018. Gerard López, his first Barca B coach, was impressed by the speed of his transition. 'McGuane is a hard worker, good in the air, arrives in the box from deep. I can use him in a lot of positions and at his age he still has a lot of room for improvement. Perhaps he just lacks that calmness on the ball, that pause in terms of our positional play, but he has everything else we need in the middle of the pitch.'

Ariedo Braida, the former AC Milan technical director who, at 72, is Barcelona's head of international scouting, preached patience. 'He can play in the 6 [defensive midfield] role but we would like to develop his knowledge and positioning in order to play in other midfield positions. At Arsenal he played for three years with the ball in front of him. We want him to work with the ball behind, or outside him. It is our responsibility to improve him as a player, and that is what we will do.'

A miniature trophy and a heavy gold medal, on a narrow shelf alongside a propped-up postcard depicting Gaudí's unfinished masterpiece, La Sagrada Familia, testify to his progress. They were won in the Catalan Cup final against Espanyol, when McGuane became the first English player to represent Barcelona's first team since Gary Lineker, who scored 42 goals in 103 La Liga appearances between 1986 and 1989.

Sensory overload is understandable as, in an affecting, almost childlike devotion to his trade, he pads around his first floor apartment with a green-and-gold sponge ball at his feet. He first visited Camp Nou at the age of two and a half; a photograph of him in a red England shirt, beside a cardboard cut-out of Ronaldinho, was taken on a tour of the stadium two years later.

'My first impression was that the stadium was so grey. I thought, that doesn't look that nice, but when I got inside it was Oh … My … God. We went up to the top tier and looked down. It was so steep. Mum was talking about how scary it would be, walking out to play in front of 100,000 people. I was so excited all I could say was "Yessss".

'It's funny. The first thing I remembered when I walked into the first team dressing room for the first time was sitting with my brother on a train when I was twelve, coming back from a game. I was a diehard

Arsenal fan and he asked me if I had to leave, what club it would be for. I said Barcelona, because Pep's team in the Champions League was crazy. I should have been in bed but I used to hang around by the door and watch them on TV, hoping Mum wouldn't see me.

'I was literally walking into the unknown. This is every kid's dream, right? I've got butterflies, thinking shit, I am here, it is real now. There's Messi, Iniesta, Suárez, Coutinho. These are players I used to watch day after day on YouTube, studying combination videos. Yet in their environment they are just normal people.'

It is a large dressing room, square, with lockers on one side. Unlike at Arsenal, where young players are required to join the first team squad on the training pitch, supplementary players from the B team are expected to change into their boots alongside the stars, beside an underground stairway that leads up to the mini-stadium on which sessions are staged.

McGuane took a deep breath, said 'Hola' to the group and sensed, with momentary alarm, shock at hearing an English accent. Messi set the tone by walking over to shake hands, followed quickly by Coutinho. Goalkeeper Jasper Cillessen and Paulinho, the former Spurs midfield player who embodies the pragmatism of Segura's short-term recruitment policy, offered to translate drills.

'There seems more opportunity to impress at Barcelona. Their players seem more open and cool, where some at Arsenal were stand-offish. There is a good energy. I tried to learn from the way they act. There is no persona, no "I am the best". No one tries to be different or flash. They come across as natural guys, just playing football.

'If you go with them you need to be sharp, mentally. If you receive the ball not knowing what you are going to do with it, it doesn't matter how good you are technically. You must have the picture in your head. Iniesta always seems to be one step ahead. Messi is doing things I don't even think are possible, getting out of small gaps.

'He's going through one, two or three players, doing these crazy things against world-class defenders. When you see him drop the shoulder it is too late. You think you know what you are going to do but you don't get the chance to put it into practice. There were times training with him I was just smiling, thinking, oh my God, this is Messi.'

Xavi Hernández, a powerful figure even in exile in Qatar, describes Messi as the quintessential La Masia product. 'Technically he is unbelievable. It doesn't matter where he plays, if it is cold or hot, he always proves he is the best. He simply goes one way with his body and another with the ball. You either have to guess right or foul him.'

Rodolfo Borrell, Messi's first coach in Barcelona, admitted to a crisis of conscience when he watched the tiny, self-contained boy of 13 who had been transplanted from Argentina to Spain. 'When I saw him I thought he was extraordinary, like now,' he said. 'At this time, the problem was not his quality. The dilemma was whether it was right to take him from his own environment.'

The small boy, who from the age of 11 injected himself with human growth hormone in either leg, on alternative nights, is thought responsible for 20 per cent of the club's commercial income. His contract, signed in November 2017, runs until 2021, with the option of another year. He received a signing-on bonus of €100 million, has a basic annual salary of €70 million, and owns exclusive image rights.

Yet McGuane was struck by the lack of materialism, the ease with which the dressing room self-regulates. The captain, rather than the coach, deals with minor disciplinary issues, such as time-keeping or incorrect kit. Since ostentatious shows of wealth are frowned upon, his first act was to buy a Fiat 500.

'In England I had a Merc, but when I came here I instantly saw the culture, how people dressed and carried themselves. There seems to be more respect for the game. Everyone is focused on football, not the things that come with it. Obviously people have different reasons for playing the game: my family mean a lot to me but predominantly I play football because I love it.'

Xavi describes playing for Barcelona as 'a final exam for a footballer. He will learn to think faster, in a few thousandths of a second. You have to be mentally strong, have convictions.' His words provided a poignant subtext to the struggle of André Gomes, the Portuguese midfield player who articulated the 'hell' of his struggle for self-justification.

'You have fear of going on the street out of shame,' he told *Panenka* magazine. 'I close myself off. I don't allow myself to get rid of the frustration I have. I don't talk to anybody. It's like I feel ashamed. Thinking too much has hurt me. I think about the bad things and what I have to do.'

The odds are against McGuane thriving in such demanding circumstances, but he believes principles passed down from Cruyff, through Guardiola, will sustain him. 'I didn't come here for any other reason than to get in the first team, but Barcelona is Barcelona,' he acknowledged. 'They can get anyone in the world. All I can do is put a marker down, show my authority in the B side, and be ready at the right time. If I can do that, doors are going to open. I've already learned so much about my positional play.

'It is so important to respect your position, and your teammates' space. You can't drift or drop because if you don't get the ball you will get in the way. You need to know where you need to be in transition, when you are attacking or defending. If you are positionally aware, you will win the manager's trust. You need to prove you have mastered the job of helping the team.'

This challenges convention, that modern football is about the individual, the brashness of the brand. McGuane is close to former Arsenal teammate Chris Willock, who is thriving in a similar environment at Benfica; both believe more young English players will prioritise their long-term development at leading European clubs, rather than taking the candy of a lucrative Premier League contract.

The wealth of the Premier League, together with the strategic concentration on the importation of teenage talent to the Bundesliga, has created an economic micro-climate, where agents demand around £1 million for facilitating the move of a star 16-year-old, seeking his first professional contract. Compensation fees to the developing club, in the region of £130,000, are negligible.

Perhaps perversely, and in contrast to City's £200 million youth academy, Barcelona has an open-door policy on academy match day. It is possible to walk in, past a solitary steward, and watch matches at Ciutat Esportiva Joan Gamper, the club's training complex in Sant Joan Despí, a featureless municipality five kilometres from Camp Nou, on the left bank of the Llobregat river.

This can have comical side-effects – a Japanese tourist entered club lore when he asked a young player to pose for a selfie as he prepared to take a corner – but its functionality is best expressed by the new La Masia, a concrete residential block, housing 85 players, that matches the drabness of surrounding estates.

Despite aesthetic imperfections, it has a magnetic mystique. Five Barcelona players represented Spain in the Under-17 World Cup. Six form the backbone of Spain's Under-16 team, and were responsible for the crowd gathered behind one goal on pitch number eight, a heavily rubberised artificial surface, on a grey, blustery Saturday morning.

I joined scouts clustered behind heavy red plastic barriers on one side of the pitch until the halfway line, and attempted, unsuccessfully, to avoid puddles of caramel-coloured mud. My companions had the air of birds of prey, circling pasture. Faces and traits were familiar; some filmed sequences on their mobile phones, others instinctively shielded scribbled notes from prying eyes.

Barcelona's Cadete A, their 2002 age group, conceded two early goals to Girona, the Catalan club co-owned by the City Football Group and Media Base, the agency operated by Pere Guardiola, Pep's brother and business manager. They control 88.6 per cent of shares and underpinned a successful first season in La Liga by sanctioning the loan of five Manchester City prospects, three of whom – Spain Under-21 internationals Pablo Maffeo and Aleix García, and Brazilian playmaker Douglas Luiz – proved pivotal.

Manchester United's interest in Barcelona's number nine, Pablo Moreno, was well established, but difficult to justify. A squat, heavily muscled young man, from an extended family of travellers in southern Spain, he scuttled where others glided. His physicality caused problems, but at 16, consensus suggested his development had stalled.

Robert Navarro, a tall midfield player with a fashionable blond buzz-cut, who played with his head up and circulated the ball intelligently, attracted most excitement. Days away from his 16th birthday, he was being courted by English and German clubs led, inevitably enough, by Manchester City.

Segura, involved in contract negotiations with the family and their representatives, was wearily familiar with the situation. 'This is the life. Obviously, everyone watches these players. They say, "this is good, this is good, this is fantastic". We cannot do anything about this. I am in discussion with my president, with my members, because they say, "This is impossible. The English and German teams should not be able to come here." OK. Do you want to pay the same as them? Then these players will stay here. If we pay, our budget will be unbelievable.

'I can't pay, I don't want to pay, the same. What is the best thing to do: win games, make money or develop young players? If one family thinks more about the money, then, OK, this is not our idea. I respect what

314

they need to do, but when parents ask me to equate the salary with what they will get in England I ask them to look at why the English clubs can't produce the same level of talent.

'Their players are strong, athletic, clever, but they have no idea. They play for themselves. Here you look at the right way to play. Watch any game and you will recognise the model. It is possible this year that we will lose two or three players at sixteen, who will go to England, but this is the price of our model. If we did not know how to develop, these people would not be here.

'We need to accept the reality. We offer a unique sporting project. Our way is good but I am losing players to work towards my first team. They are the best, but OK, in the end, many young English players will want to come to Barcelona. This is the logical thing, if they want to really learn the game.'

McGuane, then, may be a pioneer. Just as City understandably use Guardiola's reputation as an element of their sales pitch, Segura can trade on La Masia's standing as the most celebrated finishing school in the world game. The moral maze is well trodden, and short-cuts are left open to interpretation.

Football is a marketplace, raucous and unkempt; the defining issue is at what age the youngest products should be bought and sold, and whether the market incorporates even a modicum of respect for clubs and coaches that develop the raw material. Defeatist sentiment, that money wins every argument irrespective of professional merit, is common.

In the words of one agent, 'logic dies when money is involved'. The phrase seemed pertinent in March 2018, when the social media team around 14-year-old Xavi Simons announced he had reached one million followers on Instagram. Named after Xavi Hernández, he has elfin looks, long curled hair, a corporate logo, a Nike boot deal and a dispiriting sense of destiny.

His father Regillio, a former journeyman striker in the Dutch league, left his coaching role at Ajax's academy to concentrate on his son's career. Mino Raiola, the agent who purportedly made £41 million from Paul Pogba's transfer to Manchester United, suggested his son was 'un gran futbolista y con mucho futuro'. Translated simplistically, in football's Esperanto, that meant 'show us the money'.

Villarreal wanted Xavi to board with them at the age of six. Barcelona signed him the following week. 'The football world has become really "quick",' his father told Vice NL, in an interview translated by the La Masia Twitter account. 'A lot of money is involved and that attracts a lot of wrong people with wrong ideas. The beautiful thing is – and it saves us a lot of work – is that he is way too sober to get carried away. He is not concerned with attention or fame. He switches quickly. He really knows what he wants but is reserved. He feels out situations first.

'I remember asking him, "Aren't you bothered by the amount of people who want to take your photograph or have your signature?". Xavi, thinking he was correcting me, said "but that's part of football, right, Dad?". I once said that attention was all part of the name Barcelona, but they aren't really sure about how to deal with it. This is a new age. In Lionel Messi's time it wasn't as bad as it is now.'

Loyalty is an empty concept. As Barcelona captain and a one club man, Carles Puyol became a Catalan folk hero. He and his business partner, former Spanish international Iván de la Peña, spirited two of La Masia's most promising players, central defender Eric García and attacking midfielder Adrià Bernabé, to Manchester City in the summer of 2017 and 2018 respectively.

The sensitivity of the relationship between City and Barcelona reflects a broader undercurrent of resentment. A chief executive of a rival Premier League club was contemptuous of what he termed City's 'Death Star' model; another, quoted by the *Financial Times*, spoke of the City Football Group as 'a hall of mirrors'.

Attempts to broker a peace deal with Barcelona foundered at the time of Bernabé's transfer, which highlighted the difficulty of anyone claiming the moral high ground. Espanyol president Joan Collet threatened to sue when Bernabé left his club to join their lofty neighbours in the summer of 2013, and subsequently inserted a specific anti-Barca clause in youth contracts.

Youth development has become an unseemly scramble for trinkets of unquantifiable value. The world's biggest clubs operate in a low-yield economy; it is extremely unlikely a generation will produce more than a couple of first-team regulars. Bernabé must compete against emerging talents like Taylor Richards, tiresomely dubbed 'The New Neymar' when he was recruited from Fulham, and the midfield combination of Tommy Doyle and Joe Hodge.

City employ the best-connected youth scout in the UK, Joe Shields, yet still made several unsuccessful attempts to entice Barcelona's best talent-spotter, a deliberately low-key figure known to a small circle of confidants across Europe as Maestro. He has a photographic memory, encyclopaedic knowledge and an extraordinary ability to project the trajectory of a boy's progress. I met him at La Masia and complied with his request not to use his name because his tutorial was unique.

A small, soft-voiced man aged 50, whose close-cropped black hair is flecked with grey, he worked in a hospital before Segura took over and insisted he take up a full-time post. We watched the first half of the Cadete A match together; he stood in rapt concentration, much of the time with his right hand spread across his mouth. In a world of self-protective conformity, he chose the path less taken.

Other scouts stood in groups at half-time, amplifying whispers of Arsenal's interest in Navarro and speculating about Manchester City's pursuit of Moriba Kourouma, a midfield player in the mould of Yaya Touré known as Ilaix, but he had seen enough. Before driving to Montpellier for a game that night, he retreated to a small café, bought strong black coffee, and revealed his morning's case study, a boy celebrating his 16th birthday.

Jaume Jardi was small, skilful but hardly startling. 'He might have a difficult eighteen months, but he will be Barca,' said my companion, before heading to the car park. 'Watch.' Uncannily, Jardi ran the second half, dictating the pace of play and working across midfield, into a number ten role. When he scored the equalising goal, it was impossible not to smile, and toast an absent friend.

Jardi quietly signed a professional contract in June, when the Catalan press were up in arms about Navarro's decision to join AS Monaco, whose £17.5million signing of Willem Geubbels, Lyon's 16-year-old striker, signalled an escalation in the auction of precocious, but unproven, talent.

The last crop of La Masia players has fallen short. Sergi Samper, the anointed one, has regressed; Gerard Deulofeu has shown, at Everton and Watford, that his natural limit is that of an impact substitute. Segura was pained to lose Sergio Gómez to Borussia Dortmund, and is steeling himself to fight to retain the majority of the new generation.

Progression of home-grown players remains an article of faith, and much is expected of Barcelona's Juvenil A group, the under-19s who defeated Manchester City 5–4 in the semi-final before winning the Uefa Youth League, 3–0 against Chelsea. Buyout clauses worth up to €50 million have been inserted in their contracts. Juan Miranda, a left back of rare promise had a €200 million clause written into the long-term contract he signed in July. He is climbing assuredly the stairway to heaven.

The chosen few weep when they descend, and reconnect with normality. One of the motifs of Barcelona's 2018 was the pale-faced, red-eyed Andrés Iniesta, confirming his departure for Japan. Even a transcendent player, one of the planet's favourite footballers, has a finite shelf life. Nothing is for ever, and Segura admits revolution is in the air. 'Traditional clubs with traditional mentalities will have to change. Another concept has arrived. We have the country clubs, PSG and City. Who is behind these clubs? The cheque for Neymar was not from PSG. It was from Qatari Investments. These clubs have big capacity with respect to others, like Barcelona, Bayern, United and Madrid.

'Football evolves constantly. It will not stop. It is not normal or logical that the biggest and best games in the Champions League are played in the middle of the week. They produce a lot of money, yes, but in the future people will want these games to be played at the weekend when there is a greater capacity for the audience.

'At the moment, everything is being moved economically. Resistance to change is being led by the governing bodies, who tell us we need the Premier League, or La Liga. Barcelona and Real Madrid understand the attractions of a European league. It might take five or ten years but who knows? This could be the future. More money for us and for them.'

PART FOUR

The People

CHAPTER FIFTEEN

Men in Black

'Referees are the law. They have a whistle. They blow it. And that whistle is the articulation of God's justice.' – Harold Pinter

Ryan Atkin sees the good in people, but occasionally bridles at the bad. The insults are ugly, repetitive, demeaning and largely incoherent. He makes a conscious effort to remind himself that references to 'poofters', 'queers' and 'faggots who have no place in our game' do not reflect the tolerance and civility of the majority.

He is comfortable in his own skin, as football's first openly gay referee, and recognises his responsibility to help create a climate in which a prominent player can summon the courage to admit his sexuality. He knows gay footballers who mask their preferences, understands their reticence, and seeks to be a voice for the voiceless.

His social significance is ironic, since had he made the same personal statement in his capacity as a senior manager for the temporarily renationalised East Coast mainline rail service, his coming out would have merely provided a passing office watercooler moment. It is only by placing his sexuality in the manic, macho context of the football industry that it becomes a matter of public curiosity.

Tabloid prurience remains a huge obstacle, despite disingenuous claims that so-called 'kiss and threat' stories from emboldened boyfriends of 'secret Premier League lovers' are a serious attempt to address an important social issue. Sly, speculative and ultimately pernicious, they fuel below-the-line bigotry and restrict the personal freedoms they purport to defend.

Media attention is inevitable, but not necessarily negative. When Atkin came out, aged 32, in August 2017 his call for inclusivity was carefully choreographed. He had spent three months preparing for the moment of revelation, with assistance from the FA, Football League, Mike Riley, head of PGMOL, the referees' organisation, and Stonewall, the LGBT charity.

The catalyst was Jon Holmes, an online journalist for Sky Sports, who made initial contact through a WhatsApp group and had the sensitivity to tell a typical story of slow self-discovery. Atkin first suspected his sexuality as a 14-year-old Plymouth schoolboy, when, coincidentally, he began refereeing in the Devon Junior Minor League.

Football helped disguise his inner struggle to rationalise 'feeling slightly different'. He moved to London at 22, was liberated by the self-determination of the LGBT community, and worked his way up to become a Football League linesman before dropping into the National League to build a body of work as a referee.

Over time, his personal and professional lives aligned. 'Obviously, before I came out publicly, there were people who knew I was gay. I'd spoken to people a few years earlier and been advised it probably wasn't the best thing to come out at that particular time, but I was in a comfortable place and wanted to tell my story. It was a managed event, because I wanted to ensure everyone bought into the plan and understood my reasons.

'Sometimes, people don't consider the shock factor. You owe it to family, friends, to say, "This is what I'm doing. You might get calls." I told my mum to be prepared, to either say nothing to reporters or be careful what she said. It was important that the bodies I worked for understood the implications. Mike Riley, in particular, was a great advocate and supporter.'

He believes Riley, more commonly caricatured as a corporate automaton than an emotionally engaged employer, has 'the hardest job in the world'. A professional referee's requisite self-assurance often edges into self-regard; theirs is a cloistered culture, in which ambition, ego and envy fuel subtle factionalism.

'Nothing has been said to my face, but I would be blind not to see that some of my colleagues could potentially feel that I'm using the gay card to promote myself within the refereeing fraternity. If I'm there or thereabouts for promotion, are the FA going to positively discriminate? Well, I've already been told no, they won't, which is exactly the right thing to do.

'I'm not in it to get promoted because I'm gay. I'm in it to be promoted because I'm a good referee, a good person and a good professional. I honestly don't think players care about my personal circumstances. Even supporters haven't got involved. The only comment I remember was when I was refereeing at Wealdstone. I gave a free kick, and someone in the crowd said, "Oh, you can tell he's one of those, because of his haircut".

'I just turned and smiled. I thought, well, at least that's half polite. What would I do if I heard something stronger aimed at me? Probably get on with the game normally, because rightly or wrongly, it doesn't bother me. I'm quite a thick-skinned person. I think you have to be to be a referee. We are a different breed. It's weird isn't it? I'm the first openly gay person in my family, and the first referee. I work for the railway. What else could people hate me for?'

His laughter is lost in the hubbub of a restaurant filled with tourists and co-workers clustered around bottles of Prosecco. There is a sense of transience; slim-shouldered, with a strong jawline softened fashionably by carefully manicured stubble, Atkin blends naturally into the background. The first Premier League player to break the taboo will not enjoy such privacy; a culture of intolerance, aggression and distorted masculinity will poison the debate.

Self-repression and fear of judgement by a small, claustrophobic community, drove Atkin's hero, Welsh rugby referee Nigel Owens, to a mercifully unsuccessful suicide attempt. He has since become a symbol of enlightenment, a quiet inspiration to those who seek nothing more than the basic right to be themselves.

'I've never thought about taking my own life because of my sexuality. And that's maybe because I have grown up in a different time. When I was sixteen, things were starting to change. You had people on telly who were effeminate or whatever, and they were accepted by the public because they were on telly.

'I'd probably say I knew myself around fourteen or fifteen but made every effort to try and hide it. When I was eighteen, nineteen, I had a girlfriend who had a child – not with me, but had a child. You do everything to try and change what you think. You ask yourself, is it a choice? Why do I find a male attractive rather than a female?

'People in football are emotionally stunted to a point. One of the best things that could help LGBT people in the game is the dilution of the whole masculinity thing by a through-the-keyhole documentary on players. They're normal human beings, have a wife, a partner. They go to the theatre, whatever. They turn up with their washbag, which now has moisturiser in it.

'What is masculinity, in the modern day? Ten years ago putting moisturiser on your face was a no-no. Now you go to Boots and there's a whole section of stuff for men. You've got make-up for men. You've got pressure from magazines like *Men's Health*. They never put an average man on the front, it's somebody who is ripped, beautiful looking, this god of a man we should all look like. Male plastic surgery has gone crazy.

'I hate the word homosexuality. It's horrible. We're just people. In the privacy of the dressing room, there are players who know of other players who are gay. I think it is quite open and genuine. But nothing comes out of that changing room. It is a safe environment. At the moment it would be alien for a player to pop his head above the parapet and all of a sudden come out, because he will have been conditioned to be private.

'Perhaps a younger person, who comes from a more open generation, could be the catalyst. He would need the strength, attitude and personality to say, "I don't really care what people think", but is football in the right place to welcome someone willing to come forward? I'm not sure. We have made great strides when it comes to racism, ethnicity and religion, because campaigns associated with those issues have been around for a long time.

'I'll say the word in the context in which it's meant. If you say the word nigger in a game, red card, you're gone. In the crowd, you're escorted out, probably arrested. In the street, you're probably thumped or challenged. If you said, get up, you queer, or get up, you poof, it doesn't resonate the same way, purely because of the timeline of education. We've only just begun to concentrate on the unacceptability of certain words.

'I've heard players say "get up, you fucking queer". Years ago I turned my back. Obviously at that time I identified myself as gay, but you're not going to put yourself forward. Now, the first thing I would do is challenge the person. Then I'd have to really think hard about what action I was going to take. Do I send someone from the field of play for foul and abusive language? Is that going to be a media story? "Gay referee sends player off because he uses this word." Is that a double-edged sword?'

Research by Stonewall suggested that 72 per cent of football fans had heard homophobic abuse in grounds over the past five years, but trends are encouraging. Only 12 per cent admit they would be hostile if their favourite player came out; 50 per cent would be proudly supportive, the rest neutral. Sixty-three per cent agree more should be done to ensure inclusivity. Two-thirds of those polled in the 18 to 25 age group concluded that gay players would have a positive impact on football's culture.

Society is being reshaped by a new generation. An Ipsos Mori poll conducted for the BBC and quoted by Jon Holmes suggested that only two-thirds of British people aged 16 to 22 identified as strictly heterosexual. Yet the timeless context of coming out in modern sport was best expressed by John Amaechi, before a DCMS select committee. 'Identity is one of the most precious and fragile things that we have, so what you are doing when you come out is not just a statement about you, it is a statement about the people around you,' he said. 'You are saying to them, "Here is the most precious thing I have. I am entrusting you with it, knowing that you will take as good a care of this as I would."'

Atkin tells those who approach him for insight to concentrate on the establishment of a core support network before making a final decision. It is a delicate process, since he recognises the danger of unintentional alienation. 'There are secrets and cliques. One of the things I had to weigh up was whether I would move outside the circle of trust by telling my story.'

On a broader level, he is lobbying football's modern funding agencies – television companies and sportswear giants – to be more assertive in linking their support to a more inclusive approach. He recognises the potential of their marketing reach, and the aspirational, youth-focused nature of their branding strategy.

'This is not about the pink pound, or whatever you want to call it. It's about ensuring that sports brands, like Nike and Adidas, promote and engage people in a positive way. People buy into their ethos; if you could see those brands come together, and unite for a cause, you would start to create movement.

'Can you imagine if they start asking to see diversity policies, and being prepared to pull sponsorship? I'm not sure that will happen to be honest, but we'd all like to think that at the top of those companies there is a human being that is thinking through the moral implications of business decisions, like Steve Jobs did at Apple.

'I'd like to see the game fully inclusive within ten years. There will be states where anti-LGBT laws are in operation, but Fifa and Uefa need to get to the point where when you step across the ticket barrier into that stadium, you are in an environment where racism, homophobia, anti-Semitism, whatever, will not be tolerated. Football should be neutral ground, where you can be who or what you want to be.

'That might take fifty years. For me it is about basic tolerance. I appreciate and respect people being influenced by their religion and their culture. Disagree about two men, or two women, being together, so long as you treat us as human beings. Don't persecute us. Don't discriminate against us. In return we don't need to bang people over the head until they start bleeding rainbows. It's just about a general tolerance.'

333

Referees can't change the world, although Mark Clattenburg, arguably the world's best before he resigned from the Premier League in February 2017, aligned himself with an increasingly influential, if politically and socially repressive, nation when he succeeded Howard Webb as head of refereeing for the Saudi Arabian Football Federation.

His career had reached its zenith the previous year, when he refereed the finals of the FA Cup, Champions League and European Championship. At the age of 43 it is jarring that he should speak so often in the past tense of his expertise and experience. Exile on a one-year rolling contract may be financially rewarding, but it comes at the price of absence from his family, and the face-pressed-up-against-the-window frustration of media punditry.

We met at the Youdan Cup, an international youth tournament held annually in Sheffield, on a blustery day with high clouds and intermittent sunshine. Tanned and lean, with deep-set eyes and a surprisingly tremulous voice that revealed his roots in the North-East of England, his understated nature challenged a cuttings library littered with references to his tattoos, hair transplant and recurring conflicts with authority.

Below us, in the under-14 final between Sunderland and Sheffield United, a young referee was undergoing a rite of passage. A United defender, seeking to turn quickly to clear from the penalty area, accidentally collided with his goalkeeper. The subsequent injury, a double leg break, was grotesque and accompanied by a primitive howl of pain.

The referee ordered the players to the halfway line to allow the paramedics scope to operate without hindrance, liaised with the organisers and abandoned the game with two minutes remaining after the player was taken to the local children's hospital. By any standards his conduct was impressively mature, impeccably self-controlled.

'I can give advice about how to manage a game, but young referees have to go through experiences like that,' Clattenburg reflected. 'They will make fundamental mistakes, but they have to be allowed to be themselves, to develop under pressure. At this stage, they do not need the insights that made me one of the best referees in the world, because they can't be expected to understand that environment.

'Once you are at the high end of important competitions, the final stages of the Champions League and World Cup, it almost doesn't matter what you do because you are going to be criticised from someone's perspective. That's the life. I was refereeing the big sides five or six times a year. Their fans bases are bigger. The fallout, if you make a mistake, is worldwide.

'The club chairman puts pressure on the manager, who knows he has a two-year lifespan. He puts pressure on his players because he needs to survive as long as possible. They put pressure on the referee because they need to win. It is a spiral effect. The problem is that the poor guy at the bottom of the pile, the referee, takes the criticism. Of course, you feel that pressure.

'My wife would leave me alone when I got home after games. If I'd made a mistake I wouldn't be able to sleep. The game would be going through my head until three or four in the morning. My wife would come downstairs and I'd still be wide awake watching the TV. I can't switch off.

'It is only the day after that you try to evaluate. Two days on and you try to move on, concentrate on the next game. There were times when I wondered, is this worth it? That's why I made the decision to leave the Premier League. It is the best league in the world without a doubt, but leaving felt like a complete pressure release. My family tell me I am different.

'A referee has his medical treatment, but his mental health is not checked, unless he speaks to a psychologist. I thought I was mentally strong, so I didn't use one. Yes, there would be a phone call to see how you were doing, but no one comes round to the house. You try to manage situations on your own.

'There were times when it felt like it was the world against Mark Clattenburg. I felt very isolated. You haven't got day-to-day interaction. It is not like being in a football club, when teammates are in every day, together, wanting to win for one another. I could go six weeks without meeting a referee because I would be away, doing games.

'Referees are perfectionists, for sure. They want to get every decision right. There's a natural competitiveness, though there are certain referees who are quite happy not to get the big games because they don't want the scrutiny, the added pressure. It can be a very lonely job at times.'

Subsequent praise for his erstwhile international support team of Jake Collin, Simon Beck, Andre Marriner and Anthony Taylor ('they all wanted to do finals as much as me') does not entirely dispel the impression of a one-man culture clash. Certainly, a referee who refers to himself in the third person is anathema to the enclosed nature of the organisation Mike Riley has moulded in his image.

Just as only the lawyers tend to benefit when there are three people in a marriage, the self-appointed arbiters of authority study the fine print when the 23rd person on the playing field is regularly perceived as a central character. They prefer their referees to be backstage beavers rather than front of house performers.

Ironically, as chairman of Fifa's referees' committee, the original celebrity referee, Pierluigi Collina, has the freedom to wield ultimate power. Career-defining images of his bald dome, and thin face energised by ice blue, bulging eyes, regularly led to comparisons with the tormented figure in Edvard Munch's *The Scream*.

The whistle gripped between narrow lips carried the threat of a policeman's Taser.

Clattenburg becomes animated when he speaks of the Italian as 'by far' the biggest influence on his career. 'Without his support and experience I wouldn't have reached the level I did. His knowledge, desire and ability to read a player's mind made him the best. He gave me goals to achieve, and always got the best out of me. I'd die for that man.'

Collina went beyond his traditional duties as match observer at a key moment in Clattenburg's career, the 2015 Champions League semi-final between Bayern Munich and Barcelona. He shared a tactical ruse that had worked six times in the first leg; Thiago Alcântara, playing for Bayern against his old club, would ease himself into an offside position from an attacking free kick before deliberately blocking off the run to the ball of Gerard Piqué, Barcelona's biggest defender.

'Fourteenth minute. This is next-level stuff. I see the blocking tactic go into operation when the ball is floated in, and blow up. Piqué applauds me. I can see the players thinking, wow, this guy is on another level. At moments like that you get a true understanding of the game. No one else had noticed, but Collina sees everything.

'He encouraged me to man manage, get the best out of players. I won't speak to them in the manner of a school teacher. You have to pick your time to make a joke, but I would always take time to explain my decision. Even if they don't agree with it at least they can understand why I have given it. English is the spoken language in football. If a player doesn't understand I use body language, little signs. You communicate to get the best out of people.

'A top referee has to think like a top player. It isn't relevant how far he runs during a game. It is far more important to have a sixth sense where the ball is going to be. You move almost before a pass is made. So, for instance, once a full back shaped to hit the ball over the top I was gone. I tell my people in Saudi that I want to be able to see them on screen. It is not about being the centre of attention; you simply can't make the decision if you are too far away.'

Referees are fallible, vulnerable to the practised deception of the modern diver. Clattenburg has 'been conned more times than I can remember' by players who collapse under imaginary contact, and has some sympathy for those whose agility enables them to ride tackles at speed, creating the suspicion of illegitimacy. 'You have to back your judgement,' he says. 'You're angry when you make a mistake, but you have to put it away in a box and deal with it later.'

Clattenburg embodies a fundamental contradiction. His job is to uphold the laws of the game while removing the handcuffs of their precision. He admits to being a pragmatist, who makes decisions of different gravity in different areas in the pitch. There is greater scope for error outside the penalty area, so decisions are easier to give.

He enters dangerous ground, however, when he argues that the best referee is conditioned by context, and the game's natural equilibrium. He came close to playing God several times during his career, most notably in the 2016 Champions League final, 'where some of the things going on were nigh-on impossible to control'.

Most contentiously, he admits that if Real Madrid hadn't benefited from a poor call in the first half, when Sergio Ramos scored from an offside position, he would not have given Atlético Madrid the penalty Antoine Griezmann missed in the second half. 'That was possibly the best decision of my career, because I helped to get balance back in the match.'

They go where angels fear to tread. Michael Oliver was offered police protection after awarding a stoppage time penalty, converted by Cristiano Ronaldo, that put Real through to the 2018 Champions League final. His courageous decision to send off Juventus goalkeeper Gianluigi Buffon for protesting too vigorously alerted the vigilantes.

Lucy Oliver, the referee's wife, was on her own, watching the game on TV at home. Her mobile number was quickly posted on social media, leading to death threats. When someone shouted 'your husband is a cunt' through her letterbox, she tearfully summoned the police. For the next five days she was accompanied either by an officer, or a family member.

Police decommissioned her number and changed her social media settings to avoid filth like this: 'Your husband got himself into some deep shit. Am on your ass. Both of you have to pay the price. What am gonna do will teach your dumbass husband a lesson he will never forget (if he lived.) And don't think about going to that restaurant again. FUCK Y'ALL.'

All referees have their war stories, but they must not be cheapened by their ubiquity. Clattenburg is a visible personality, a lightning conductor. He attempts to appease those who feel they have the right to criticise him to his face, but is wearied by the ritual of rudeness and ill-considered contempt. He is, or was, merely doing his job to the best of his ability.

He urges the FA 'to create a controlled environment at the grass roots'. He has never forgotten a formative experience in Sunday morning football, when a player threatened to break his legs after the match. 'I had no support and had to walk off not knowing what was going to happen. Luckily enough he was talked around, but I was going to quit. You shouldn't feel that fear.'

Abuse leads to assault, and the case studies multiply. Ryan Hampson, only 19, organised a strike of 2,000 grass-roots referees after being head-butted, spat at and punched. He is an ambassador for the charity Ref

Support UK, which is campaigning for officials to be allowed to wear body cameras as a form of protection.

The value of video evidence was underlined in May 2018 when a camera phone captured a referee being chased by a group of players, punched and kicked as he lay on the ground, following a Turkish Football Federation cup final in Wood Green, north London. It prompted an immediate FA and police investigation, and added to the pressure on IFAB, the game's law-making body, to modernise.

County FAs, hidebound by tradition and an astonishing lack of social awareness, have been reminded of their responsibilities after the Lancashire FA pressurised Max Ormesher, a 15-year-old taking charge of only his third game, into giving evidence against three allegedly abusive adult coaches involved in the match, an under-11 friendly in Preston. Despite being scared to do so, he was warned he faced a misconduct charge if he did not appear at the disciplinary hearing. He eventually testified via a video link, and the case was found 'not proven'. His father Graham suggested Max had been 'treated very shabbily' and struck a chord by concluding 'they talk about protecting refs but it is just lip service'.

Parents and coaches see a uniform rather than a child, since they are conditioned to seek a scapegoat. Veteran referees like Rod Pimlott have a paternal concern for those they mentor and come closest to the original view of Sir Stanley Rous, the first Fifa president, that referees 'are doing a service to the country'.

Just before Easter 2018 Pimlott sent the following email to the football community he began serving in Derbyshire in 1966, before moving to Cheshire. 'The Diabetic and Cancer specialists have advised this week that it will be a further 12 months before I am fully recovered, so I have decided to finally hang up my whistle. I am hoping to raise some monies for cancer charities for everything they have done to help both myself and my daughter towards recovery.'

His is the quiet selflessness that raises the spirit, and plenty of cash. He has already collected more than £50,000 for children's hospitals. In addition, he donated each match fee until his retirement at the age of 74 to children's charities in memory of his late son Simon who, like his son Ryan, was also a referee. He organises teams of referees to act as Father Christmas in hospices caring for terminally ill children.

Emerging referees like Harry McDermott, a student who officiates at the Woodley Sports Village in Stockport each Saturday morning, will forever be in his debt. Pimlott has taught them the value of humour in a confrontational situation, and been there when doubt strikes, and the abuse becomes overwhelming. Have faith, he tells them, before delivering his most effective life lesson: 'Some things are more important than football.'

CHAPTER SIXTEEN

Colour Blind

'I have witnessed first-hand how football can literally save lives. Growing up surrounded by gang
violence, and having that label attached to you
automatically because of where you live, shapes
your mindset. Suddenly, someone places a football
at your feet, gives you a kit to wear and a badge to
represent. The game teaches us the fundamentals
of how to treat each other.' – Tajean Hutton

Quamari Serunkuma Barnes was stabbed three
times with a kitchen knife outside his school,
Capital City Academy in Willesden. Tamsin Nathan, a
mother of three, came across him, lying alone in a slowly
expanding slick of arterial blood. She held his hand,
feeling him grow cold even as she implored him to concentrate on his breathing. He died after identifying
his murderer.

Quamari was 15, the same age as his attacker, deemed too young to be legally identified on conviction at the Old Bailey in September 2017. He had worn a mask, with a hood pulled over his head, and was captured running away by CCTV. 'I'm not a waste, man,' he told the court, before being sentenced to 14 years' imprisonment. 'I want to have a different life but I don't know how.'

It was one of nine murders in the London borough of Brent that year. The sense of loss, of a community turning in on itself to seek answers to the death of a popular boy who excelled in the performing arts, was familiar to Tajean Hutton, an activist who works from a bare, borrowed ground-floor office due to be demolished as part of the regeneration of the area around Wembley Stadium.

The Metropolitan Police's Operation Trident suggests there are 15 main gangs in the borough, including the Church Road Soldiers, St Raphz Soldiers, Machine Gun Murderers, Money Motivated Fam, Stonebridge Gang Bangers, Wembley Fornia Dons, Thugs for Life and Chalkhill Blue Boys. The average age of a member's first arrest is 14.

The names are stereotypical, almost theatrical, yet according to Hutton, official statistics are too simplistic and out of date. He has seen street culture develop in the six years he has been running the Corner League, in which he uses football as a tool to combat dysfunction, created by a lack of education, leadership, mentoring and facilities.

It was a concept taken from Jamaica: a demilitarised zone where teams from surrounding estates, identified as historic enemies, pay a token £1 to play each other in hour-long, ten-a-side matches. These are staged on summer evenings, on an artificial pitch at Wembley's Ark Academy, a school in the shadow of the arch that symbolises football's delusion of grandeur.

'There are no gangs as such any more,' says Hutton. 'There are literally just packs of people who have grown up together. That's their family basically. Unwritten loyalty drives them to roam around together. With the Corner League we realised that when they come together, there's a huge possibility it could go downhill. All it takes is for someone to pull out a weapon and then everything goes pear-shaped.

'It's not like we're bringing fabricated or diluted versions of gang culture to the league. This is the real deal. If you were to see that person on the other team on the street, it's going to be an issue. But because you're both now in football kits it's OK. We're competitors but I respect you because you're on a football pitch. Automatically the mindset has changed, because of the environment.'

Yet grass-roots football is inherently aggressive and young men have a heightened sense of bravado among their peers. Emotions are tinder dry and lead to the type of confrontation that tested Hutton to the limits of his natural authority while he was refereeing a game between estate teams from Chalkhill and Wembley Central.

'It was very heated. I had to stop the game a lot of times and say "look, calm down" because I could see where it was heading. One player went in for a rough challenge and I saw the way the other player got up and thought, he's about to react. He clenched his fists, pulled his arm back, and wham. From that point, it all went in slow motion. I felt I was in a scene from *Game of Thrones*.

'So many things were going on. It was a full ten-on-ten brawl. Thankfully, the estate teams on the sideline came in to help stop it. So I'm doing the best I can, and I get this from my dad – when I raise my voice, it is loud enough for everybody to hear above the commotion. They started stopping. I pulled apart the last few people and made them all sit down in the centre circle.

'At that point, the manager of the sports centre came out. She's got a look on her face that's saying, "this is exactly why I didn't want you here in the first place". I told them they were robbing themselves. If that brawl had happened in another setting, with police officers around, a lot of them would have been put into custody. Some of them could have been given prison sentences, because of offences they had on file.

'I didn't need to give the reasons why it was wrong because they knew. They were feeding a stigma that was

347

already attached to them. I simply said, "All the people that are writing you off, all the people that look at you negatively based on how you look, you're proving them right when you act like this".

'Having that discussion was one of my proudest moments. They listened to me with respect and then got on with the game, in the appropriate manner. That gave me the insight that these kids are not out of control. They just need the right guidance by the right people. The reason why they do what they want is because you don't open your mouth and tell them to stop.'

Tajean has a soft, high-browed face, and poise beyond his 25 years. He has inherited his father's street wisdom and innate dignity. Trevor Hutton was only 52 when he died suddenly, in April 2014. Thousands lined the route of his funeral cortege, as his coffin was borne on a white horse-drawn carriage through streets on which he was revered as a man who held true to the values of respect, integrity and unity.

Once a PE teacher at City Academy, Quamari's old school, he became a coach, mentor and anti-discrimination campaigner. He organised refereeing courses for the Middlesex FA, helped found the Black and Asian Coaches' Association, and formed the Community Football Federation with his son to promote initiatives harnessing the game's social power.

'I have dozens of people I consider my brothers because of the impact my dad had on their lives, people who can confidently say, if it wasn't for that man's intervention I would be in a much worse place. I didn't expect to lose my dad at twenty-two years old. It makes you appreciate that life can literally be taken at any moment.

'His death gave me urgency. It's no longer enough to say, OK, I'll give back to my community in ten years' time. It's so important for at least one person to be out here representing the growth of young people with no fabrications and no ulterior motives. Because in the end, what can you say your legacy is?

'Your legacy can't be material things you leave behind for your family. Your legacy is in the knowledge and the love that you imparted on other people. I was fortunate enough to see the impact my dad had on other people, through his funeral alone. If I can get half of that, I'll know that I've done a great job with my life.

'I've got god-kids and nephews. My loved ones are toddlers. If they are to grow up in the area I want them to be around a safer environment. If we're not standing up for things we believe, then what's going to happen to future generations? People have to stand up and fight for what they believe in otherwise the streets are going to be a free-for-all.

'I don't have anything to lose, so only great things can come from me starting this at a younger age. The terminology of giving back is very clichéd. Yes, I'm sacrificing a lot in terms of the usual things that a twenty-five-year-old would be doing but I have a vision of contributing, making where I live a better place.

'Times are changing. Grass-roots football is changing, heavily. It is very business-oriented now. Ten, twenty, thirty years ago, it was just the local shop-keeper, the fireman, the police officer, the teacher, picking up his bag of balls, going to the local park on a Saturday, and that's a football team. Everybody was doing it for the love of it.

'Now you'll find a lot of people starting organisations with the term "academy" in it. So you have Hotshots Academy, or whatever. They are charging the kids astronomical amounts of money, in areas where the parents can't really afford two pounds a session as it is. They're selling them this dream. It's ludicrous, but that's the way the industry is going.

'The beauty of football is you can tell the motives of the coach. You can tell when the coach is there for the money or for the love of the kids. I find now most are more loyal to the money. You're talking a minimum of fifteen pounds an hour for a Level 1 coach, so it's a very well-paid job. Yet here your impact has nothing to do with how much you earn. You can actually save a child's life.

'I know people who would be dead if it wasn't for my dad's intervention. I've seen them turn up to training sessions with knives and guns. I've seen eleven-on-eleven fights where they go away to get weapons and come back. I've seen the worst of the worst. That's why, for me, the role of the coach is so important. You have to do it for the love of it.

'There's so much depth to football. That two-hour period, playing the game, might be the only time a child feels comfortable in learning, or able to express him or herself. At the same time it is easy to see when a child is vulnerable, struggling. There's that sudden outburst, which just comes. It is up to the coach to delve deeper.

'There is so much unrealised talent out there, hundreds of players undiscovered because of their attitude, which is something the professional clubs can't or won't deal with. These boys know they are very talented, but the dream is over. What now? Dad's not there. I see Mum struggling with bills. I'm going to stop doing football and start doing other things to get money.'

The charitable foundation established by Jason Roberts, the former Bristol Rovers, Blackburn, Reading, West Brom and Wigan striker, delivers social inclusion programmes in Stonebridge, the estate in north-west London on which he grew up. The lack of strong male role models is addressed by Father Figure, an organisation founded by David Mullins that seeks to educate absent fathers.

The Tottenham Hotspur Foundation stages community coaching sessions in the borough as part of the tenancy agreement at Wembley Stadium, but they are transitory. Austerity has bitten to the bone; local authorities' youth engagement programmes have been reduced to the point of practical irrelevance. Pitch fees are increasing yet record numbers of matches are being postponed because they are ill-tended.

Hutton's response has been to stimulate the community's instinct for self-sufficiency. Programmes are being run from the local barbers and convenience store. His most productive alliance has been with Kick It Out, football's anti-discrimination body, which he joined as Grassroots Manager in June 2018. Its education officer Troy Townsend has become an informal mentor.

Hutton describes Townsend as being 'genuine of heart, and that's very rare'. They work, in different ways, on the margins of a fragmented society, in which racism and exclusion are everyday realities rather than an academic, political or cultural construct. There are small signs of progress – the FA has just employed an officer to reach out to the community in Brent – but the overall picture is bleak.

Kick It Out's latest survey revealed a 75 per cent increase in abusive incidents in the professional game, to 131 in the first half of the 2017–18 season. That underplays the problem, since the vast majority of cases are not reported. A more measured piece of research, conducted in April 2015, unearthed 134,400 bigoted social media posts directed at Premier League players and clubs in the previous seven months.

Townsend, father of Crystal Palace and England winger Andros, runs workshops across the professional game, focusing on equality in race, gender and sexuality. One such presentation, to senior coaches at the FA, became a cause celebre when it prompted England manager Gareth Southgate to suggest domestic football should 'get its own house in order' before condemning other nations and institutions.

The response to an Instagram post by Steven Gerrard about an England Under-16 team that featured Bobby Duncan, his cousin, put the issue into sharp focus. The slurry of below the line commentary was understandably described as 'disgusting' by Southgate: 'Seven black players, ha, ha, ha' ... 'England squad or the Senegal squad?' ... 'It looks like Nigeria's team' ... 'Seven out of 11 are non-English, what's happening to this country?'

Domestic strictures are well directed, but football's self-serving moral incoherence is best illustrated by its global governing body, Fifa, which disbanded its anti-racism task force in September 2016 because it had 'completely fulfilled' its mission. A generation of black players, forced to dodge bananas and endure monkey chants, turned its lonely eye towards the heavens in resignation.

English football's below-stairs ambivalence towards Kick It Out, its 15 full-time staff and network of volunteers, is telling. The organisation's annual budget, in the region of £900,000, would fund little more than four months of the salary taken by one of its original supporters, Gordon Taylor, the chief executive of the PFA.

Townsend is unequivocal: 'I think the game is actually frightened of the impact Kick It Out can have, frightened that it has certain power, but I'd probably put that word in inverted commas. We can touch people, communities and players. They would rather have conversations and work with us, than those at the top level of the game.

'I sense an apprehension from the FA, Premier League and EFL to embrace that and really put us out there in the open. Sometimes people go over us rather than through us, at the highest level. If that was ever to change, and they were to utilise the respect and experience we have within our organisation, you would see the progressive nature of the game.

'We deal with players better, especially the young. They get dismissed in this game. It doesn't think they are of any value, apart from the one or two they pick from the cohort. If the governing bodies really wanted to learn a little bit more about equality, diversity and inclusion and what we deliver, wouldn't you tap into us a little bit more? Wouldn't you ask us to produce research from all levels of the game, commission us to provide advice and guidance on how it could be better structured with a diverse workforce?

'Football doesn't know how to utilise its power properly. It utilises its power in the wrong way. The power stays with the power. It doesn't support and educate downwards.'

The setting for such stridency, a tea room in the House of Lords, is incongruous but subtly uplifting, because it testifies to social progress against forbidding odds. Our host, Herman Ouseley, founded Kick It Out in 1993, 38 years after he arrived in England from Guyana, via the Italian port of Genoa and the rail networks of northern Europe, as an unaccompanied ten-year-old.

A dapper man in a finely cut grey three-piece suit, Lord Ouseley had escorted us through the Royal Gallery, dominated by two huge paintings of the Napoleonic wars, and along the Peers' Corridor, where panels depict the reign of the Stuart kings. He paused at the doorway to the Lords' chamber, where the senses are overwhelmed by gold engraving, deep blue carpeting and rich red leather, to reflect: 'Not a bad place to work.'

Though stereotypes were reinforced by two peers chatting in a corner over a fluted glass of champagne and a Bloody Mary, history has a modern resonance. Ouseley stopped at a gallery of paintings of the Tudor dynasty, to point out that Queen Elizabeth I had ordered the deportation of 'blackamoores' in 1596. She demanded something similar five years later, when she referred to 'Negars' as 'infidel'.

An arched eyebrow reinforced the point: 'The reason why I'm mentioning that is because black people feel that they are here as guests, or here under sufferance. It's almost like the slave mentality is still out there, somewhere. If you're not politically radical, you're almost compliant. My mother did three, four, five jobs a week just to pay the bills. It was almost the norm to be abused.'

A meritocrat in a place of privilege as a crossbench peer, he has never forgotten his mortification at his mobile phone going off during the first debate he attended. 'I apologised, went out of the chamber, kept walking, and didn't come back for a week.' That was in 2001; the ornate Tardis of the Palace of Westminster ensures he is still occasionally reminded of his indiscretion by attendants.

Football may not be a unique repository for hatred but the virulence of personal abuse, encouraged by the anonymity afforded by a crowd, indicates the mood of the time. Ouseley has seen racism and intolerance mutate since attending his first match at Arsenal, with an uncle, in the late 1950s. He fell in love with the game, destroying cardboard-soled shoes in the playground before his mother purchased a pair of hobnail boots from an army surplus shop.

When the family moved to Peckham, he formed an enduring association with Millwall. 'Of course, it was rough and ready, but they looked after me. We went to a part of the ground where banter was rife, but there wasn't any racism. It was more violent than anything else; you could get your head kicked in, people were car-rying knuckle-dusters, bicycle chains and flick knives.

'As a black guy you had to have survival instincts. There were parts of south London I wouldn't go, pubs I wouldn't enter even when my friends swore I'd be all right. You develop an awareness of the guy who wants to break your legs because you're black, or because he thinks you're better than him. I played amateur foot-ball to a good standard, and there were times you knew you were going to get savaged. We changed together. You'd hear people saying, "we're playing the niggers and we'll give them a good fucking kicking" and had to swallow it.

'As a black person in a white environment, you had to absorb yourself into the culture to be seen as someone who could be trusted. There is an element of suspicion, because people carry perceptions and stereotypes about a person like me, so you make that adjustment. Through-out that period, I was schizophrenic; I had one personality at home, another on the street, another when I went to work, and yet another when I went out with certain friends.'

Ultimately, racism and tribal violence drove him away from football for two decades. His misgivings hardened during two matches at Stamford Bridge, the first of which involved West Bromwich Albion's 'Three Degrees': Laurie Cunningham, Cyrille Regis and Bren-don Batson.

He was under no real physical threat, since he was accompanied by his brother-in-law, a nightclub bouncer, but the experience remains vivid. 'The warm-up was really vile. There was this barrage of fruit, and the abuse was incessant. When the game started the three black boys were booed every time they touched the ball. Laurie went through the Chelsea defence, scored twice, and they went mad. There were two big guys in front of me being obnoxious; one looked at the other and said, "Mind you, the nigger's fucking good isn't he?".

'Although it was foul, and to an extent I was attuned to such racism, it told me the black guys would win out through their character, skill and personality. They were announcing they were there to stay. It was only when I went back, soon afterwards, when there was a lot of blood, broken glass and bottles that I thought, I can't do this any more.'

Coincidentally, our initial conversation occurred the day after the passing of Cyrille Regis in January 2018, aged 59. His last tweet was unbearably poignant; it featured the simple comment 'Says it all' over a photograph of Cunningham captioned, 'Laurie being booed there, but continues unperturbed. Away again to show that grace and pace and control.'

The outpouring of love and respect from his peers, and those who followed his example, triggered a re-evaluation of his influence, and the indignities suffered by other pioneering black players like Howard Gayle and Clyde Best. Regis was of my generation, a familiar figure, wry and warm, yet it struck me how little his struggle had registered with me, as a white, broadsheet sportswriter.

There is a tendency to be desensitised by statistics, which highlight the paucity of BAME managers in English football – 8.7 per cent, compared with more than 30 per cent of players supplied by under-represented groups. Perhaps we should all dwell more immediately on the quality of the individual, the nuances of humanity hidden by the spotlight's glare.

Eulogies tend to be soft focus, yet those paid to Regis had an edge of defiance and regret. Contemporary black players celebrated his influence, identified him as the individual who carried them, consistently if metaphorically, on his shoulders.

Townsend, typically, was touched by the personal relevance of his life story, and the pathos of his premature death. 'When I was growing up, I used to research the black players who were my heroes – Cyrille, Laurie, Brendon – to see if they looked and sounded like me. I'd go as far back as Paul Reaney, Ces Podd, Clyde Best, Ade Coker. Vince Hilaire was part of my Sunday team and went to Crystal Palace. He made it all real. I glorified the way they played, the way they looked different.

'That empowered me. Very few people in my school, my social surroundings, were like me. Mum only rarely allowed me to watch football on TV, but when I did I saw someone I could immediately look up to. I bunked in to watch my first match, Tottenham against Nottingham Forest, and saw Garth Crooks score. Over time, my hero became my friend, and told me what they went through.'

A bullet was sent through the post to Regis, in sinister reference to potential recrimination. Ouseley had excrement pushed through his letter box, and feared petrol would follow. 'These guys had the worry of someone targeting them,' Townsend said, sadness merging with admiration. 'I'm not sure today's players could put up with what they had to go through to help the second and third generation to make it.'

His son Andros has forced himself to blot out the monkey chants; he was, however, deeply affected by the systemic racism his England Under-21 team endured in Serbia in 2012. Troy advised Rhian Brewster, the emerging Liverpool player whose case against Leonid Mironov, a Spartak Moscow player, arising from a game in December 2017, could not be proven by a Uefa investigation.

'I got fouled,' Brewster told Daniel Taylor of the *Guardian*. 'I was on the floor and I had the ball in my hands. One of their players started saying stuff in Russian to the ref. I said: "It's a foul, man, what you playing at?" I was still sitting down at this stage. Then their player leaned over me, right down to my face and said: "Suck my dick, you nigger, you negro."'

Jürgen Klopp praised him for speaking about racism 'with the same power, command and composure that he shows when playing'. Before paying tribute to Townsend's work, the Liverpool manager added, tellingly: 'That it takes a seventeen-year-old boy to do this is as frustrating and depressing as it is inspirational and uplifting.'

Brewster was resigned to the verdict, telling Townsend: 'I didn't think it would be any different.' His innocence died at the age of 12 when he was first abused on the pitch. Little wonder that 63 per cent of black players polled by ITV London admitted they hadn't bothered to report the abuse they had suffered; 57 per cent of them believed racism is not taken seriously by football's authorities.

The growing mood of militancy was captured by the intervention of Chris Ramsey, QPR's technical director, at a Kick It Out forum. He called for collective action by black players, arguing: 'It may be a time for martyrs. The younger, more wealthy generation can afford to suffer the media backlash. Players are now worth too much to suffer in the game by taking a stand.'

Townsend senses a tipping point will soon be reached. 'Some in the room didn't like it, but Chris was keeping it real. Players have so much traction. It might be that two or three will say, you know what, enough is enough. They'll be joined by twenty or thirty more. Football has to be careful. Victims are being victimised by the process, which is too open-ended.'

Ouseley, an older soldier, is more circumspect. 'I hope it doesn't happen, because that will mean we've made progress. It doesn't necessitate that.' However, history tells us unless we challenge the system, and challenge it as hard as we can where it's resistant, things are not going to change. People don't give away power and influence.

'We have a debt to people like Howard Gayle, whose career was destroyed because he said he wasn't going to put up with it any more. Clearly, if black players say they're not going to play, there will be no football. Football can't deny their right to be treated equally. Looking to the future I think you've got to look at the roles and responsibilities of the players.

'The dominant force in the game, organisationally, is money. Should you be taking Qatari money, if they are oppressing their own people? Look at the big sponsors, Nike, Adidas, or whoever. Where is the morality there? If you are a sponsor will you be saying to clubs, "show us your equality policy before you get a penny out of us"?

'We haven't set out a revolutionary process. We've worked, tip-toeing around the system. I could call the lot of them a bunch of racists. Some people would like me for it, and others would say I am very crude. Will I achieve anything? Sometimes you have to work with and within the system to change the system.'

I have long believed that a man of Ouseley's foresight, balance and rigour would be a transformative FA chairman. His reply to my imaginary invitation was cryptic but cutting. 'One of the things my mum taught me was, don't covet what other people have got. Try and build things for yourself. And the other most important thing is, don't go where you're not wanted.'

The FA has promoted BAME coaches within the national team structure, yet is conflicted between a duty of care to the game and the crassness of its senior management, best illustrated by Martin Glenn, the gaffe-prone chief executive, mentioning the Star of David in the same breath as the swastika as a symbol breaching laws banning religious and political imagery in football.

Townsend has attempted to be consensual, with little impact. No action was taken when FC Peterborough, a team drawn from the Muslim community, endured continual vilification. When he assisted the West Riding County FA in an attempt to foster better relationships with a team of black players in Chapeltown, Leeds, he was aghast that the primary concern was whether their officer should wear a suit and tie while watching them play.

Grass-roots football in London and the South-East has 'horrendous' racial issues to deal with. Townsend has twice taken youth teams to play in Essex, where players have been racially abused by opposition parents. He intervened when a 15-year-old boy was asked, during a disciplinary hearing, to describe the sound of a monkey, directed at him during a match.

This is the shadow world in which Tajean Hutton works, a hundred metres or so from the FA's £800 million stadium. His view of the FA is similarly jaundiced, and dates back to a letter of condolence, given to him by Roisin Wood, Kick It Out's chief executive. It was from former FA chairman, Greg Dyke.

'When my dad was alive, I saw the struggle that he faced week in and week out to try and create opportunities for people. He was looking for support, and there was no correspondence from someone like Greg Dyke. But now that he's passed, and there's a whole load of noise and commotion about the impact he made, now you want to acknowledge it? That, for me, was one of the most disrespectful things ever.'

Dyke's letter was doubtlessly well-intended, but when compassion is easily misconstrued as condescension something is clearly wrong. Hutton is not a bitter young man; his instinct is to see the best in people however daunting their circumstances or damaging their reputation. It was approaching Easter, a time of reflection and redemption. He had more pressing matters to attend to.

A One Love Memorial Festival, in honour of Quamari Serunkuma Barnes, was being organised at the school where he met his death. Its theme was a celebration of the ethos of non-violence. If football helps Hutton to save another star-crossed child, it will require no further justification.

CHAPTER SEVENTEEN

Heartbeat

'I have been to eight different countries with Everton this season. I've seen social cohesion in action. Sit down with someone who doesn't speak your language or share your culture, and quote names of teams and players. Football brings you together. That's why it really is the beautiful game.' – Dave Kelly, co-founder, Fans Supporting Foodbanks

The young couple slept on the streets of Liverpool when the relatives with whom they lived moved away. Winter was endless and the chill gnawed their bones. They somehow held down their jobs, on little more than the minimum wage, but were held back by local authority bureaucracy and a lack of paperwork. To all intents and purposes they were left to fend for themselves.

Their lives changed one Sunday in early April when they attended a homeless drop-in at the Wirral Deen Centre, part of the network served by the Fans Supporting Foodbanks movement. They poured their hearts out to Dave Fitzpatrick, a volunteer who offered 'hot food, warm clothes and warm words'. They feared losing their jobs and being sucked deeper into a cycle of decline.

The Deen Centre is an Islamic initiative that seeks to honour what it calls 'the authentic concept' of a mosque, as a place of worship and a centre for communal activity, regardless of faith or background. The vision 'is to create a local community in Wirral where all people come together as one, living in peace, love and harmony'.

It was established by Ibrahim Syed, a deputy head teacher, in 2016, in a run-down row of three empty shops, 500 yards from Tranmere Rovers' Prenton Park ground. Four such mosques contribute to the North Liverpool foodbank, which is served by the FSF, a combination of two supporters' groups, Everton's Blue Union and Liverpool's Spirit of Shankly.

Fitzpatrick approached the elders, who contacted an existing network of local landlords and found a property developer willing to help by waiving the normal deposit and identity checks, on the proviso that his identity remained private. The couple had just finished eating a roast dinner when Fitzpatrick returned with the keys to a flat.

'The look on their faces was a combination of shock, tears and unbridled joy. It was like life, captured in a single snapshot. They had been in despair and didn't know how to react. We all have a down day in this job, when we think what's the point, but a moment like that is why I do this, seven days a week.'

The FSF began with a wheelie bin for donations, outside the Winslow Hotel before an Everton home game against Manchester United in December 2016. It has taken a conscious decision not to have a penny to its name, or a bank account, but now has access to warehouse space and logistical support for the distribution of 30 tonnes of food a year.

Dave Kelly was its co-founder, with Ian Byrne. 'I am a community activist, not a political activist. I have never joined a political party but I care deeply about my community. This might sound like a big thing to say, but we are capable of eradicating hunger on Merseyside. That is the power of football. People who normally say no when they are asked to help say yes, because it is Liverpool, or Everton.

'You need a can-do spirit. Our largest donation was forty-seven thousand pounds' worth of Jaffa Cakes. They arrived on seventeen pallets on the back of an HGV, and were getting close to their sell-by date. If they had not been given to us, they would have incurred costs, either for putting them into a landfill site or being ground down for animal food. The donors were amazed how quickly we distributed them all over the city.'

Social need in the hinterland around two great football clubs is urgent. According to the latest Index of Multiple Deprivation, the Anfield ward is the 48th most deprived out of 32,844 in the UK. In the neighbouring ward of Everton 48.7 per cent of children live in poverty. Life expectancy is 74.7 years, compared with the national average of 81.3.

'We have a unique set of circumstances here. Walton is the only English constituency with two football clubs in its boundaries. It is home to a socially and economically deprived community. The reality is that football is intensely tribal, but if we work collectively the potential is enormous. To use the trade unions' slogan, "unity is strength".

'We have tried to build bridges with other faith groups, in part to undermine what the Football Lads Alliance is trying to do in demonising the Muslim community. Hunger doesn't discriminate so why should we? I am not doing this as an Evertonian, but as someone who wants to help someone who is hungry.'

The clubs were initially tentative when approached, owing to doubts about the project's infrastructure. These were dispelled immediately when the fans worked their way through a checklist of 26 priorities. Season ticket holders are now contacted strategically, to source donations. By the spring of 2018 supporters' groups from

20 clubs were affiliated to the Merseyside initiative, under a 'hunger has no colours' banner.

Millwall players and supporters have been servicing a local foodbank for seven years. Newcastle fans help to feed 1,000 people a week. Celtic supporters have been working in conjunction with Glasgow North East Foodbank for four years; one collection after a home game against Ross County, reported by *When Saturday Comes*, realised almost five tonnes of food and 600 pairs of trainers.

Huddersfield Town fans are following the Merseyside model, with eight donation points at home matches. Jim Chisem, of the club's Supporters Association, strikes a familiar chord: 'I find it absolutely abnormal to have foodbanks in the 21st century in an industrial world power. It shows a broken system. Now, football clubs are the only real working institutions in town. We need to help each other out, help the man and the woman next to you.'

On the day we spoke, Fitzpatrick had just taken delivery of food parcels from Hartlepool supporters, dressed as clowns on their traditional fancy dress day out, their last away match of the season, at Tranmere. This is compassion on an industrial scale, founded on a single act of humanity, the willingness to help others who are worse off.

That simplicity of purpose breaks down barriers between those who watch and those who play. It is an echo of football as a working-class game. The lives of successful players may be tattooed by materialism, but those insulated from the excess by enduring values, fostered by a strong sense of family, tend to have a natural gratitude and generosity.

Republic of Ireland international Jonathan Walters regularly serves meals at the Deen Centre and has purchased a chest freezer to store donations. Robbie Fowler and Jamie Carragher, through his 23 Foundation, provide quiet support. Joe Royle and Sam Allardyce, Everton managers from different generations, are engaged.

Liverpool's Andy Robertson has a historic link with the foodbanks movement; he requested that all his 21st birthday presents be in the form of donations. When he discovered that Alfie Radford, a seven-year-old schoolboy, had given his pocket money to the cause, he wrote to him directly and sent him a signed Roberto Firmino shirt – 'because, let's be honest, no one wants the left back's shirt'.

Kelly momentarily allows the supporter to speak over the social activist. 'I was sixty in February. I've been an Evertonian, home and away, all my life. I never even asked for an autograph but I am humbled when the legends of my club come to me with their donation. When Robbie Fowler comes in, he doesn't want to be thanked. He's not there for the photoshoot.'

Many clubs enrich their community and are unabashed in claiming credit. This paradox, of making benevolence measurable and marketable, helps to explain why the intensity of fans' emotional commitment to their teams is exploited in the form of ticket price increases that bring in loose change. Like a scorpion, clubs are conditioned to sting, whenever the opportunity arises.

Kelly, a board member of the Football Supporters' Federation, isolated the problem during a meeting with the Premier League. 'They were implying we were being greedy and unrealistic in seeking price caps for ticket prices. Richard Scudamore kept telling us that football had its hand in its pocket. There seemed to be a degree of empathy in what he was saying, but when he told us solidarity for good causes extended to giving the PFA seventeen million pounds it made us laugh.'

This is not a question of personal principle, but institutional hauteur. The instinct of football's ruling class is to patronise supporter-run clubs, such as AFC Wimbledon and Exeter City, where fans paint the ground, wash the kit and cleanse the spirit. The idealism of such institutions will come under pressure in the near future because, in the words of Exeter chairman Julian Tagg, 'the market place doesn't change'.

Ownership by an uninterested party is inevitably malign and usually self-destructive. The nuances of loyalty in such circumstances guided Doug Harper who, as head of Leyton Orient Fans' Trust, led a successful fight against Francesco Becchetti, who took the club into the

Conference from the verge of promotion to the Championship.

Harper did so despite the handicap of so-called 'chemo brain', a legacy of successful treatment for breast cancer, which led to difficulties in concentration, short-term memory problems and an inability to remember conversations. 'When I'm feeling tired or feeling like shit because my medication is pretty mixed up, football is a wonderful distraction. It works to my advantage.'

Becchetti demanded servility and went rogue as the challenge to his authority was mobilised and his losses mounted. His was a fundamental failure of understanding; he had acquired an institution that lived through, and for, the support base. Following a club like Leyton Orient is not a fashion choice; it is a personal statement.

Leyton Orient's first home game and last away match of a transitional season under new ownership provided cameos of devotion. This was a club with a different set of heroes, most notably secretary Lindsey Martin, whose kindness kept the club running in adversity, and her husband Ada, the kit man, who worked without pay when the chaos was at its height. A poster above Lindsey's desk proclaimed, 'Money doesn't make the world go round'.

The 3–1 home win over Solihull Moors had the feel of a family reunion; aniseed twists were passed down my row in the main stand by a fan who had given himself nine hours to make the four-hour journey from his home in Dorset because he didn't want to miss a special occasion. 'It's good to be back,' he said, to murmurs of assent. 'I didn't think we were going to be here this season.'

The 3–1 away win at Gateshead united the family in mourning. Bert Crow, one of nearly 500 Orient fans who made the long trip to the North-East for a meaningless match, was taken ill during the game and passed away 48 hours later. He loved the camaraderie he found in the South Stand bar at Brisbane Road, and in return was loved as a friend and fellow sufferer.

He and two sisters inherited their allegiance from their mother. He passed on the torch to his son, grandson and nephew Paul, who summed up their sense of loss. 'I am so proud of his passion and loyalty, which resulted in him being in Gateshead for a "nothing" game. For the moment I can't face returning to Brisbane Road without him, but ultimately it will have to happen, because it is LOFC that brought us closer in the first place. We have to continue the Orient Family.'

Harper plays bass and sings in the appropriately named Protest Band. He watched Arsenal in the late 70s but was struck by how few supporters spoke to one another. 'At Orient it was so much more personal. It is a completely different mentality. I suppose it is down to there not being so many of us, but we are all in it together.

'I remember years ago, being in Clacton and seeing a car with an Orient sticker in the back. I really wanted to find out who the driver was, so I could make contact. So many of my friendships have come through the club. That's why when Becchetti left I ran around my house punching the air. No one could see me but it felt good.'

The most revealing case study of the necessary fusion of campaigning zeal, native cunning and commercial pragmatism is that of Portsmouth. They have taken the next step and transferred power back from the fans to Michael Eisner, the former chief executive of Disney. His media investment vehicle Tornante paid £5.67 million for a controlling stake and committed £10 million to infrastructure improvements.

Crowds have remained high and Portsmouth are favoured for promotion to the Championship in 2019. Such relative stability would not have been possible without the street sense and persistence of supporters like Bob Beech and Micah Hall. There is an easiness between them, born of years of friendship and struggle. They talk over one another, stories spilling into surrealist commentary on the plight of a football club prey to opportunists, fantasists and criminals.

We met just before the fifth anniversary of their ultimate achievement, enacted in room 30 of the High Court's Rolls Building on 10 April 2013. The fans, through the Pompey Supporters' Trust, prevented the club's liquidation and stemmed a five-year decline from the high water mark of winning the FA Cup under the ownership of French-Israeli businessman Alexandre Gaydamak. PST assumed control of the club nine days later.

They sat, on a chilly evening, on a trestle table in the garden of the Shepherd's Crook pub, once the command centre of a distinctive resistance movement. Beech, a taxi driver and boxing aficionado, oversaw what he calls 'black ops' with his 'SOS Pompey' group, which incorporated 'a few of my mates who used to get up to skulduggery on a Saturday afternoon'.

He is of medium height, wiry and compulsive; Hall, a corporate relationship manager who has retrained as a lawyer, is taller, erudite and more reserved. He suffered the consequences of being the most prominent member of a group of bloggers, including Nick Bain, Colin Farmery, Sue Maskell and John Lish, whose investigations exposed a bewildering succession of would-be saviours, whose fates, when woven together, form a barely believable narrative.

Gaydamak, who convinced the Premier League his wealth was the result of property dealing in Russia, suffered similar financial difficulties to his father Arcadi, who was sentenced to three years' imprisonment for tax evasion and money laundering after presenting himself to the French authorities in 2015. Gun-running charges had been dropped; there has never been any suggestion his son has been involved in criminal activity.

Portsmouth, £65 million in debt, came under the control of Emirati businessman Sulaiman Al Fahim on 26 August 2009. The front man for the Abu Dhabi United Group's purchase of Manchester City the previous year, he promised to recruit Diego Maradona, Roberto Mancini and Sergio Agüero but left after 41 days. He was sentenced to five years' imprisonment in his absence by the Dubai Criminal Court in February 2018 for stealing £5 million from his wife to fund the purchase.

No one is entirely sure of the provenance of Ali al-Faraj, a Saudi citizen who became the next owner on 5 October following a deal involving Falcondrone, a company registered in the British Virgin Islands. Hall has seen the blurred photocopy of a passport in his name, all the documentation the football authorities required. 'I think there is someone who exists, but whether he knew he bought a football club, who knows?'

Portsmouth, saddled with debt that had somehow risen to £135 million, were in freefall. Their next owner, Hong Kong-based financier Balram Chainrai, loaned £17 million and placed the club in administration on 26 February 2010. The following month Rob Lloyd, a property developer apparently acting for a South African consortium, lodged a bid to take control. This came to nothing. Lloyd's company, Eatonfield Group, posted losses in excess of £26 million following the collapse of the housing market. His last public incarnation was as a participant in a reality show, *The Real Housewives of Cheshire*. Another would-be owner, Tom Lever, aged 21 when he bid £16.2 million in August 2010, was declared bankrupt in June 2017.

Vladimir Antonov, a Uzbekistan-born banker purported to be worth $300 million, took over through his company Convers Sports Initiatives on 1 June 2011. On 24 November he was arrested in his London offices after the issue of a pan-European warrant by Lithuanian prosecutors, investigating alleged asset stripping at Bankas Snoras, 68 per cent of which was owned by him. Operations in another bank with which Antonov was associated, Latvijas Krajbanka, were suspended. He appeared in Westminster Magistrates' Court the next day and after an unsuccessful four-year attempt to avoid extradition to Lithuania he broke bail. In September 2015, *Forbes* magazine reported he was living in Moscow.

He had resigned as Portsmouth chairman soon after his arrest, propelling the club into administration for a second time on its descent into League One. More strange suitors emerged; Keith Gregory, whose interest was revealed in February 2012, presented himself as a millionaire clothing salesman. He would be cleared of criminal damage to a Thomas Gainsborough masterpiece, *The Morning Walk*, in December 2017 due to insanity. He had been sleeping rough for four months before his arrest after absconding from a mental institution. Southwark Crown Court heard three psychologists unanimously agree he was suffering 'severe symptoms' of paranoid schizophrenia when he slashed the £24 million painting at the National Gallery in London with a drill bit.

In September 2012, after a close season in which the entire playing staff had left the club, Laurence Bassini, the former Watford chairman, expressed his interest. He was found guilty of financial misconduct and dishonesty by an independent disciplinary commission the following March, and banned from involvement with any Football League club for three years. He was declared bankrupt the following summer.

Another potential buyer, Harry Kerr, gave administrators documents that suggested his investor group Portco had funds of £6.47 million to underwrite a purchase. He admitted fraud in November 2017, when he was sentenced to two years in prison, suspended for a year, as part of a case that led to the jailing of two men for stripping gate receipts during a takeover attempt at Hartlepool United.

Once Chainrai abandoned his plans to resume control, the Pompey Supporters' Trust faced down opposition from a consortium led by Keith Harris, who would become an Everton director in the autumn of 2016. A second member of the group, Pascal Najadi, a Swiss citizen living in Moscow, remained in Russia following the murder of his father Hussain in a car park in

Kuala Lumpur in July 2013. Four years later, Malaysia's High Court sentenced tow truck driver Koong Swee Kwan to death for the gang-style killing, after a retrial. The third member of the consortium, veterinary surgeon Alan Hitchens, has no formal association with football.

'To start off with it was comedy stuff,' Beech recalled. 'We'd chase one lot out and another lot would come in. It got so that it was a bit like the Seven Dwarfs. No one could remember all the names. There was an unholy alliance between us and Sky. They interviewed me at the ground and asked what we were going to do about things.

'I said, off the top of my head, that we were going to protest outside the Premier League offices. I had about half a mile to walk home. Before I got there I had someone from the League on to me, wanting to negotiate terms. He asked whether a meeting would suffice, because they were obviously worried about us making a scene. We were the first fans' group to so do.

'They obviously thought we were a rabble but it turned out we were an educated rabble. We were expecting to meet the tea lady but were able to give Richard Scudamore a pretty forensic cross-examination. We talked about the fit and proper test, gave them our ideas. They seemed to be listening because when they came out with their plan a year later it looked very familiar.'

The tone might be jaunty, but the fight was deeply personal. Supporting a football club is a kaleidoscopic experience, in which fragments of memory are cherished, and have their relevance regularly renewed. Beech refused to watch Portsmouth when it was a stranger's plaything, because of the debt he owed to his father.

John Beech, a former youth team goalkeeper at Portsmouth who passed away just before the 2008 FA Cup final, first took Bob to Fratton Park on 16 March 1974, when he was eight. They stood on the Milton End, with his brothers and cousins, as Portsmouth beat Hull 3–1. On the walk home, his father told tall tales of groundsman Duggie Reid, a Scottish inside forward known as 'Thunderboots' whose goals helped win the First Division title in 1949 and 1950.

Bob's campaigning spirit was initially stimulated by the death of his daughter Charlotte, who was 15 when she succumbed to an asthma attack in 2009. He addressed MPs and assisted Asthma UK in a drive for better education, based upon the development of the online 'Triple A Test', designed to provide an early warning of susceptibility to a fatal seizure.

He was revealingly reflective. 'Getting the club back was the biggest achievement by any fan base in this country, ever. We set a benchmark. No matter how big or small your club is you don't have to take that shit. My wife said, "You can have a row with anyone. You need this." It literally saved my life. Looking back I can see the spiral I was in after we lost Charlotte.'

Hall captured the confessional mood and interjected: 'It nearly destroyed mine. When you start to mess with the wrong type of businessmen, which clearly some of them were, there is a price to pay. I was sued, unsuccessfully, once we had saved the club. I was in a bad way. I lost my house and my marriage broke up.

'Irrespective of whatever you have gone through, once you find yourself on the other side of the fence, there's a load of shit coming your way. People start saying, "What are you doing with my football club?". Part of the problem is you are trying to run a business when everyone thinks you are sitting there in the pub, whirling a scarf around your head.

'Once the trust took over I went in there with Mark Catlin, the chief executive. We walked into a mess. There was no commercial staff, no sponsors, no ticket holders, no kit deal. The place had been stripped of its history: trophies and mementoes had just disappeared. We'd saved the jobs of many of the staff but they didn't really like me because of my background as an activist fan.

'The second problem was the make-up of the board. You had successful businessmen, guys who were running merchant banks and understood the need to get money into the club quickly, and fan advocates who understandably wanted everything run so ethically they would have opposed any kit deal unless it was knitted in hemp by people from Pompey.

'On weeks where we won I could sit there, with my feet on the desk, blowing smoke rings at the ceiling from a big fat cigar. When we'd lost, nothing I did was good enough. The phone never stops ringing from people telling you what a shit job you are doing. That's the way it is. It's wonderful to be able to go back and be a fan again.

'If I had to advise another set of supporters I'd tell them to think of themselves as a consortium of all the talents. Don't worry about what is going to happen in five years. Worry about bringing stability to the business and draw a breath. You will be fighting with one arm up your back if you cannot raise the money to invest.'

Beech raised £12,000 towards Hall's legal fees after the defamation case was thrown out of court. He is using £19,000, accrued from club shares bought by contributions from regulars in the Shepherd's Crook, to set up a Pompey History Group in conjunction with his research into the Pompey Pals regiment in the First World War.

He laughed, sardonically. 'Most fans are liars. They will tell you they want their football club to be as pure as the driven snow, with a great academy producing local boys for the first team. Brilliant. What they really want is to win on a Saturday. If that happens they don't really care whether a Colombian drug cartel is running the place.

'They'll look for excuses. They'll tell you, though they deal drugs, they don't cut them with poison. They'll tell you they are good people, really. It's nonsense. We were linked to one of Gaddafi's sons, and when we objected, some supporters were trying to tell us "he's the good one". As if that meant anything . . . .'

The defence of the indefensible has become a reflexive action, usually from a younger, more disparate and distant generation of fans less likely to attend live games. They view even reasoned criticism of their club as treasonable and personally offensive. Social media allows them to explore persecution complexes, reinforce perceptions of bias without the defence mechanism of objectivity. They tend to be shallow, nasty and sociopathic.

Football has not developed in a vacuum. Political discourse has been cheapened by similar examples of blind faith and bitter recrimination. The temptation is to hit the mute button and avoid the grief of delivering forthright opinion but, for those of us who seek balance and decency, a line was crossed in the Carlsberg Lounge at Crewe Alexandra on the evening of Monday, 26 February 2018.

All 250 tickets for the event, leadingly entitled 'Let's Talk Football', were sold. The club's apparent intention to defuse debate led to a security guard screening attendees at the door. His request for identification involved checking an A4 sheet of paper, containing photographs of journalists who were to be refused entry.

John Bowler, Crewe's chairman and a director throughout the period that convicted paedophile Barry Bennell was employed by the club, faced three questions about its association with such evil acts. He insisted it was 'inappropriate' to comment; the final enquiry, to a low groan from the audience, was announced as being on behalf of the BBC.

Graham McGarry, BBC Radio Stoke's sports editor, has been a highly respected match-day commentator on Crewe Alexandra games for 25 years. This was no dispassionate outsider, caught in the act of perpetrating a hatchet job. He has personal and professional affinity with the achievements of a small club, but recognises its diminishment by the impression given, of a culture of denial.

He was clearly nervous. The tape of the evening reveals an audible tremor in his voice, as he questioned Bowler over the allegation by former managing director Hamilton Smith, that he had warned the club about Bennell's behaviour. McGarry drew his thoughts to a conclusion by asking: 'I know you answered what you wanted to say to the gentleman before, but is there anything to add?'

When Bowler brusquely answered 'none at all' he was applauded. Some supporters even laughed. What sort of warped tribalism causes people to make light of issues raised by the employment of a coach jailed for 30 years for sexually abusing 12 junior players, and facing further charges relating to 86 other boys? How can the shirt he wore, while representing Crewe and Manchester City, be prioritised over a child's terror and a lifetime's shame?

I do not seek to imply these Crewe supporters and the board to which they profess loyalty are somehow devoid of human warmth. They have families; they would doubtless demand action if a similar dilemma touched their personal lives. I would only ask them to dwell on the experience of someone who knows the gravity of their misjudgement.

Alan Fisher is an award-winning author. Together with Martin Cloake, a fellow fan and member of the Tottenham Hotspur Supporters' Trust, he produced a people's history of the club that sought, successfully, to articulate the emotional bonds formed, often by chance, in football fandom.

Fisher is also a social worker, who has personal experience of dealing with sex offenders. 'Abusers thrive on the security of secrecy,' he says. 'They rely on silence for protection. I have seen them one on one and they wield enormous emotional power. Dealing with them is a conflict because you know they seek to dominate and impose their will. Child sex abuse is such an awful thing, so far outside the ordinary experience and reality of vast numbers of people that when something like this comes up people are challenged by it.

'It is easy to look at a football club as a happy family. Barry Bennell had success and helped develop a great team so it must have been fantastic. Well, it wasn't. That should make you question what some people are doing, but it also completely challenges a basic tribalism. You are attacking personal relationships, understanding of the world around you.

'We often say that football is escapism, ninety minutes' release for the working man. That's still true, but football actually enforces reality by sharpening the senses, the joy, pain, pleasure and agony. You are part of something that is a cushion, a safety net. Tribalism is something that gives you a refuge. People say this is my team, thick and thin.

'That's where the problem lies. Support is defined by saying, "This is my team. I am behind it come what may." That's not my idea of support, or my idea of a reasonable society. The Crewe supporters who applauded were part of a coalition of denial. They didn't see the implications of their actions. The laughter and applause that greeted the non-answer to the question was appalling.'

Is the system listening? There are times when doubt strikes, like a dagger in the heart.

CHAPTER EIGHTEEN

Cracking the Code

> 'Young People: Football acknowledges that public confidence demands the highest standards of financial and administrative behaviour, and will not tolerate corruption or improper practices.' – Code of Conduct, Football Association

The boy was 15 when given stretching exercises by academy staff to increase flexibility in his back. An acute injury had apparently been misdiagnosed and he was barely able to use the stairs without the aid of a banister during two wasted years as a scholar. He should have been given an MRI scan within 48 hours of the problem becoming apparent, but he waited six months.

Section 6.5 on the third page of his scholarship contract with a Championship club confirmed its responsibility for ensuring prompt medical and dental treatment. He was initially taken to the wrong hospital, in Stevenage. A staff member dropped him off at the correct venue in Chelsea and told him to call when the procedure, which involved an epidural injection, was complete.

The player's parents found it difficult to source information about his welfare. Internal lines of communication within the club were so confused they suspected intransigence, and a conspiracy of silence. They are seeking legal redress, but nothing can save their son's career. At the age of 18, his dream has endured a painful, protracted death.

'That's as bad as it gets. The boy is never going to be a player. The duty of care process has been horrific. If it was your son how would you feel? Devastated. No one would listen to the family's perspective. Things in this game have to change. I have thought that for a long time. There are things going on that deserve to have the lid blown off.'

The face of the speaker, Pete Lowe, is creased by a strange combination of empathy and distaste. He leans forward, dark eyes searching for understanding. As managing director of PlayersNet, he has overseen more than 30 cases of systemic failure and individual distress in the past year, while remaining true to the organisation's founding values of integrity, impartiality and transparency.

He has spent 25 years in professional football, rising from development coach to head of education and performance management at Manchester City. His case load ranges from an 11-year-old, traumatised by being bawled out in an academy dressing room, to a young professional in a contractual quandary because he signed for an agent operating during an FA suspension for previous misdemeanours.

The FA employs 35 full-time safeguarding staff, who handle an average of 60 disclosures each month. Yet a long-standing bullying allegation, taken to the FA after intervention by the Premier League, led to a Kafkaesque situation in which the player's father, who made the original complaint, was denied information about the investigation's progress because of confidentiality concerns.

His father, who wishes to remain anonymous because he is worried his son will be persecuted, is disgusted. 'How can there be progress when the FA don't seem to be taking abuse seriously? They just don't reply to complaints now. A head-in-the-sand job. My son's doing OK, but his experience at the hands of the bullies has left its mark.'

Lowe's exasperation is palpable. 'You feel almost paternal. People put their heads above the parapet and are told they can't know what is going on. Clubs are supposed to have policies and procedures in place, but too often they are just paper exercises. I come from stock where you are taught to fight hard for a principle. I have got to believe we can make a difference. People deserve to be treated thoughtfully and transparently.

'Would a first-team player have gone six months without a scan? Of course not. Why should a young player be penalised because he placed his trust in an unscrupulous agent? It is a bloody big issue if you are eleven years old and you don't know how to walk into a dressing room, where you know you will have the shreds ripped out of you by an excessively aspirational coach.

'Why should that boy suffer? If you're the coach, don't rant just because it makes you feel better. Parents don't want to go to the club, because they are concerned about creating a point of conflict. An independent process, using quality people who deal with these issues on a daily basis, is required. Football convinces itself it has all the bases covered but it doesn't.'

I must, at this point, declare an interest. I supported Lowe's aims when the initiative operated under the guise of the Players Trust. I spoke on its behalf at a House of Commons reception, having had first-hand experience of the effectiveness of its mentoring programmes and confidential counselling service. Lowe helped a family of my acquaintance by extricating their son from a Premier League club that was attempting to coerce him into signing his first professional contract by falsely claiming they had the right to demand an inflated transfer fee for his services. Twelve months later, following a brief stint in German football, he is on the verge of the first team at a leading club in the Championship.

The fact the trust was encouraged to change its name in the spring of 2018 by Martin Glenn, the FA's chief executive, as part of a broader attempt to realign the game's response to an impending safeguarding crisis, signals the wider significance of a campaign that highlights the practical difficulty of enacting meaningful change in a system shaped by veiled suspicion and naked self-interest.

This story begins in October 2004, when Simon Andrews met Sir Alex Ferguson, who had released him from Manchester United 14 years earlier. Andrews had built a successful secondary career in financial services after a season at Wigan Athletic and saw, from personal experience, the need for a more integrated, independent matrix of player support.

David Gill, United's chief executive at the time, gave strategic advice in early 2005 after being assured this was not just another opportunistic sales pitch. Gary Neville, Ryan Giggs and Ole Gunnar Solskjær provided practical examples of problems facing callow players confronted by sudden fame. Edwin van der Sar shared the lessons of a similar programme at Ajax.

First-team coaches Mick Phelan and René Meulensteen fed into the process, but perhaps the most telling observation came from Paul Scholes, an acidic commentator on football's exploitative culture. 'I don't need this advice now,' he told Andrews, 'but I did when I was sixteen or seventeen. Back then I needed all of it.'

It was not until the summer of 2006 that a programme reflecting the holistic, socially aware nature of Sir Alex's management was ready for implementation. Ferguson led an initial session with parents, outlining the pitfalls of an anarchic system of player representation, before calling a meeting of 80 players and associated staff at United's training base at Carrington.

He stressed Andrews' credentials as a former player and left no one in any doubt about the strength of his personal endorsement. He helped create the capitalist citadel of the modern Manchester United by winning 49 trophies, but this was a fusion of his working-class faith in family and community and his sardonic overview of the football industry.

An extract from his second autobiography, brilliantly co-written by Paul Hayward and reproduced in a persuasive *New Statesman* piece by John Bew following Ferguson's retirement, echoes the softer side of the Govan firebrand. 'People try to apply to football the usual principles of business. But it's not a lathe, it's not a milling machine; it's a collection of human beings. That's the difference.'

Andrews, approaching another career crossroads because of the increasing time he was obliged to devote to the roll-out of United's support plan, found a kindred spirit in the blue half of Manchester when he met Lowe in 2007, following an introduction by James Cooper, the Sky Sports reporter.

'City were really successful in terms of youth development at the time, though they had no money. I thought the barriers would be up as a result of our involvement at United, but Pete [Lowe] and Jim Cassell, who ran the academy, identified with what we were trying to do. They weren't like the others, who'd tell us the system wasn't broken. They were keen to promote change and wanted to help in any way they could.'

Influential advocates like Gill and Richard Caborn, the former sports minister, helped to persuade the Premier League to give Andrews an 18-month contract, leading up to the 2010 World Cup. It was a piecemeal concept; clubs like Chelsea and Everton took up their option of rejecting the chance to be helped in two specific areas, lifestyle management and media training.

The social media bubble was just starting to form. Players from participating clubs were given practical advice on the nature of the news cycle, and the best way to respond to journalistic scrutiny, especially in the unsettling environment of a post-match mixed zone. They were also given an insight into the warning signs of an addictive personality, and the social pressure that so often derails a promising career.

Yet, scratching beneath the surface, it did not take Andrews long to detect poor practice and paranoia.

'One coach came up to me and said, "You're just after my job, aren't you?". Clubs gave us a random couple of sessions before shutting down. There were so many individuals with closed minds. To be honest, I began to wonder, is this too soon for the game?'

Then, to use his wry phrase, 'it was welcome to the world of football politics'. The inquest launched by England's failure at the 2010 World Cup in South Africa concentrated minds and crisis management strategies. The Premier League prevaricated before, in May 2011, it launched the Elite Player Performance Plan in conjunction with the Football Association. It was a long-term initiative, but short-sighted in its creation of institutionalised inequality and administrative servitude. As the Football League allowed its clubs to be bullied into submission, the idea of an independent player-support system began to be marginalised. For two years, Andrews became engaged in a futile turf war with Gordon Taylor, chief executive of the PFA.

Taylor's claim to own the so-called 'education space' was never tested stringently. By 2013, having sunk £500,000 of his own money into his initiative, Andrews assured his former employers St James's Place, a FTSE 100 wealth management company that invests more than £85 billion of client funds, that he was committed to returning to a senior role.

'The whole process had been mentally unsettling for me. It was the darkest place I have been in. I still believed in what we were offering football but felt I had nowhere to turn. Once they came under fire for youth development after the World Cup, everyone at the Premier League disappeared into their bunker.

'I had a series of meetings with Gordon, who kept telling me "we do all this". I kept some things back from my wife because I didn't want to worry her, but I did tell her how strange those meetings felt. Gordon was quite nice about it, but I could tell he thought I was his worst nightmare. In my eyes I represented what he probably wasn't doing.

'Core people around me, like Pete Lowe, Richard Caborn and Phil Townsend at Manchester United, were telling me not to give up. But it tests your belief, desire and sanity. Just when you think you have cracked the code, football goes quiet on you. I thought that was because of me, but the more people you talk to in the game, the more you realise that this happens to everyone.

'There is a certain type of person in football who concentrates on constantly defending his corner. Clubs and administrators like to tell you how busy they are. There is a culture in which it is seen as a sign of weakness to offer encouragement, rather than a strength. The gradual drip, drip, drip of negativity wears you down.'

Andrews concentrated on a demanding day job while remaining in touch with Lowe, who had established First Team, a performance management consultancy, after leaving Manchester City in the summer of 2013. His friendship with Michael Appleton, another Manchester United alumnus who became Oxford United manager in July 2014, was to prove significant.

Appleton is progressive, intelligent and, like many of the best coaches, informed by adversity. He had been forced to retire at the age of 27 in November 2003 after two debilitating years attempting to overcome a posterior cruciate injury to his right knee, sustained in an accidental training ground collision with West Bromwich Albion teammate Des Lyttle. Frustration lingered, and could not be purged entirely by five years' developmental coaching before he was appointed as Albion's first-team coach. Impatience subsequently led him to poor career choices, which involved brief spells attempting to manage basket-case clubs like Blackburn Rovers, Blackpool and Portsmouth, but his basic principles were sound.

He had dealt with the insecurity that assails young footballers, judged at a susceptible stage of their lives. He had endured the chaos of a club in a tailspin, where each day is an assault course. He had never forgotten the essential humanity of Sir Alex Ferguson's approach. He recognised that promotion from League Two in 2016 with Oxford presented a deeply personal opportunity.

'You never really recover from having your career taken away from you. I was twenty-five when I last kicked a ball in anger. I spent two years in rehab and had three major operations without getting on the pitch before realising I was done. The six months after that were bad. I wasn't prepared to admit it at the time, but speaking to people around me, my character changed.

'I became quite aggressive, short with people. I wanted my own space and wouldn't give them the time of day. The doctor thought I was a horrible, angry little shit. When you've been in football you don't see a future outside it. You try to block it out and not think about it, but if you do not have a purpose you can end up staying in bed until midday, feeling that your life has gone.

'I was depressed, but I was one of the lucky ones. I kept busy, doing the under-thirteens and fourteens. I got my badges and spent six years working my way up to assistant manager. You learn a hell of a lot as a youth coach. You work with a broad base of players and you understand just how vulnerable they feel.

'If I was releasing a player it was my duty to do everything I could for him, even before I told him the bad news. I'd see him having already spoken to six or seven clubs about potential trials, or opportunities for a contract. I'd want to give someone a second, third or fourth chance to have a career before he takes that huge step that everyone dreads, into a world of work.

'We all need help and support. I like to think, slowly but surely, people are recognising the need for young players to be mentored and monitored, especially when they may have to weigh up options outside football. I understood what the trust was trying to achieve, and was happy to work with them.'

Sessions overseen by the Players Trust at Oxford dovetailed with the work of Chris Gooder, a protege of acclaimed sports psychologist Dr Steve Peters, who operates in football, golf, tennis and motor racing. In addition to advising a range of players from youth level to the first team, Gooder provided a sounding board for Appleton, who sought respite from a leader's loneliness. 'In many cases it comes down to how long you've been in the game. Some old-school coaches don't feel they need that type of help. I like to think of myself as being open-minded. I ask a lot of questions. I would spend half an hour with Chris before I did the opposition analysis on a Thursday morning. It is good to talk to someone who doesn't have an angle.'

Self-improvement was part of Ferguson's credo. Appleton was not academic at school, but acquired sports science qualifications as a player at Preston and educated himself as he worked towards his Uefa Pro Licence. He earned the LMA's diploma in management and was in the first cohort of graduates from the master's degree course in sporting directorship at Manchester Metropolitan University. The two-year part-time programme, the first in the UK and the world's only academically validated course serving a role that is slowly reshaping domestic football, is designed to develop executive competence and confidence. Appleton qualified in July 2017, just before he left Oxford for an eleven-month spell as Leicester City's assistant manager; he had learned to delegate, and dilute instinctive obsession.

'I would spend Wednesday and Thursday studying there once every month and had to trust my staff to deliver a session in preparation for the Saturday game. It was refreshing because I wasn't thinking about players, formations, group dynamics or dwelling on something that had gone on at the club. It got me reading again and had to have my sole concentration. I had to clean my mind and give my studies my full attention. It improved me as a manager because of the discipline it instilled and the ideas it generated. This job beats you up. It is there all the time. If you are not careful it can send you senseless.'

Football, meanwhile, was facing an existential crisis. The sexual abuse scandal was starting to play out in the courts, and administrators struggled to retain public trust. A series of distressing case studies posed fundamental questions about standards of care provided for young players. Lives had been scarred and responsibilities had clearly not been met.

Allegations of a culture of racist bullying at Chelsea in the 80s and 90s, revealed by Daniel Taylor in the *Guardian*, were a secondary tumour, threatening the game. Legal papers served on the club by three former players alleged one was so traumatised he ended his career, despite having a professional contract. Another painted a picture of a 'feral environment'.

Gwyn Williams and Graham Rix, the coaches implicated in the scandal, deny all allegations and, after a seven-month investigation, police decided there was insufficient evidence to take further action. Chelsea offered the complainants counselling and took the initiative by calling in FA safeguarding officers.

The details of the case remain profoundly disturbing and are outlined in the language of the slave plantation. When a player speaks of being referred to as a 'black bastard', 'wog' or 'jigaboo' and ordered to 'pick up your lip, it's dragging on the floor', it reignites the debate about whether football is a reflection of a flawed society, or a law unto itself. Lawyers have been approached by former players from other clubs, citing similarly abhorrent behaviour.

Concurrent concerns about the conduct of coaches and clubs at youth level highlighted the value of the Players Trust in 2017, when Pete Lowe was approached with increasing regularity by players, concerned parents and club staff members, who requested anonymity because they feared for their jobs if they were overt in their complaints.

Simon Andrews, resigned to the fact that he was 'back to square one', helped in his spare time. It took two years for an important ally, Colin Bridgford, chief executive of the Manchester County FA, to secure an initial meeting with Martin Glenn in February 2018. They discussed three main areas of influence, which the FA chief executive asked to be fleshed out in preparation for a meeting with Richard Scudamore, the Premier League's executive chairman.

Andrews sought to formalise the relationship by pitching the idea of an independent service to support whistle-blowers, provide advice and education about agents, and develop a player passport, an online CV recording a boy's time in the game, designed for use as part of an exit strategy in the event of rejection.

Glenn, though originally sceptical, was fully engaged ten weeks later, when presented with a business plan that required a mandate to push through significant change. An advisory board including Appleton, Caborn, Falklands hero Simon Weston, parental representatives and senior executives from local government had requisite credibility.

Ripples spread across the political pond. In what was seen as a self-defensive move, the PFA simultaneously 'launched' Safety Net, an online portal offering young players advice on mental health issues. The timing was intriguing since they were first approached with the idea by brothers Lee and Nick Richardson in 2009. According to the PFA website the scheme had been introduced in June 2015.

Glenn, though hapless in some of his public pronouncements, had gained internal respect for his gradual overhaul of the FA's culture. At his next meeting with Andrews and Lowe, in mid-May, he was accompanied by Andy Ambler, the former Millwall chief executive whose role as the FA's director of professional game relations identifies him as a unifying figure.

The business plan for the newly renamed PlayersNet had been augmented by a series of case studies highlighting increasing anxieties. Ian Braid, former chief executive of the British Athletes Commission, drew on the lessons of working closely with Tanni Grey-Thompson on her Duty of Care in Sport review, published in April 2017. He stressed: 'Athletes need access to an independent organisation that gives them confidence they will be genuinely listened to, and that a genuine grievance will be properly investigated and acted upon without fear of recrimination or reprisal. They need to have trust in a system and, based on my experience across a number of sports, that does not exist.'

Baroness Grey-Thompson's suggestion that the advisory board include a duty of care guardian, an FA Board member designed to reassure FA councillors, was accepted. In return Ambler asked Andrews to consider aligning with Kick It Out as part of a collaborative approach. He intended to meet Scudamore to confirm a joint approach, involving the FA, Premier League and Football League.

Momentum was beginning to gather. Paul Elliott, Chelsea's first black captain and the first former player to be an FA Board member, proved to be an influential ally. He secured the support of Herman Ouseley, Kick It Out's founder, during an informal conversation at the FA Cup final. Troy Townsend was similarly enthusiastic.

Football's instinct is to seek the hidden agenda, the ulterior motive. But as Andrews remarked: 'If we wanted to make money we would have become agents. We've not done all this, merely to milk the game.'

All concerned knew that the consensus would be meaningless without Scudamore's buy-in. The FA is in the invidious position of being obliged to maintain the pretence of authority while the real power is wielded by the Premier League's wealth and political influence.

Even when confronted with a potential windfall, in the sale of Wembley to generate a £800 million pot for a revival of the grass-roots game, the FA hierarchy were poorly treated as Scudamore's useful idiots. Those complaining about the sale of football's family silver conveniently overlooked countless park pitches, waterlogged, ill-tended and unusable between the months of December and March.

Central government has shredded the nation's social fibre by an evasion of responsibility in an age of austerity. Local government's hostility to sport was summarised by Wandsworth Council in London, which threatened to impose £80 fines on anyone caught playing football and cricket in 39 designated parks. For good measure, officials also promised to pursue kite fliers and tree climbers.

At the last election the manifestos of the main political parties ignored or glossed over football's totemic status. Scudamore has his hand firmly on the tiller through his chairmanship of the Sports Business Council, alongside Sports Minister Tracey Crouch, whose office has the political gravitas of the Downing Street cat.

Football's resistance to accountability is hardening. Both Glenn and Scudamore declined to be interviewed for this book. They are extremely busy men and have the right to keep their counsel. Refusing an interview is hardly an affront to the democratic process, but the Premier League in particular prefers to communicate through sanitised channels.

Scudamore's surprise announcement of his intention to stand down by the end of 2018, after 20 years in charge, had the air of a monarch's abdication. He responded to the possibility of football's fragmentation by portraying a 'strong' Premier League as 'the biggest antidote to chaos' and predicted further growth through the exploitation of international TV rights. Things look different outside the bubble. Exploitation and expedience will become more pronounced as the game becomes more elitist. His successor, likely to be even more acquisitive and corporately driven, will seek to enhance globalisation of the product, most logically through a cross-continental round of matches.

Young players represent an opportunity for Scudamore to deliver a lasting legacy. They deserve greater protection. Lowe has shared their tears, sensed their fears. He is not optimistic. 'This is a game covered with great complexity by a modern media, but too many things are hidden away. The image of English football, as a brand, would be amazing if it is seen to work together in such an important area. It would be seen as inventive, creative and proactive. That's not rocket science. It is common sense.'

But is it realistic? Watch this space.

CHAPTER NINETEEN
New World Order

'I cannot accept that some people who are blinded by the pursuit of profit are considering selling the soul of football to nebulous private funds. Money does not rule. We are not the owners of football. It is not for sale. I will not let anyone sacrifice its structures on the altar of a highly cynical and ruthless mercantilism.' – Aleksander Ceferin, Uefa president

Mohamed Khalib stirred from a fitful sleep in a fetid room, G10 in Block 54 of the Asian Town labour complex on the western fringe of Doha. He opened the thin yellow cotton curtain surrounding his bed, over which hung a grubby white vest and flaccid grey socks, to find two television cameramen focusing on his face. The human zoo was open for business.

His narrow shoulders flinched as he recoiled, attempting simultaneously to pat down his dark, unkempt hair and smooth his brown nightshirt. He smiled nervously and glanced at the Qatari officials standing at the doorway. They encouraged him to speak openly to the strangers who had gatecrashed his life. Rarely has football felt more like grief tourism.

Khalib, one of an estimated 1.75 million migrant workers in the gas-rich, austerely conservative emirate, had been allotted a ten-square-metre room, shared with three other men. Their humanity was expressed through fraying photographs of loved ones, taped to the wall beside their bunks. They were convenient props, used to make a point by World Cup organisers who wished to address welfare concerns.

It emerged that he was 35. He had worked away from his family in India for a decade. His day shift as a painter began at 3.45 a.m., when he was bussed to a World Cup construction site. He was one of the lucky ones, paid £380 a month by a responsible employer for the sort of menial job that would realise £30 in the South Asian labour market.

Many are impoverished and exploited, having paid an extortionate recruitment fee in their home nations. They exist in far worse conditions than the 50,000 housed in Asian Town, where security guards control nine entry points to a 272-acre site that lies behind forbidding high metal fencing. An external compliance audit found some went 148 days without a break; one worked 402 hours in a single month.

The cameramen left quickly, dispassionately seeking more content down a narrow corridor that smelled faintly of antiseptic. Out of common courtesy, and deeply ingrained Western guilt since I conspired in the inquisition, I lingered to shake Khalib's hand and thanked him for his forbearance. 'All is good,' he said, in what came across as the verbal equivalent of a shrug.

To those involved in the rebalancing of world football, he is a fleeting reminder of a public relations problem. If Qatar's Supreme Committee for Delivery and Legacy, an appropriately Orwellian title for the organisers of the 2022 finals, thought their difficulties were limited to the occasional death on associated building sites, they were wrong.

The English-educated Anglophile Hassan al-Thawadi, who is leading preparations, has a carefully rehearsed, endlessly rehashed response to enduring suspicions of corruption. He insists he has 'answered a million questions about dirty money' and has 'co-operated fully with the relevant authorities, in a very transparent manner'.

When we first spoke, two years ago, he saw his definitive challenge as embracing sport as a catalyst for profound social change in the region in the manner of South Africa during the transition from apartheid. By the time his advisers failed to fulfil repeated promises that he would expand at length on his aspirations, in late spring 2018, the world had changed.

Saudi Arabia led a campaign of destabilisation, involving a coalition of regional partners, designed to isolate and intimidate. Football's prominence, and susceptibility to financial manipulation, enabled them to target Qatar's sphere of influence and application of soft political power. The great World Cup heist was under way.

Fifa under Sepp Blatter, a deceptively comedic, ultimately delusional figure, was defined by early-morning FBI raids and overt venality. Under his successor as president, Gianni Infantino, the butler who inherited the palace, greed was more covert and the culture more insidious. Football was under renewed threat from a mixture of personal ambition, geopolitical priority and commercial opportunism.

Infantino, requiring a financial windfall to add momentum to his campaign for re-election in 2019, led secret negotiations over a proposed $25 billion deal for two new tournaments, an expanded Club World Cup and a biennial Nations League. Simultaneous discussion of an accelerated programme for a 48-team World Cup, a fundamental challenge to Qatar's capacity, also suited the Saudi strategy.

The Fifa president withheld the identity of investors from his own council, citing confidentiality agreements, but details of the initiative, teased out by the *Financial*

Times and *The New York Times*, were revealing. Masay-oshi Son, Japan's richest man, sought a 49 per cent stake in the new ventures; his consortium was underpinned by the sovereign wealth of Saudi Arabia and the United Arab Emirates. He made a specific play for rights to Fifa's video game.

This power grab, inevitably undercutting Uefa's Champions League, emphasised the increasing attraction of the club game over international football. Infantino used traditional divide-and-rule tactics, telling a private meeting of seven leading clubs, including Manchester United, Liverpool, Real Madrid, Barcelona and Bayern Munich, that their involvement would be worth up to $150 million.

Richard Scudamore's central involvement in opposition, through his leadership of an obscure lobbying group, the World Leagues Forum, was poetically predictable. The Premier League was, after all, under threat from its formative force, avarice. Juventus chairman Andrea Agnelli duly promoted his counter-vision of what amounted to a European super league.

Aleksander Ceferin, Uefa's Slovenian president, took a populist stance, arguing for a radical distribution of funds to restore competitive balance. His ideas, especially the imposition of luxury taxes to curb reckless or indulgent spending, were sound but delivered with sacrificial innocence. Such idealism tends to be extinguished by bitter experience.

Intriguingly, Southampton's Les Reed was comforted by the incongruities of the system: 'Modern ownership, or the trend that ownership is taking now, is highly linked to non-football global activity, whether it be political, business, oil, whatever. They are so interlinked that it would be a big jump for the people that have bought clubs for those reasons to sanction something like a global league, or pan-European league. There's a hell of a lot of risk in that.'

The game-changer, quite literally, is Fifa's evolution from a supposedly independent arbiter of professional standards to a self-interested agent of change. Its advocacy avoids the prospect of any breakaway being complicated in the manner of Kerry Packer's short-lived cricket circus, which led to those involved being temporarily ostracised.

Football's future has never been more fluid. Its nature changed, fundamentally, once it accepted Roman Abramovich and his opaquely acquired wealth. The Chelsea owner's acceptance of Israeli citizenship, following difficulties with the renewal of his UK visa, piqued the interest of a senior executive in a London-based private bank. 'It looks like the bubble could burst,' the banker said. 'I'm not sure it is sustainable. The banks love the investor visa process. I know from experience it is a big money-spinner. Football likes to think it is insulated by the huge income it receives from television, but the minute the banks question their involvement the industry comes to a grinding halt.'

This is not intended as a reflection on Abramovich, who reinforced his power by pointedly postponing plans for a new Chelsea stadium, but in elite banking circles investors from Russia and central Europe fall into a higher than average risk category that requires enhanced due diligence. There is a widely held belief that financial systems in China, South America and Africa have inadequate safeguards against money-laundering.

Constantine Gonticas, an Athens-based financier who has been a Millwall director for the best part of a decade, has double vision. On a personal level, he is captivated by the intimacy of his association with the English game. Professionally, he understands its attractions to a new breed of owner, from rapidly-developing markets. 'Many from emerging economies are finding a viable and visible place to park their assets offshore. The Chinese, for instance, are selective investors. They are all about brand extension, rather than the collection of trophy assets. English football sells global eyeballs to Asia for more than nine months a year. That power is impossible for an Asian investor to ignore.

'Football has always attracted funny money. Historically, with bungs and things like the chairman's gate, we've no need for lessons in sharp practices, but whatever nefarious things have gone on we are here because of the integrity of the product on the pitch. If that gets lost the new money evaporates. The guy tuning in from Timbuktu wants to know his team is doing its best. The integrity of the sporting outcome is paramount.'

On a broader level, regimes and individuals have been allowed to use football with impunity to 'sportswash' their image, to use the phrase applied by Kate Allen, director of Amnesty International UK. They seek presentational opportunity rather than profit; the impression of tolerance and transparency is invaluable.

Russia's president, Vladimir Putin, knew he had a supine partner in Infantino. To no one's great surprise, Fifa found there was 'insufficient evidence' of doping among Russian players, scheduled to compete. Its announcement of an encrypted, anonymous online method of registering complaints about human rights violations during the tournament was, frankly, risible.

Putin welcomed Blatter, who is halfway through a six-year ban from official football duties, imposed because of financial misdemeanours, to the Kremlin as an honoured guest. The sight of Iranian women being allowed in Tehran's Azadi Stadium for the first time in 40 years, to watch a beam-back of the Group B game against Spain, may have been a reminder of the World Cup's capacity to engineer social change, but Fifa's moral bankruptcy endures. It took greater offence at ambush marketing than an England player, Danny Rose, finding it necessary to warn relatives against travelling to the World Cup in Russia because of fears of overt racism. It fined the host nation £22,000 for abuse endured by France's black players during an international in Moscow in March 2018, only £6,000 more than the sanction applied to the FA because an England Under-20 player used an unofficial energy drink.

Rose did more good, in one interview, than Fifa has done in years of empty expressions of social concern. Searing candour about his fragile mental health did his and future generations a huge service. In speaking from personal experience about a range of fundamental issues, from racism to gun crime, Rose proved it is possible to cry, and to care.

His caution about the setting was misplaced, since Russia 2018 provided joyful reaffirmation of the World Cup's ability to transfix the planet. The tournament had an epochal feel, with the fall of old empires and the arrival of new stars.

Gareth Southgate, England's emotionally-engaged manager, crystallised the mood. 'We have the chance to affect something bigger than ourselves. In England we have spent a lot of time being lost about what our identity is. We are a team with diversity and youth that represents modern England.'

Football's beauty has long been in the eye of the beholder. It is capable of lyricism and cynicism, artistry and banality. It is shaped by reckless romanticism and bloodless calculation. Its essential contradictions are embodied by its most acclaimed coach, Pep Guardiola.

The splendour of his teams, and the authenticity of his personal principles, are undeniable. Yet his passionate espousal of the Catalan cause left him exposed to accusations of hypocrisy, since he has profited from an Abu Dhabi-owned club, Manchester City, and an ambassadorial role with the Qatari World Cup. Neither Gulf regime is noted for its liberalism.

Football is not fussy about its bedfellows. It has allowed betting companies literally to shout the odds, despite growing concerns about the normalisation of gambling through sport, especially in the young. The Institute for Public Policy Research estimates the annual burden gambling places on the UK public purse is £1.16 billion.

Agents, as a breed, understand the universal language of money. Uefa's investigations unit calculated £2.5 billion was paid in commission on transfers to European clubs between 2013 and 2017. Despite the natural linguistic caution of the bureaucrat, they described the figure as 'eye-watering'. Fifa, having effectively surrendered control in 2015, took three years to respond to the subsequent anarchy.

Infantino convened a 'consultation workshop' in Zurich, involving 24 prominent agents, in April 2018. It was tempting to dub it the Day of the Jackals, yet three who did not deign to attend – Jorge Mendes, Mino

Raiola and Kia Joorabchian – wield some of the greatest individual influence over clubs, managers, players, and elements of the media. Mendes, whose empire was founded on Cristiano Ronaldo and José Mourinho, is the human equivalent of a creeper vine. Raiola, memorably described as a 'shit bag' by Sir Alex Ferguson, at least has a sense of humour; he named his company Maguire Tax & Legal, after the film *Jerry Maguire*. Joorabchian, a defender of third-party ownership who made his name with Carlos Tevez, is more sensitive about his public image.

Jonathan Barnett, the most successful agent to respond to the Fifa president's invitation, co-owns the Stellar Group. Prone to bombast, yet honest enough to admit he has no emotional attachment to the sport that enriches him, he is renowned as a brilliant negotiator who has an intuitive understanding of a client's market value. All four fill a void, and are very good at their job.

Theirs is a hard world, often condensed into crude terms. Very few agents wish to go on the record about the realities of their trade, but I informally asked an experienced industry figure briefly to describe two of his major competitors, with the protection of anonymity. He paused for effect before dismissing one as 'a dog' and the other as 'a psychopath'.

This is not language designed to echo around boardrooms, where risk-averse modern decisions are made. Their business will never be entirely sanitised, since it inevitably involves the more base human failings of covetousness, duplicity and vanity, but its future lies in a more refined, strategic version of wealth harvesting.

North American sports agents like Scott Boras in baseball and Tom Condon in the NFL, are iconic figures in the business community. They provide the template for a more corporately reassuring model, which football will be forced to adopt, as the chancers and shysters are pushed to the margins over the next decade.

To survive, smarter agencies will need to be recreated in the all-encompassing example of the Wasserman Group, whose promotional literature speaks of '360 degree management'. It represents more than 600 players across Europe and the US, and advises clubs and rights holders on everything from image rights to brand identification.

Owned by Casey Wasserman, grandson of Lew, historically one of Hollywood's most powerful figures, it helps market major corporations like Microsoft. Individual agents essentially operate as internally competitive franchises under its umbrella. Clients have social media strategies enacted by the artfully named Laundry Service. Unsurprisingly, it inspires fear and loathing.

'Of the big agencies, Wasserman are the most detached from reality,' said a rival who specialises in the European market. 'They're a bunch of estate agents and marketing dildos. It's like listening to

Prince William telling you he likes rap music. Their people are competing for the same players. They hate each other as much as they hate me.'

Such invective is a backhanded compliment to an organisation that turns over in excess of $200 million annually. Wasserman's 800 staff members operate in 14 cities across the globe; the football operation is run from London, in a modernistic office in the Strand, close to the Old Bailey.

The furniture in the reception is angular and achingly fashionable; the office layout is aspirational. Senior agents operate from a series of glass-walled, centralised pods. Their hourly schedule is recorded on small, rectangular electronic consoles for all to see. Each oversees a personal team of junior agents or consultants, profiting from the proceeds of their work through an internal bonus system.

Around 90 top representatives from around the world gather each autumn in a London hotel for a series of seminars. The last, in October 2017, featured sports psychologists, nutritionists, book publishers and a Premier League club chairman. Presentations, led by marketeers from Beats by Dre and Adidas, reflected football's increasing cultural relevance.

We are conditioned to regard agents as barrow boys rather than bankers. It is, after all, a trade that quietly tolerates chicanery and client-stealing. Wasserman's sensitivity to perceptions of greed was highlighted by denials of football's conventional wisdom, that Paul Martin, one of their leading operatives, earned £7 million from Ross Barkley's £15 million transfer from Everton to Chelsea.

Martin is a low-key figure, averse to personal publicity. Dean Baker, one of his senior colleagues, is more inclusive and willing to take practical steps to challenge stereotypes. Over more than two hours, starting in his pod and finishing around the boardroom table, he built a picture of consistent diligence to counter assumptions of cartoonish ducking and diving.

He oversees the careers of four leading managers, including Bournemouth's Eddie Howe, and more than 30 players. He estimates he has completed in excess of 700 major deals over 20 years. He has lost only five clients along the way; three subsequently re-signed with him. He is measured, even-toned and plays a straighter bat than Geoffrey Boycott.

Agents earned £211,011,187 in fees from Premier League clubs in the year to 31 January 2018, an obscene sum by any standards. Baker conventionally takes 5 per cent of a player's basic guaranteed salary and signing-on fee. That doubles in more complicated deals, which require time and additional internal input. He has access to two in-house lawyers.

'Do I get the public's dismay at transfer fees, players' wages? Yes, yes, yes. Do I cut corners? No. I haven't got any juicy stories to tell my mates. We don't dangle carrots for parents, or anyone else attached to a foot-baller. We don't buy them. If they want our services, great. If they are looking for something else, then it's not going to be for us or them, because we just don't do it.

'When I first joined, the chief exec said you attract the wife you deserve in life, and footballers attract the agents they deserve in life. I kind of know what he meant by that. We attract a certain type of footballer. We are a very corporate structure. I worked for five banks in the City before I worked for a football agency. Walk through our office and, barring a few bits of memorabilia, this could be a bank.

'The reason why I've been in this industry for as long as I have is because I've got a good reading of people. It's all very well saying, I'm going to set out a player's earn-ing potential, but let's do it in a way that they are motivated. I've had players in the past interested in fish-ing, so my job was to go out and not just get them free fishing gear but get them on the front cover of the Crafty Carp magazine or whatever it's called. They were very proud of that.

'There aren't set rules and there probably isn't a right way of doing it, but I've certain rules that I've lived by. Tell the truth, because an awkward conversation is much better in the long run than being caught out for doctoring the truth or out-and-out lying. Never give players a false impression; don't tell them what they want to hear, tell them what they need to hear.

'There is no choice – if you want to be successful you've got to work at it. This is a job you give your life to. Within three minutes of waking up I have been on the BBC News website and put Sky Sports News on. I'm scrolling down, saving texts. My diary is already in hand, and I'm going through the day. You've got to be extremely self-motivated.

'I have an element of guilt if I don't make around seventy or eighty phone calls in a day. In the transfer window that's over a hundred. Days intersect. I'll fire out fifteen or twenty text messages around nine o'clock, which I think is an acceptable time of the day to start work, for most people. Do they want to be receiving them at ten to eight in the morning when they are getting on with their family life? I'm not so sure.

'I work in small windows of opportunity. Call players probably between nine and nine-thirty, managers between nine and ten. Most of them are then on the grass for a couple of hours, so I'll pick up my deals with chief execs, chairmen, sponsors, press, whoever it might be. Around one-thirty you're back on the phone to players as they are leaving the training grounds. You can speak to managers, no problem, up to midnight.

'It's all-encompassing but that's expected. Friday afternoon is fairly quiet. I have that as planning time. Managers are focusing on the game, or travelling. I don't want to disrupt a player's routine. Invariably if I'm getting a phone call from one at that time it is not good news. It's normally to say, "I've been dropped". There's never a great way to deliver that bad news, and some managers are better at it than others.

'Some players act impulsively, on emotion. There will be agents who rub their hands together after that phone call. I try to give sensible advice, "OK, let's settle down, talk this through rationally. Let's pick it up again on Monday once you've slept on it. We've got the game tomorrow, things can change. The guy that's taken your position could get injured, sent off, have a stinker. Many problems in life solve themselves. So, you might be back in the team by Tuesday."'

He has to be assertive – one emerging player, who had complained of not getting his desired move to the Premier League, was forced to sit with Baker when he called eight leading managers, who explained, over the speakerphone, why they were not interested – but it is not a natural process. The cold caller needs to conquer himself. 'You've got to take yourself out of your comfort zone. It's not natural for me to walk into a room and start introducing myself, for example. I'm still not comfortable walking into a players' lounge. It's just not in my personality. I grow in confidence with familiarity. So if I've got one or two people in the room that I do know, I'll make the most of it.

'Even after twenty years when I'm cold calling a footballer I'll still plan and visualise that conversation in my head. Maybe I'll press the button to call, and then press stop, before it's started to ring. If the player knows I'm calling, it's totally different. I say to all the guys that work in my team and I remind myself of it; if I'm going into a negotiation, I'm totally comfortable with every word that I'm going to say.

'There's no lying, blagging. It's "this is the market rate for my client. The reason I know that is because we've got an office with four thousand contracts in it. I know what the market dictates, what the market is saying about my client." And if I'm ever questioned, I'm happy to give three or four examples.

'I'm not a good poker player. Other agents might be. I'd rather work harder to cover more ground, to have more of a solid argument to present to a football club, a brand, a sponsor, whoever it might be. I'm probably still the original agent that I set out to be, which is: sign a client, work for the client, negotiate with the other side. I'm always the exclusive representative of that client.

'There are not just middle-men these days. There are middle-middle-men, brokers. Relationships I have fostered over the years mean I will occasionally broker a deal on behalf of a football club, who need to shift certain players off the books. They ask me to search the market, see if there is a way in anywhere, and try to put a deal together.

'Principally, though, I'm about my players. I want them to learn about life as well as the game. I want them to learn the business of football. I'm a shoulder to cry

423

on, but I always say, "learn how to do things for yourself. Understand what you're going into, don't just let other people do everything for you. You will be a greater human being for it, and you'll understand the world around you.'"

That world is changing, irreversibly. The future player will have an instinctive respect for knowledge, and an appreciation of the complexity of his or her body. He or she will have learned from the curiosity and rigour of an innovator like Kirk Cousins, the quarterback who signed a record $84 million, three-year contract on joining Minnesota Vikings in March 2018.

According to an intriguing *Sports Illustrated* profile, Cousins consults with a brain coach, biochemist, kinesiologist, naturopath, fitness coach and physical therapist. He funds his own saliva testing, tissue rejuvenation, blood profiling and massage therapy. He rests in a hyperbaric chamber and measures his heart rate and breathing during deep sleep and REM sleep cycles. He evaluates hormonal, adrenal and testosterone levels. He records theta and high-beta scores on an EEG, which measures electrical activity in the brain. He trained on a computer program that slowed down films or restricted the screen when it sensed high levels of brain activity. He analyses the left side of his brain, because it controls his internal speech, which he seeks to control in times of stress.

If that is a paradigm shift from the days of the magic sponge and a restorative Woodbine at half-time, the nature of managers will change accordingly. Trends in Major League Baseball hint at things to come: the six new managers employed in 2018 were up to 12 years younger than their predecessors.

AJ Hinch is 44 and the manager of Houston Astros, World Series champions in 2017; he has a psychology degree from Stanford. He's positively old-school compared to Gabe Kapler of the Philadelphia Phillies, who is 42, and encapsulates his philosophy accordingly: 'All of the various departments around a baseball organisation are the soil, and our players are the plants and the trees that are going to grow in that soil. So as I think about managing a ballclub, I think about being really nutrient-dense soil.'

Managing upwards, towards a foreign owner, is becoming a definitive skill. Vetting processes must be improved radically, to identify unscrupulous and unsuitable individuals. Greater thought has to be applied to macro-politics; Chinese owners, for instance, have struggled because of their government's rapidly changing political and financial priorities.

The arrogance of the self-elected elite, the so-called top six clubs, is stultifying. Their braying, bullying style, justified in their terms by the acquisition of a greater portion of the Premier League's global TV revenues, is accelerating alienation. They wish to impose serfdom on a game that needs to become more civilised than commercialised.

The sanctity of Arthur Hopcraft's working-class communion has been destroyed by infantile public address announcers and exploitative practices, such as West Ham's policy of charging a child £700 to fulfil the timeless dream of being a mascot. The urgency of the search for equality was emphasised by a Women in Football report, highlighting a 400 per cent increase in cases of sexual discrimination and harassment in the 2017–18 season.

Antipathy towards female observers and commentators is an irrational denial of the professionalism of such pioneers as Amy Lawrence, Anna Kessel, Vikki Orvice and Janine Self. It is a reflection of male social inadequacy, and overlooks the common denominator of a passion sustained since childhood. The example of Jacqui Oatley, for instance, is universal.

She began by kicking a ball, purchased from a sports shop in Codsall, against the garage door. Her love for Wolverhampton Wanderers was consummated 'in the choir' on the South Bank at Molineux, where 'it was a lovely whiff of a Saturday afternoon, chicken Balti pies and urine'. At the age of 27, she 'devoted my entire life to making my way in journalism'.

She split up from her boyfriend, moved from London to Sheffield to do a one-year post-graduate journalism degree, and slept on the floor of friends' flats. She progressed from voluntary work on Hospital Radio, collecting requests for Frank Sinatra songs from elderly patients, to earning £21 a week, doing non-League reports for Radio Leeds.

She survived the intimidating silence of the enclosed press box at Bradford Park Avenue, 'where a load of gentlemen who had been there for years were looking at this blonde woman with a massive mobile phone and a clipboard'. Negotiating shared toilets at Bury and Shef- field United involved stepping over suspicious puddles and 'giving thanks that I'd been doing my pilates'.

The 'surreal' controversy that greeted her appearance as the first female commentator on *Match of the Day* seems even more absurd, given her development into an incisive interviewer and seamless presenter. Her work with Women in Football is a conscious attempt to reas- sure a new generation about the authenticity of their ambition.

'It's really important to show women coming through that you don't have to choose either football journalism, working in football, or motherhood. You can do both. I can't pretend it is easy. It really is one heck of a juggle. I don't really care about attitudes. That's never really bothered me because for me, it's always been about the love of the game, pure and utter love of the game of football.'

Intolerance increases the importance of other pro- foundly impressive figures like Baron Ouseley, founder of Kick It Out. 'Where will we be in ten years' time?' he asks. 'We are looking for change, for football to become a better environment for training, for watching and being influential to the rest of society. That is our bottom line, or certainly mine.

'I would say to those at the top, come out of your hospitality box and go and mix with the proletariat on the estates and understand. It's not about a football club creating a foundation, giving them some money, doing a programme and boasting about numbers. It's about who's in there and what they are getting out of it. What are their hopes and aspirations for the future?'

For all its faults, football still offers a reliable insight into the human condition. It can reduce wealth or social prominence to an afterthought. A successful businessman like Constantine Gonticas may rationalise his passion for the game by suggesting being a club director 'is the closest to competing I get' but, at heart, his devotion is an extension of a childhood love story. He was captivated at the age of seven by yellowing, out of date copies of the *Roy of the Rovers* annual. He was educated by Brian Moore, host of ITV's *The Big Match*, shown at his grandmother's house, a week late, in black and white, on Greek television. At the age of nine, transplanted to a British boarding school, football represented continuity.

'Though I was born in England I had only visited there once before. It was a mythical world of perfect grass pitches, swaying stands and a brand of full-on football that featured guys covered in mud. It anchored me, when I was down and homesick. It was the one thing in my life I could latch on to.'

Now he is permitted only 90 bed nights in the UK. He has planes on stand-by, cars ready to whisk him to games 'because the more you taste, the more you want'. His companion, Nick Blackburn, the former QPR chairman, attends 160 games a year. Their ambition is to watch a match in Transnistria, an enclave between Ukraine and Moldova.

My journey has been as much in the mind as on the road. Having begun in Jeff Astle's armchair, it ends in a deserted non-League ground, Twerton Park, home to Bath City since 1909. It might be situated in a working-class enclave of a gentrified city that prefers rugby union, but it had the feel of an empty country church, and the fascination of a rural graveyard.

'Beautiful isn't it?' said my companion, Carole Banwell, the club's general manager, as we looked out on a bare, sloping pitch from a steeply angled set of steps leading into the main stand. I knew what she meant. The small, shallow terrace to our right, sheathed by nets that have prevented generations of mis-hit shots sailing into surrounding streets, spoke of half-remembered dreams and fleeting pleasures.

The community-run club is losing money and has debts to clear from a previous regime. Proposed ground improvements, including a new stand, dressing rooms, social club and artificial 3G pitch, form part of a regeneration plan centred on the provision of low-income housing and purpose-built student accommodation.

I was there for a literary event that was a promotional fiasco, but an uplifting occasion. Since there was no pre-publicity, the audience for broadcaster Danny Kelly and authors James Brown and Tony Evans consisted of six passers-by. We bought them all a drink and discussed the simple joys of football for an hour or so.

James spoke of the seductive power of a five-a-side footballer's inexplicable moments of perfection. Tony dwelt on the importance of identity. Danny, like the rest of us, confessed to being a compulsive spectator of park football. I was transported back to the gymnasium at my grammar school, and a pick-up game that enlivened a drab PE lesson.

I had a modicum of speed, and enough agility to be a decent long jumper, but as a footballer I had the co-ordination skills of an infant. I found myself trapped against the wall, my back tensed against would-be tacklers who took great joy in nipping at my ankles. Suddenly, something clicked, and I came the closest I have ever come to an out-of-body experience.

I deliberately kicked the ball against the wall bars, calculated its exit angle, and backheeled it beyond my markers with just enough pace to enable me to turn and get off a shot, which struck the bench, turned on its side, which acted as the goal. Even now, nearly half a century later, I can remember the audible intake of breath from boys waiting their chance to play.

That thrill has not left me. It never will.

Homecoming

'We might live in a time where sometimes it's easier to be negative than positive, or to divide than to
unite, but England: let's keep this unity alive. I love
you.' – Kyle Walker

Waistcoat Wednesday had given way to Trump
Thursday when, at 12.50 a.m. Moscow time on
12 July 2018, Gareth Southgate emerged from the tunnel
at the Luzhniki Stadium to pay a final act of homage to
England supporters who had amused themselves for
the previous 70 minutes by singing the chorus of
'Whole Again', a seventeen-year-old dirge by Atomic
Kitten, reworked in his honour.

He paused, as if dutifully looking for a waste con-
tainer, before dropping a water bottle behind his back,
on to the scuffed turf. He responded to the acclaim by
waving first with his right hand and then with his left.

He exuded the bashfulness of the bank clerk who went to war, massaging his forehead as if nonplussed by the fuss he had created. Finally, before turning on his heels, he twice bowed low, in supplication.

Semi-final defeat by Croatia was not the end for Southgate's England, merely the end of the beginning. Unlike in previous World Cups, there was no anger, no anguish, in the aftermath of elimination. There was no shame, no scapegoating. The poison would instead be laid down later that day by US president Donald Trump, at the start of his state visit to the UK.

Though conflating sport and social progress is precarious, it seemed appropriate to compare extremes of leadership. The toxicity of the times was captured by Trump, a narcissistic, racist ideologue who dishonoured his hosts by offering a deeply and deliberately divisive commentary on Brexit Britain. The pomp and ceremony afforded a man whose immigration policy resulted in children being caged provided a jarring contrast to nationwide protests against his presence.

Trust in the political class has never been as low, or as routinely betrayed. Southgate and his squad, half of whom came from immigrant stock, were a blessed distraction, the boys of a long, hot summer. The players, empowered by a manager who combined empathy with integrity, and honesty with humility, were unafraid to address their social significance.

They seized the moment, using interactivity to radiate positivity, an act that felt almost counter-intuitive. Southgate understood why: 'The players have a voice, too. They can influence young people, especially from the areas where they came from. They can give hope to them. We're not a team that just turns up, waltzing around, strolling around, thinking we've got an entitlement.'

As we have seen in these pages, football holds a mirror to ourselves. Millions saw in Southgate a reflection of a bigger, better person. He came across consistently as someone unafraid of expressing emotion, of acting with common decency towards others. His achievement had substance beyond silverware, since it involved the return of respect, and re-engagement with strangers.

Expectation will intensify as his squad evolves. A cosy narrative, of England winning the 2020 European Championships in a final staged at Wembley, has already been set. The FA's widely derided digital clock, counting down to the 2022 World Cup in Qatar, suddenly seems eerily prescient. Yet a note of caution needs to be struck.

Premier League clubs do not owe Southgate a living, and will ration game time for England's best young footballers as they see fit. Money continues to overwhelm idealism. Journalists who covered England's progress with authority, insight and intelligence will remain powerless, should their editors or owners decide to make commercial or political capital through a change of tone and a return to impulsive criticism.

Only the hopelessly naive expect FIFA to change. Gianni Infantino preened throughout his final presidential press conference of the tournament, in which he disingenuously wore a red volunteer's hoodie for effect. He was blind to the contradiction of proclaiming, 'We are not here to talk about politics' while ingratiating himself with Vladimir Putin and insisting the expansion of Qatar's World Cup to forty-eight nations could stimulate the resolution of regional tensions.

Recent history teaches us that politicians disengage once sport has served its purpose. Britain's Olympic legacy, from 2012, is a more indolent, less physically engaged nation. For England's Russian revival to have enduring relevance it must act as a turning point in administrative resolve. Participation in football has plunged by 19 per cent over the last decade; the Football Association will not be forgiven if they recoil from the challenge of restoring the grassroots game. By their own admission, 150,000 matches were called off last season because of poor facilities.

The young have a reason to believe. Now they need a place to play.

Author's Note

Since this book begins with a reflection on a father's love, it seems appropriate that it ends with a reminder of a father's gratitude. My family helped carry the weight of this project's ambition; they knew not to disturb me when my study door was closed, and did their best to get back to sleep when I disturbed them, getting up to write at my most productive time, 4 a.m.

Thanks, then, to my wife Lynn, and to my children Nicholas, Aaron, William and Lydia. The love my dad lavished on Marielli, his great-grandchild, would surely have been shared with her brother Michael, had he been alive to witness his birth. Yes, dear reader, he was named after me, and I cried my eyes out at the privilege.

Caroline Flatley, the Angel of the Keyboard, has transcribed countless hours of interviews. I give thanks to her, and to everyone who spoke to me, on and off the record, during my research. Occasionally, truth is coaxed out by confidentiality; the trust invested in me is deeply felt and will be honoured. David Manton and Ognen Bozinovski are not the real names of the prisoners mentioned in Chapter 3.

I am in the debt of Andy Walker, Greg Demetriou, Jonathan Wilsher, Antoni Fruncillo, Jo Tongue, Alan Redmond, Paul McCarthy, David Jackett, Jock Waugh, Merv Payne, Neil Allen, Dan Silver, Simon Hughes, Ian Watmore, Tom Boswell and Phil Townsend. I have endeavoured to mention all sources, though with my notes running to more than 700,000 words it is prudent to apologise for any unintentional oversight. The quote at the start of Chapter 12 is taken from Graham Taylor's autobiography, co-written by Lionel Birnie.

I'm still proud of my battered old trade. The media, like football, has changed fundamentally over the last half century, but Arthur Hopcraft would, I am sure, recognise the authority and empathy of contemporary sports columnists and senior football writers. Breadth of insight from such online outlets as Football 365, The Coaches' Voice, and Training Ground Guru complements enlightened work by such academics as Professor Simon Chadwick.

I value, hugely, the advice and enthusiasm of Rory Scarfe, my literary agent. Ben Brusey, my publisher, is a source of constant support and inspiration. The team at Century, headed by Selina Walker and Susan Sandon, is stellar. Special thanks to Glenn O'Neill, Tom Monson, Rachel Kennedy, Fergus Edmondson and Ajda Vucicevic.

I'm consumed by sport's humanity, and have never lost the buzz of seeing my words on the printed page. Writing is certainly better than working for a living, so thanks, above all, to you, for being with me.

Michael Calvin, June 2018

Index